All the

KING'S
FATHERS:

*The Paternal Ancestry of King Charles III
and the House of Glücksburg*

E D W A R D   H I L A R Y   D A V I S

PALFREY
PRESS

For my grandfather

Wing Commander
ARTHUR EDWARD ROY DAVIS
OBE RAFVR(t)
(1926 –2002)

Contents

Acknowledgments

My grateful thanks to Brady Brim-DeForest for helping to make this publication possible. I should like to thank the Royal Danish Library; the Museum of Sønderjylland; the Fredericksburg Hillerod Museum; the Pushkin Museum of Fine Arts; Corpus Christi College, Cambridge; the Palace of Versailles; the National Portrait Gallery; the archives of Britannia Royal Naval College; Christiansborg Palace; the BBC; the University of Cambridge Library and the collections of Nyborg, Sonderburg, Fredericksburg and Rosenburg Castles.

Special thanks also to Capt. Katharine Clare RN, Joanna Vaughan, Alex Wolgar-Toms, Antonia Cosby, Roan Hackney, Dr Craig Paterson, Quentin Peacock, Professor Kate Williams, the late Prince Michael of Greece, the Society of Antiquaries and my long-suffering mother. I should also like to apologise to anyone who sat next to me at a dinner party in the last couple of years and had to listen to me talk about this book as a captive audience.

I STARTED WRITING THIS book in 2022 several weeks after the death of Queen Elizabeth II. Her late Majesty's death was announced on 8 September, the day before the UK book launch of my previous book, *The British Bonapartes: Napoleon's Family in Britain*. In light of the sudden plunge into national mourning, I took the decision to postpone that book launch until January 2023. On the morning of Queen Elizabeth II's death, I had been recording the audiobook of *The British Bonapartes* in a studio in North London. Throughout the day, everyone in the studio had been receiving texts and calls from people 'in the know' in the royal household or armed forces regarding The Queen's health. Having finished recording the book, I went to meet my oldest friend, Edmund Mortimer, whom I have known since we were toddlers, for a drink in St James's. After finishing up, we were walking along The Mall towards Buckingham Palace discussing the rumours of the sovereign's health when subtly, slowly and with no warning the flag was lowered to half-mast. Having seen this, I exclaimed, *"Has she gone?"* And in true 2022 style, a passing bloke waved his phone and the BBC News app at me and said, *"Yeah, mate, just now."* I paused in silence for just a moment.

She was the same vintage as my grandfather. It seemed like the last of a generation had gone, the last generation to have served in the Second World War. It felt like we'd lost a direct link to our past. She was, after all, the granddaughter of the man who led us through WWI and the daughter of the man who led us through WWII.

Upon arriving at the theatre-like flower beds and god-like monuments in front of the palace, it became clear that a number of people must have known before we did. There were audible gasps and a touch of eerie silence around the palace – like the calm before an inevitable storm. The stillness was only broken by banks of bustling journalists (yes, I suppose they are people too) who were already set up, while more were arriving. We decided not to get too close to the palace, knowing that it might soon get overcrowded. We hung back by the flower beds, people-watching from a calm reflective position. We continued our quiet observations until I was forcibly elbowed out of the way by a short yet determined young woman who said, "*Sorry, we need this position – we're Lebanon News,*" as though that somehow justified bad manners and something akin to assault.

Some weeks later, it was the start of a new term at Cambridge, and I found myself needing to give the first lecture of the year to the Cambridge University Heraldic and Genealogical Society. Now that we had a new king, I thought this was an apt moment to observe that, technically, the royal house had changed. Visibly, the House of Windsor remained, but technically, it was the end of the reigning House of Saxe-Coburg und Gotha (The Queen's 'real surname') and the beginning of a new one. But what is the new reigning house in Britain? What is the 'real surname' of the monarch – if he has one at all? After some research, I put together a presentation on the patrilineal ancestors of our new sovereign, King Charles III. I found it far more interesting that I thought I would – from mythical warriors to Scandinavian and even Mediterranean kings. I was determined to investigate further. This is the product of that interest and those investigations.

This book tries not to assume too much prior knowledge of British history or royal family history, which is why there are some family trees provided and there are chapters which briefly explain the passage of the English crown from the Anglo-Saxons to the present day. The passage of the Scottish crown (pre-1603) has not been deliberately ignored, it would just deviate from the main theme of the book, which is the direct male-line ancestors of King Charles III. This work looks at The King's ancestors, not The King himself. The main section of the book follows each paternal ancestor of HM The King from his twenty-fourth great-grandfather to his father and his heirs to come, preceded by a brief history of all the previous royal houses of Britain and England since Alfred the Great.

The Two Halves of the Royal Story

I N THIS BOOK, we will tell the story of the two halves of The King's lineage. We will first seek to examine the origins and passage of the Crown of England/Britain to its current owner – from King Cerdic of Wessex through to the late Queen Elizabeth II, mother of The King. Then, in the second part, we will discover the origins of The King's direct male-line ancestry. There we will briefly explore the individual men from Count Elimar I of Oldenburg to King Charles III of Great Britain. These two halves of the same story explain how a man of Saxon/Danish/Greek extraction now sits on the throne of the United Kingdom.

History Comes Full Circle – Saxon to Saxon

When Queen Elizabeth II of the United Kingdom of Great Britain and Northern Ireland died in 2022, the ruling House of Windsor ceased to occupy the throne in the traditional sense. Her 'house' or family name was Windsor, a name which she inherited from her father like most still do in western society. The name Windsor was adopted when Elizabeth II's grandfather, George V, for political, anti-German and self-preservation reasons, dropped his own family's real name of Saxe-Coburg und Gotha – a name he in turn had inherited from his German grandfather, Prince Albert, who married Queen Victoria. Saxe-Coburg und Gotha became Windsor from 1917 onwards.

If we take the basic tradition of individuals inheriting their surname purely from their father, then King Charles III is neither a Windsor nor a Saxe-Coburg – these were his mother's family.

At this point, the uninitiated might begin to mention the name Mountbatten. After all, King Charles's father, prior to marriage, was

Lieutenant Philip Mountbatten (Royal Navy), later Prince Philip, Duke of Edinburgh. However, Mountbatten is a name that was also changed during the First World War to sound less German. It is a simple anglicisation of Battenberg. Yet neither Mountbatten nor Battenberg were the real names of Prince Philip; they came from his mother's family. He too changed his name to sound less German in the wake of WWI. Mountbatten was not Prince Philip's 'real surname' name. The princely family of Battenberg changed their name to Mountbatten (a direct translation) at the same time as the royals changed their own. Thus the Mountbatten surname rose to prominence in Britain as two men from this family served as First Sea Lords in the Royal Navy. However, these two names of Battenberg and Mountbatten were the maiden names of Prince Philip's mother. So, what was his 'real surname' and what therefore is the surname of his son, King Charles III?

Put simply, King Charles III is technically neither a Windsor nor a Mountbatten. Traditionally speaking, and based on him inheriting his name from his paternal line, his family name is Schleswig-Holstein-Sonderburg-Glücksburg. This may be a mouthful, but it is the original 'surname' of The King's father and many of his fathers before him.

Much has been made of the House of Windsor and the House of Mountbatten over the last century or so. From a historiographical point of view, the focus has long been on either the change from Saxe-Coburg und Gotha to Windsor, the abdication of Edward VIII in 1936, or the exploits of the Mountbatten family, particularly Prince Philip's maternal uncle – Lord Mountbatten of Burma. This has (partially deliberately) diluted almost all public knowledge or understanding of King Charles III's paternal ancestry. So, does The King descend from a line of military officers, or does he too come from a line of ancient kings?

The King's father, Philip, was a Prince of Greece. The King's great-grandfather was King George I of Greece from 1863, but prior to that, he was a Prince of Denmark and second son of King Christian IX of Denmark.

The House of Schleswig-Holstein-Sonderburg-Glücksburg, though famously connected to Denmark and Scandinavia, has its origins south-west of the border in modern-day Germany. It is itself one of the many cadet branches of the older House of Oldenburg – which takes its name from the town of the same name in Lower Saxony around the year 1108. King Charles III's direct male line ancestor was Elimar I who is regarded as the first Count of Oldenburg who founded the family. The location of the original ancestors of The King in the area of Saxony is in itself interesting.

The Saxons and the First House of England

After the fall of the Roman Empire in Britain (in the early fifth century AD), Saxon raiders, mercenaries and settlers were becoming more frequent in the southern and eastern parts of Britain. Much of the history of these times comes from traditional stories and accounts written by men who lived centuries later. The Saxons were pagan, the remaining Britons were largely Christian like their old Roman masters. In some mythical traditions, it was the legendary King Arthur who led resistance against the invading Saxon settlers. Much of the west of Britain held out against the invaders in Wales, Devon and Cornwall (Dumnonia). Traditional Welsh songs sing of fighting *"Saxon foemen, Saxon spearmen, Saxon bowmen".*

The foreign, pagan, Germanic settlers (Saxons and Angles) successfully gained control of much of the south of Britain. Having gained control of large swathes of what would later be called England, they founded tribes and kingdoms: Essex (East Saxons), Middlesex (Middle Saxons), Sussex (South Saxons), and Wessex (West Saxons). Wessex was to prove the greatest and longest lasting as well as the first house to rule England. The first King of Wessex was King Cerdic from 519 AD. Nearly all Kings of England are descended from Cerdic, Alfred the Great, and the original Saxon invaders who became Kings of Wessex and, centuries later, England. The Anglo-Saxons ruled England until 1066.

Full Circle

Whilst King Charles III does not descend from King Cerdic in the direct male line, he almost certainly descends from the same Saxon warriors living around Oldenburg or Lower Saxony in the male line. Their kin likely made the journey across the seas to invade and settle England. One could therefore argue England began with Saxon kings and, nearly a thousand years later, a Saxon sits upon the throne once more – if only by descent!

The title of the book is *All the King's Fathers;* therefore, a detailed biography of HM King Charles III is not necessary. As The King started the most important part of his life only a few years ago – in a job which is for life – it would be unfair, indeed premature, to give a detailed history of his reign and life at this early stage, and it is not the intention of this book.

Introduction

THE PATRILINEAL TRADITION

W HAT'S IN A NAME? Specifically, what's in a surname? Even today when ideas about gender roles and gender identity are constantly changing or being challenged, one thing still remains roughly the same: in Britain, surnames are passed down the male line of a family. Of course, not everyone chooses to do this nowadays. With the rate of divorce being what it is and the increasing number of single-mother families (by choice or by fate), naturally the father's surname might get switched out in favour of the mother's maiden name for young children or newborns. That said, it is more likely than not that the mother's maiden name came from her own father. It is safe to say that the majority of people in the world (from many different cultures and traditions) take their family name, which we now refer to as a surname, from their father's side. For centuries it has been virtually automatic or assumed that any child will bear the name of his father and his father's fathers. It is certainly surprising that in 2025, in our world of great social change, this tradition largely remains intact throughout most of the world from the Far East to the Americas.

Traditionally, in Europe as well as other places, property and aristocratic titles (as well as the name) are passed down the male line. This was particularly customary before the mid-twentieth century. Of course, there are a myriad of exceptions, all of which have individual explanations, but speaking generally, it is more common for the patrilineal lines to pass down great wealth and one common name through many generations.

Most of us usually know who our grandparents are and, if we bother to check our old family photos to remind ourselves, our great-grand-parents too – even if we never knew them personally. Far fewer people can go beyond this. However with the current fashion in do-it-yourself online genealogy websites, that number is growing fast. Given even a little bit of information, almost anyone of British descent may be able to easily trace their native forebears as far back as the 1830s – when centralised birth certificates were introduced. Beyond that, one starts to become more reliant on regional sources such as individual parish records.

1 – *The Line of Kings (and Queens)*

ROYAL HOUSES OF ENGLAND/BRITAIN
FROM 802-2022 AD

THE HOUSE OF WINDSOR was an invented name. The patrilineal ancestry of George V and his granddaughter, Queen Elizabeth II, is of course German. King George V, in 1917 during the First World War, changed his family's name in an effort to sound less German – changing Saxe-Coburg und Gotha to something more British. This was a way of seeming less German to a war-weary British public who were sick of the long war and full of extremely anti-German sentiment.

More recently, the name Windsor has been combined with Mountbatten, the adopted surname of Prince Philip the Duke of Edinburgh. However, his surname was also changed in the wake of the First World War in order to sound more British – and therefore Mountbatten is also invented. Prince Philip was born a Prince of Greece and Denmark, but his mother was Princess Alice of Battenberg. Her parents were Prince Louis of Battenberg and Princess Victoria of Hesse (one of Queen Victoria's granddaughters). Prince Louis was at one time First Sea Lord and an Admiral of the Fleet. Following the example of the British royal family, he too anglicised his name in 1917, opting for Mountbatten (an English translation of Battenberg) and gave up his German princely titles. His grandson, Prince Philip, later became a Royal Naval officer. Shortly before Philip's engagement to Princess Elizabeth (the future Queen Elizabeth II), he relinquished his Greek and Danish titles and adopted his maternal grandfather's invented surname, Mountbatten. Of course, as you all doubtlessly

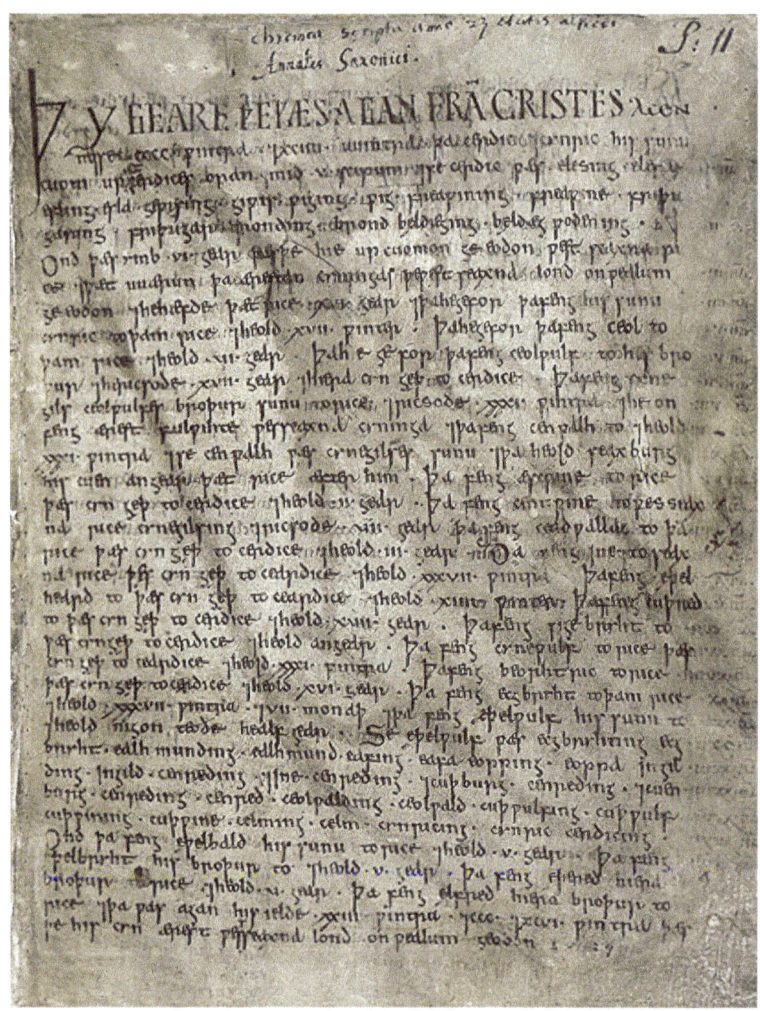

Figure 1: An early page from the Winchester Chronicle giving the genealogical preface of King Alfred the Great. It was begun during Alfred's reign (871-899) and forms part of the Anglo-Saxon Chronicle. Parker Library, Corpus Christi College, Cambridge.

know, Prince Philip's 'real surname' and house was that of Schleswig-Holstein-Sonderburg-Glücksburg (a collateral branch of the House of Oldenburg)! It is difficult to imagine British people getting on with such a name. The switch to Mountbatten, his mother's newer anglicised 'surname', like the switch to Windsor, was a sensible political move for Prince Philip. Many thought, as had been the case, that the future royal children would adopt their father's name. However, on 9 April 1952, Queen Elizabeth declared that her heirs would be of the name and house of Windsor – which will probably be the case for many generations to come, whatever their 'real surnames'. However, as per a declaration made by the Privy Council in 1960, the double-barrelled name Mountbatten-Windsor applies to all male-line descendants without royal titles or styles – such as Lady Louise Mountbatten-Windsor.

Throughout previous centuries, surnames were not always used by royals. Indeed, surnames were not commonly developed or used in the way we understand today until the Norman Conquest in the eleventh century. With royal surnames and dynastic houses, territorial designations, usually stemming from a title, were more typically used instead. This is not just a British tradition but rather a European one which continued down the centuries. Britain has been importing its royal families from Germany and other countries for generations. Prince Albert of Saxe-Coburg und Gotha became the Prince Consort when he married Victoria in 1840. Prince George the Elector of Hanover became King of Great Britain in 1714. Prior to the Hanovers, the ruling family had been Scottish. They possessed a great Scottish name, Stuart/Stewart, and prior to them, in England at least, the ruling family was of Welsh extraction with a supremely Welsh name – Tudor. Before the Tudors, the great Plantagenet dynasty ruled. Their name too is an anglicised name created from a Latin nickname given to its founder Geoffrey of Anjou. The Plantagenets' 'real surname' (if we can say that) would have been Anjou – a province in France. Indeed, they were initially known as the Angevins. Prior to them, of course, was the House of Normandy, who ruled by dint or right of conquest. Before the Normans, it was the House of Wessex which ruled England (with occasional interludes of Viking rule). One has to go as far back as the House of Wessex to find a royal family with an English 'name'. That said, in a surprising mirror of the kingdom's current state, that particular dynasty was also descended in most part from invading (and settling) Anglo-Saxons

– some of whom would likely have come from parts of Lower Saxony. Furthermore, the 'Germanic' settlers also came from parts of the Low Countries (modern-day Netherlands and Belgium) and possibly from the southernmost parts of Denmark which border, or are now part of, Germany.

So, in a convoluted way, the ruling dynasties of England have come full circle. The kingdom's first ruling dynasty, the House of Wessex, harkened from Germanic, Dutch and Danish lands. The new ruling house in England is coincidentally similar in its geographical origins. From the Frisian borders in the west, round to the Schleswig-Holstein lands in the north-east, our present monarch would appear to have similar paternal origins to that of Alfred the Great himself – if one goes back far enough. (It is perhaps fitting therefore that the title of Earl of Wessex was revived for King Charles's brother, Prince Edward – now Duke of Edinburgh.)

From 1066 and indeed earlier, the throne of England, and subsequently Britain, has been occupied by a series of different families – often termed 'houses'. (A 'house' can be defined as a family which has been or will be important for many generations, especially royalty or senior nobility.) From the House of Wessex to the House of Windsor, each had left a clear mark on the nation's history and evolution, but how are they all connected? Of course, such a question is well documented and worthy of yet more books, television documentaries and journal articles. However, for the uninitiated, this large chapter aims to shed light on the genealogy in a succinct and easily digestible way.

1a – The Old Gods and the New

THE HOUSE OF WESSEX

Kings and Rulers of Wessex:

Cerdic, 519-534

Cynric, 534-560

Ceawlin, 560-591

Ceol, 591-597

Ceolwulf, 597-611

Cynegils, 611-643

Cwichelm, c. 626-636 (sometime co-ruler with Cynegils)

Cenwalh, 643-645

(Penda of Mercia), 645-648

Cenwalh (restored), 648-672

Queen Seaxburh, 672-674 (widow of Cenwalh)

Cenfus, 674 (disputed)

Æscwine, 674-676

Centwine, 676-685

Cædwalla, 685-688

Ine, 688-726

Æthelheard, 726-740

Cuthred, 740-756

Sigeberht, 756-757

Cynewulf, 757-786

Beorhtric, 786-802

Ecgberht, 802-839

Æthelwulf, 839-858

Æthelbald, 858-860

Æthelberht, 860-865

Æthelred, 865-871

Alfred the Great, 871-886

Kings of the Anglo-Saxons:

Alfred the Great, 886-899

Edward the Elder, 899-924

Æthelstan the Glorious, 924-927

Kings of the English:

Æthelstan the Glorious, 927-939

Edmund I, 939-946

Eadred, 946-955

Eadwig, 955-959

Edgar the Peaceful, 959-975

Edward the Martyr, 975-978

Æthelred the Unready, 978-1013

(Sweyn of Denmark), 1013-1014

Æthelred the Unready (restored), 1014-1016

Edmund II Ironside, 1016

(Cnut the Great of Denmark), 1016-1035

(Harold I Harefoot of Denmark), 1035-1040

(Harthacnut of Denmark), 1040-1042

Edward the Confessor, 1042-1066

(Harold II Godwinson), 1066

Attributed arms of the House of Wessex, particularly associated with King Edward the Confessor.

I F WE LOOK back to the time of Alfred the Great and the subsequent formation of the Kingdom of England, surnames did not exist of course. The first King of all England was Æthelstan, who ruled during the early tenth century. He was the grandson of Alfred the Great and was of the House of Wessex. Before and during the Viking invasions, England had been divided into separate kingdoms. Wessex was one of these kingdoms and was predominantly governed from Winchester. To tell history more simply, after the battle of Eddington (878 AD), where Alfred defeated the Viking forces, Wessex emerged as the leading Saxon power in the land.

THE HOUSE OF WESSEX

The House of Wessex was founded by Cerdic, who became the first known King of Wessex (519-534). Cerdic was probably of Saxon origin, but he may well have been born in England and possibly even had some Briton ancestry. The Saxons came from what is modern-day north-west Germany.

The name Cerdic may have been derived from the Briton word for Celtic. Mixed heritage or not, he led the settling West Saxons – hence the name Wessex. In fact, at the time he would have been known as the chief or King of the Gewisse – a local tribe in the upper Thames valley. The Anglo-Saxon Chronicle records his ancestry back to the Germanic/Norse god Woden/Odin. The Saxon settlers of Cerdic's time came from the north-west German coast. This may well have included the lands around Oldenburg – which is relevant to our theme. It is entirely possible that Cerdic's male-line ancestors came from the same place as the present-day King Charles III. The descendants of Cerdic ruled Wessex, and latterly England, from 519 until the death of Edward the Confessor in 1066. There were, of course, several intervals of Viking invasion and short-lived rule over England in the later centuries (under Cnut, for example).

Early Anglo-Saxons

Across England, the settling Saxons consolidated themselves in England forming seven small regional kingdoms known as the Heptarchy; this included Kent, Sussex, Wessex, Mercia, Essex, East Anglia and Northumbria. After St Augustine's visit to the Kingdom of Kent in 597 AD and the founding of a church in Canterbury, the Anglo-Saxon peoples gradually became enthusiastic converts to Christianity. A product of this was the founding of monasteries up and down England, which were rich defenceless pickings for Scandinavian Viking raiders, who gradually, over the years, began to settle, not just raid, in the north of England. Over the years, Viking influence and raids pushed further south in England to the very borders of Wessex.

Alfred the Great

Several centuries and many Wessex chiefs and kings later, after four of his older brothers died or were slain by the Vikings, Alfred succeeded as ruler of Wessex in 871 AD (the twenty-sixth king as far as we know). He is credited with halting the advance of the Vikings at the Battle of Eddington and subsequently Christianising much of the Viking leadership as well as beginning to expand the dominance of Wessex in England.

During his reign, Alfred the Great collected many learned men from all parts of Britain to help make his court a centre for study and writing. He recruited a Welsh monk called Asser from St David's. Alfred and Asser met in Dean (now West and East Dean) in (West) Sussex in 887, and Alfred expressed a desire to learn and read Latin. Asser later became close to Alfred; he wrote his biography (*The Life of Alfred the Great*) and became Bishop of Sherborne. Asser recorded the ancestry of the great king; not only did he trace Alfred's genealogy line back to Cerdic but to the biblical Noah (of Noah's Ark) and further still to Adam (of the Garden of Eden). This was almost certainly a political move and merely highlighted Alfred as the leading and most senior Christian magnate in England. His 'family history' would impress both foreigners and subjects alike. Many genealogists have tried to interpret or map out these ancestral claims. In some cases, Cerdic is interpreted as the seventy-eighth or seventy-ninth generation after Adam and Alfred the ninety-third. So, according to tradition/legend, most Kings of England following Alfred the Great can trace their descent from the biblical Abraham, Noah, Adam and, therefore, God.

As King of Wessex, Alfred managed to gain paramountcy over neighbouring Saxon kingdoms and was recognised as King of the Anglo-Saxons – an attempt to unite all Saxon peoples against the pagan Scandinavian invaders/settlers. The Danes or Vikings still ruled Northumbria and minor southern parts of England. Alfred's crown passed to his son Edward the Elder. He succeeded in defeating the Vikings in the south. Only Northumbria remained under Danelaw.

ENGLAND IS FORMED

It was at the Battle of Brunanburh in 937 AD that Æthelstan, Edward's son and eventual successor, defeated the Vikings (as well as King Constantine of Scotland, King Olaf of Dublin, and King Owain of Strathclyde) and brought Northumbria under the rule of the House of Wessex. This is largely seen as the moment England was actually formed. From the northernmost part of Northumbria in the north, to the borders of Wales in the west and the English Channel in the south, Æthelstan was recognised under a new title: King of the English.

He was succeeded by his younger half-brother, Edmund I, who continued the struggle to keep all the lands of England together from rebels and Viking incursions particularly in Northumbria. Though it is disputed, there are accounts of Edmund dying during a tavern brawl in 946 at Pucklechurch in Gloucestershire, leaving his sons Eadwig and Edgar still of minor age.

Dynastic Turmoil

Because Eadwig was still of minor age, upon his death, King Edmund was succeeded by another brother, Eadred. Eadred held the throne for nine years. He suffered from poor health and eventually died unmarried in 955, returning the crown to his nephew Eadwig, who was about fifteen.

As king, Eadwig attempted to take ecclesiastical lands for the Crown. This drew him into conflict with the clergy. What is surprising is that, two years into his reign (in 957), the kingdom was divided. Eadwig ruled everything south of the Thames, while his brother Edgar became king of (everything to) the north. This may have been the result of a pre-agreed arrangement or the product of opposition and revolt against Eadwig. To add insult to possible injury, the following year, Eadwig's marriage to his wife Ælfgifu was annulled on the grounds that they were too closely related by blood. It is not clear exactly how they were related, but they may have been cousins to some degree. Eadwig died childless a year after the separation, and Edgar inherited all the realm of England. King Edgar the Peaceful reigned from 959 to 975.

His successor, partly chosen by Archbishop (Saint) Dunstan, was Edward the Martyr. His epithet is certainly a spoiler! His reign was short. Many ealdormen and nobles reacted very negatively to the Benedictine reforms being enacted in the church of the day. They felt forced to surrender lands to the church and disapproved of monks replacing secular clergy (who were often married). Edward supported such reform in the monasteries, which contributed to his undoing.

Edward was murdered in mysterious circumstances whilst at Corfe Castle. He was about sixteen. It is uncertain who was to blame. Much later chroniclers imply that it was nobles or even his own mother – but probably only because it was her residence. Hastily buried at Wareham and then Shaftesbury Abbey, the cult of a saint formed around the late King Edward over the subsequent centuries. His remains were hidden during the Reformation and are now in an Orthodox Church in Brookwood, Surrey, where he is prayed to as a saint.

Æthelred and the Vikings

Edward the Martyr was succeeded by his younger brother, Æthelred the Unready (another spoiler), in 978. Æthelred's reign was punctuated by problems with the Danes.

Vikings had been raiding and invading the north-eastern parts of England for over a century, but by the late tenth century, these raids had increased in size and intensity. An English force tried to put a stop to these invasions at the Battle of Maldon in 991; however, they were crushed by the strength of the Viking warriors, who may have numbered two to four thousand. In retribution, King Æthelred ordered the mass killing of all and any Danes in his lands, be they settlers or warriors. Many Vikings had intermarried with Anglo-Saxons and settled as farmers in southern territories such as Wessex. These people were also targeted in what is now known as the St Brice Day Massacre. In the same year as this massacre, Æthelred married (secondly) a noblewoman of Normandy – Emma, daughter of Richard I of Normandy. He could not have known how crucial to the future of England Emma and her family's influence would be. The couple had two sons: Edward and Alfred. More on them later.

The Viking response to the massacre came in 1003, and there followed a decade of heavy Viking raids in Wessex and East Anglia. In 1013, King Sweyn Forkbeard of Denmark led an invasion of England, which resulted in Æthelred fleeing with his family to Normandy.

Viking Invasion and the Ruling House of Denmark

King Sweyn Forkbeard, who invaded England, was either the son or nephew of Harald Bluetooth (King of Denmark 958-986), after whom Bluetooth technology is named. Harald united the tribes of Denmark into a single kingdom. (Thus, his name was given to the wireless specification design invented in 1997 because it united or combined other technologies to form something more powerful. The Bluetooth logo is a merging of the Viking runes of his initials: HB.)

Harald Bluetooth, Sweyn Forkbeard and Cnut the Great, who were grandfather, father and son, were of the House of Knýtlinga – which in English translates as Cnut's descendants. This family traced its origins to the semi-legendary King Harthacnut of Denmark, son of Sigurd Snake-in-the-Eye – also a semi-legendary figure – in the same way that Alfred the Great's ancestry was traced back to Biblical times, that is to say, for political reasons. Harthacnut's father Sigurd apparently had a strange looking eye that resembled the popular Danish/Viking symbol of the *ouroboros*, a dragon or serpent eating its tail, representing the circle of life and death.

Invader King Sweyn Forkbeard's daughter, Estrid, would marry Ulf the Earl and come to found what eventually became the ruling house of Denmark, the House of Estridsen, from 1047 to 1412. This house preceded the House of Oldenburg in Denmark and so is connected to the lineage of King Charles III's fathers.

Sweyn occupied the English throne (as well as that of Norway and Denmark) from December 1013 until his death at age fifty in February 1014.

Æthelred the Unready and the Vikings

Following Sweyn's death, Æthelred returned from Normandy and was proclaimed king – again. But the Vikings had not gone away. Much of the north of England (Danelaw) was still under Viking control. Æthelred died two years after his restoration in 1016. Despite the ongoing pressure from the Danes, the Witan (council of earls) chose Æthelred's son by his first wife Ælfgifu, Edmund Ironside, to succeed him. Meanwhile, Sweyn's son, Cnut, who had been defeated following his father's death, returned to Denmark to gather men and provisions for another invasion of England.

Cnut eventually amassed a great Viking force of around ten thousand from all over Scandinavia and sailed for England. As the Danes invaded Wessex, King Edmund Ironside bravely defended his lands, but there were many inconclusive battles. Eventually, King Edmund raised the siege of London and defeated the Danes at the Battle of Brentford. However, the conflict was concluded and the invasion stopped with the Battle of Assandun on 18 October 1016, in which King Edmund's forces were heavily defeated by Cnut's.

Following a possible ancillary battle in the Forest of Dean, the two men met to discuss peace. This led to the dividing of the country. Edmund retained Wessex (the land south of the Thames including London), whereas Cnut effectively had free reign in the rest of England. It was also agreed that Cnut would rule the Wessex lands upon Edmund's death. By shocking coincidence, on 30 November 1016, just a few weeks after this agreement, Edmund died! The cause of his death is not known. Saxon and Dane alike accepted Cnut as their new king, and he was crowned King of England in London in 1017. Edmund Ironside's son and heir, Edward the Exile, as one can guess by his name, went into exile for his safety as Cnut sought to hunt down anyone who might be a threat to his rule.

Cnut the Great

Attributed arms of the House of Knýtlinga (or Jellingdynastiet) and King Cnut. These arms actually first appear on a seal of King Cnut VI of Denmark (of the House of Estridsen) in 1194, who was descended from Sweyn Forkbeard via the latter's daughter, Estrid. Versions of this have subsequently been adopted as the royal arms of Denmark.

King Cnut ruled England for two decades and is generally considered to have been a good, effective monarch, despite being a Viking. He was obviously not of the House of Wessex but, like his father Sweyn, Cnut was from the House of Knýtlinga. Possibly because of Cnut's plans to invade and wage war on England, his younger brother Harald succeeded their father Sweyn as King of Denmark from 1014. However, not long after Cnut's victory in England and subsequent coronation as king there, Harald died in 1018 and was succeeded by Cnut. For the first time, England and Denmark shared a king.

To solidify his hold on England, and for dynastic purposes, Cnut took as his wife the murdered King Edmund Ironside's mother, Emma of Normandy – who had been the queen of Æthelred the Unready. Her sons were not killed by Cnut but allowed to go into exile in Normandy – where her family ruled.

By 1028, Cnut had developed something of a North Sea Empire. That year, through both bribery and conquest, he became King of Norway. Not for nothing do we have the legendary tales of his subjects believing he could actually command the sea! In either a hubristic exercise of vanity, or as an actual gesture of modesty, Cnut once took a group of his courtiers and advisers to the shoreside. There he publicly commanded the sea and tide to halt. Of course, it did not, and his feet got wet as the tide came in. This may have been a disappointment to Cnut's audience, but he was trying to demonstrate and explain to his lords and courtiers that he was not in fact in possession of god-like abilities to control the seas and tides. This story was recorded by the historian Henry of Huntingdon in the twelfth century and is sometimes still taught to children in British schools . The point of this old story is that kingly or secular power is nothing next to the power of God.

HARTHACNUT AND HAROLD HAREFOOT

Cnut died at Shaftesbury in 1035. He was succeeded by his son Harthacnut as King of Denmark and technically as King of the English. Harthacnut resided in Denmark and was greatly concerned with putting down rebellions. Meanwhile, he installed Cnut's other son, Harold Harefoot, as regent of England.

Harold filled this post for two years and governed England, but he was not content to be his half-brother's caretaker. He wished to be named King. The Archbishop of Canterbury, whose office's privileges included crowning the new Kings of England, initially resisted and refused though. As the two years rolled on, Harthacnut got bogged down dealing with rebels and establishing his control in Denmark and Scandinavia. Harold was unpopular but still able to take advantage of Harthacnut's absence. Supported by a coup of senior earls, Harold was eventually proclaimed King of the English in 1037.

The House of Wessex Wanes

During the uncertainty following Cnut's death, the House of Wessex made a daring return, hoping to oust the Danish usurpers. Princes Alfred and Edward, sons of King Cnut's wife Emma of Normandy by her earlier husband (King Æthelred the Unready), returned to England from their exile in Normandy. Sensing that the situation was perhaps ripe for an uprising against Harold, Princes Alfred and Edward came separately across the Channel with designs to raise support from the local earls and Anglo-Saxon people.

Prince Alfred landed in Sussex. Earl Godwin of Wessex, head of one of the kingdom's most powerful families and a supporter of King Harold, was in the area. Godwin captured Prince Alfred and took him by ship to Ely. Whilst in Godwin's care, perhaps on the orders of Harold, Alfred's eyes were gouged out, and soon after he died from the wounds. Neither Alfred's full brother Edward nor his half-brother Harthacnut forgot or forgave this crime. The hope of a return of the House of Wessex was crushed – for now.

The Danes Return

By 1040, Harthacnut was preparing to invade England and take (back) his kingdom from his brother Harold Harefoot. Somewhat conveniently, Harold died in March, making invasion unnecessary. In June Harthacnut returned. He was proclaimed king, and he had his half-brother's body exhumed from Westminster Abbey, beheaded and then tossed into a fen along the Thames. There are conflicting stories of the body being retrieved and subsequently re-buried by Anglo-Danes.

One such story suggests the church aptly named St Clement Danes as Harold's final resting place.

King Harthacnut had lost Norway but retained Denmark, and by June 1040, he was King of the English. Harthacnut, his mother Emma, and his half-brother Edward then sought revenge for the death of Harthacnut's half-brother Alfred. Having exhumed and beheaded Harold's body, they turned their attention to the man most believed complicit in Edward's murder – Godwin, Earl of Wessex. He was tried before members of Harthacnut's council. However, several witnesses attested to the fact that Godwin was only carrying out the orders of his king. As recompense for Alfred, Godwin gifted Harthacnut a grand and expensive warship. The ship was worth more than the traditional Danish wergild (fine or man price) for killing even a prince, and so Godwin was able to buy his freedom. It seems he survived by luck of wealth.

THE HOUSE OF WESSEX RETURNS: EDWARD THE CONFESSOR

Harthacnut reigned for two more years. In June 1042, while attending a wedding in Lambeth, he collapsed. Contemporary accounts said he had consumed much alcohol – though it was likely a stroke. By prior arrangement, Harthacnut's lands in Denmark passed to Magnus the Good (who already ruled Norway). In England, the crown passed to his half-brother Edward the Confessor, who was the last standing heir of Æthelred the Unready. The House of Wessex returned to power in England once again.

To cement his hold on the kingdom, Edward married Edith, the daughter of the powerful Godwin, Earl of Wessex, in 1045. Since Harthacnut's death, Godwin had truly changed his colours; he gave support to Edward's claim and reign.

Although crowned at Winchester in 1043, Edward the Confessor is widely associated with Westminster Abbey. He was responsible for the new building of Westminster from 1042 and consecrated it in 1065 (shortly before his death). Edward was a great patron of the church, and

Westminster was likely the first Norman style Romanesque church in England.

Though Edward the Confessor seems to have reigned England successfully and commanded respect, his lack of children created a succession crisis – perhaps the most famous in British (and even European) history. Again, it is impossible to convey all the complexities and characters of this momentous period of English history in just a few paragraphs. Nevertheless, we shall try.

Struggles with the Godwins

Attributed coat of arms of King Harold II (Godwinson) depicted in Historia Anglorum (c.1255) by Matthew Paris (c.1200-1259).

King Edward the Confessor was the ruler of the most prosperous nation in Europe. That said, he had a long-standing internal power struggle with his overly politically powerful father-in-law, Earl Godwin of Wessex. The Godwin family were too rich and too close to the throne for comfort. Perhaps to address Godwin's dominance, Edward filled his court with Norman courtiers and advisers, some of whom were kin on his mother's side. He went further in 1051 when he offered his cousin, William, the new Duke of Normandy, the succession in lieu of any issue of his own. This was not necessarily a binding offer, as Edward could change his mind at any point. However, it was an important move by Edward to manage the politics of the day in England and to keep Godwin at bay and curb his power.

Later that year, one of Edward's followers, Eustace of Boulogne, was returning to Normandy via Dover with a host of men. While in Dover, an argument arose between Eustace's party and the townsfolk. After their demand for supply of vitals was refused, Eustace and his men became rowdy and physically assaulted the townsfolk. After a serious scuffle, around twenty were dead on both sides. Eustace complained to the king, who quickly judged him to be the aggrieved party, and the king demanded that Godwin, in whose territory Dover was located, should punish the men responsible. Godwin refused. Civil war looked imminent between Edward and Godwin. In the end however, Godwin was forced into exile.

Soon after Godwin was sent away from court, Duke William of Normandy sailed to England to pay homage to Edward. However, a year later in 1052 Edward faced a backlash. He was persuaded by his advisors and English nobles to restore Earl Godwin to his position and to expel some of his Norman advisers back to Normandy.

Earl Godwin was succeeded by his son Harold (Godwinson) as Earl of Wessex. Another son, Tostig, inherited Godwin's northern lands as Earl of Northumbria. Tostig was not a good governor of his lands, and a rebellion there drove him out. He was abandoned by his brother Harold and was not supported by King Edward, so he went into bitter exile to plot and scheme a return.

Harold Godwinson, in Norman sources and English sources, is reported to have (for some reason) made a journey to Normandy during these years of peace. He may have even been shipwrecked there. He was rescued or taken in as a guest by Duke William. While with William, he (probably) swore an oath of some sort, and the Norman chroniclers insist that it was that he would help William gain the throne of England should Edward die. However, years later at the death bed of Edward the Confessor in January 1066, it is possible that Harold himself was granted succession by the dying king.

HAROLD II, THE LAST ANGLO-SAXON KING OF ENGLAND

Edward died on 5 January 1066, and the Witan promptly nominated and elected Harold as King of the English. The following day, King Harold II was crowned as king. He was likely the first king to be crowned in Westminster Abbey, where nearly all English monarchs have since been crowned. He was also destined to become the last Anglo-Saxon King of England.

Harold Godwinson's claim was based on the last-minute bequest of Edward and the approval of the Witan – and not a great deal more. He had been the brother-in-law of the king but was not a blood relative. Edward's closest relative at the time of death was his great-nephew Edgar the Ætheling, but Edgar was young, lacked any major supporters and was not nominated by Edward. Little is known about Harold Godwinson's ancestry. That said, the Godwins must have had strong noble origins to have such vast land holdings in Sussex. One theory is that they distantly descended from Alfred the Great's elder brother King Æthelred of Wessex. This is difficult to prove, however.

Meanwhile, two other men felt they should take the throne.

A Dual Invasion

Enraged by the perceived betrayal, William Duke of Normandy prepared an invasion force. William was Edward the Confessor's first cousin once removed, after all, and believed that he had not only been promised the crown but that it was his by right. He gathered the largest army of knights and men he could from home in Normandy and also from Brittany, promising as payment land, title and bounty in England (a far richer and older country than Normandy).

Meanwhile, seeing an opportunity in the wake of Edward the Confessor's death, Tostig (Harold's brother) managed to persuade the King of Norway Harald Hardrada (uncle of Magnus the Good) to invade England in a bid to take the throne and restore Tostig to his earldom.

Hardrada and his Viking invading force sailed up the River Humber and had initial success at the Battle of Fulford (20 September) in Yorkshire but were crushed by King Harold II's Anglo-Saxon army at the Battle of Stamford Bridge (25 September). Hardrada died in the battle.

Unfortunately for Harold, however, three days later on 28 September, William Duke of Normandy landed with a great Norman army at Pevensey in Sussex. King Harold marched his weary men south to try to repel this second invasion in a week. The two sides met in a field on the side of a hill called Senlac near Hastings on 14 October 1066. The Anglo-Saxon army formed a shield wall and held the hill against the Norman cavalry for most of the day, but eventually King Harold's men began to tire. False Norman retreats lured Saxon warriors off the hill in pursuit, which weakened their main army's formation. As the sun waned, the Normans were about to rout their adversary, hailing arrows and breaking the Saxon lines. Though the Battle of Hastings was closely fought, it ended with the death of Harold in battle (by either an arrow to the eye or being cut down) and the defeat and rout of the Anglo-Saxon army.

Shortly after the battle, what was left of the Witan promptly elected the young (about 14) Edgar as king, but it was too little, too late. William fought his way north where he was hastily crowned king in Westminster Abbey on Christmas Day 1066. Edgar and surviving English lords paid homage to William at the coronation – though Edgar was often a thorn in William's side for decades to come. Edgar died in or around 1125, the last member of the House of Wessex and the line of Cerdic.

As anyone who went to an English school will know, the House of Wessex and the rule of the Anglo-Saxons ended in 1066. They did not vanish from the earth, however. Norman rulers, keen to consolidate their claim on England, would marry into the pre-existing royal house. Edgar the Ætheling had briefly been proclaimed King of the English following the Battle of Hastings, but this claim is academic since the Normans were already in control of much of England. The new King William the Conqueror spared him, and Edgar led an interesting life but died with no male issue to claim the Wessex inheritance.

It is also worth noting that many displaced Anglo-Saxon warriors and noblemen chose exile in the wake of the Norman Conquest. The Varangian Guard of Constantinople largely consisted of such men – serving as the elite unit and bodyguard of the emperor. This must have made for an awkward confrontation when Frankish and Norman forces

EDWARD HILARY DAVIS

reached the gates of Constantinople on their way to the First Crusade in the 1090s seeking refuge and sustenance only three decades after the Battle of Hastings.

1b – Bastards

THE HOUSE OF NORMANDY

William I, 1066-1087
William II, 1087-1100
Henry I, 1100-1135
(Stephen of Blois), 1135-1154

Arms of the Duchy of Normandy

W E RIGHTLY CREDIT the Normans for conquering England from 1066 onwards, but as a dynasty, the house of Normandy failed and fizzled out after just two ruling generations, despite William the Conqueror having at least four sons. The Plantagenets on the other hand picked up where the Normans left off and, after a long war of succession, would hold the English crown through eleven generations. That said, the first Plantagenet King of England was himself half Norman.

What do we mean by the House of Normandy? The name naturally comes from the territorial designation of the Dukes of Normandy and relates to those descending in the male line from the Dukes of Normandy (William the Conqueror being the most famous of these). Although Normandy is south of England, etymologically the word Norman derives from 'north-man' – from the north. As the French are nowadays apt to conveniently forget, the Normans were not French. They were Vikings. From around 820 AD Viking warriors (from Scandinavia and Denmark) raided settlements up and down the River Seine. At a similar time, Vikings were raiding and settling in both England and Scotland. Nearly a century later, north-men had formed settlements along the Seine and throughout northern parts of France. Around 911, the King of the West Franks, Charles III (aka Charles the Simple), made an agreement with the leader of these settling north-men, Rollo. The Treaty of Saint-Clair-sur-Epte granted Rollo the lands along the lower Seine, which in point of fact he already controlled. The grant was really a move to appease the growing Viking threat building in the north of France. This grant to Rollo is regarded as the founding of what developed over the proceeding century into the Duchy of Normandy and County of Rouen. Intermarriage between the Franks and the northern settlers followed, and Christianity was quickly adopted by the north-men.

Rollo's descendants developed the duchy into the strongest and most powerful province in France. Though they held the land from the king, they were effectively rulers in their own fiefdom. It was these Norman dukes who helped to place Hugh Capet on the throne of the Franks in 987. The House of Capet, France's ruling family from then until 1789, was indebted to the Normans for their royal position, and the duchy continued to grow in power. As in Danelaw in England, some Viking laws, customs and traditions survived and were observed in Normandy. One such convention was that illegitimacy did not rule out someone from inheriting.

Rollo's three-times-great-grandson, Guillaume/William was the product of a relationship between his father, Robert I, Duke of Normandy, and a local girl, Herleva. The story goes that while at Falaise Castle, Robert looked out and saw Herleva toiling in the fields and noticed that she was stunning. Having caught his eye, Herleva effectively seduced the young duke or was herself seduced. Driven with lust, Duke Robert sent for Herleva to be brought into the castle. She demanded to be brought in through the front gate mounted on a white horse. Robert acquiesced, and in she came in semi-official procession as his concubine. The two did not marry, but nonetheless their son, born in

c. 1028, inherited the duchy becoming William II, Duke of Normandy. He of course is more commonly known by another number (William I) or by another epithet ('the Conqueror'). The other famous epithet often applied to him, 'the Bastard', was not at that time an insult, merely a technicality. In other lands his illegitimacy would have barred him from succeeding but not, at that time, in Normandy.

As any English nine-year-old should (hopefully) be able to tell you, William invaded England, won the Battle of Hastings on 14 October and was crowned king on Christmas Day 1066. He subsequently conquered the rest of England. Unlike his Viking forbears, however, this was not entirely unwarranted – there was a dynastic link between William and the late English king, Edward the Confessor. Edward was, after all, the son of Emma of Normandy. Emma, in turn, was wife to both a Viking king (Cnut) and a Saxon king (Æthelred the Unready) and was also daughter of Richard I, Duke of Normandy. She was, therefore, Duke William's great-aunt, and the sainted King Edward was his first cousin once removed. This fact and an assertion that Edward had promised him the crown while living was the basis of William's claim to England.

After Edward died, the Anglo-Saxon nobleman Harold Godwinson was elected by the Witan to sit on the English throne. Meanwhile, across the Channel, William the Bastard could only look on with rage, supposedly having been promised the succession by the late king. A papal blessing for William's invasion was sought and acquired. Preparations were made, and the rest, as they say, is history. In the interest of time, we will not dwell on the monumental events of 1066. However, three battles and a (possible) arrow in the eye later, a new dynasty sat upon the English throne. William the Conqueror was crowned at Westminster Abbey on Christmas Day. Effectively, he confiscated lands from the Anglo-Saxon nobles and gifted it to his Norman friends (warlords) as well as replaced the key members of the clergy with Norman clerics.

Subduing Newly Won England

William's reign was a steady progress of conquest throughout England. He did have some difficulties in gaining control of certain parts of the country such as East Anglia and the north of England – which led to a series of brutal campaigns, including scorched earth tactics, known as the Harrying of the North in 1069-70. It is possible that up to 75% of the population in some northern areas were either killed or displaced. Many motte-and-bailey castles were built just outside of towns and settlements across England not for the inhabitants' protection but to keep an eye on the disgruntled Anglo-Saxons whom the Normans now found themselves ruling. This (sometimes literal) oversight meant that any militant resistance could be forcibly suppressed if necessary.

One of the most important works during the reign of the Conqueror was the Domesday Book – a great survey of (most of) the lands of England (and parts of Wales) finished in 1086. It documented land; detailed owners and previous owners; recorded ascribed land values; documented manors; and numbered villages, villagers, slaves and live-stock – down to the last pig. Candidly, one could say that William had just acquired a prize (England) and now he wanted to know what it was worth and potentially how much tax he could squeeze out of it.

Whilst the Normans famously brought with them some new sophisticated architecture and building styles, namely their churches and cathedrals, they were less than sophisticated when it came to inheritance and succession. The House of Normandy, like many other royal houses of the time still followed the custom of partible inheritance – which was followed by their Carolingian ancestors on the continent. Partible inheritance is a system of inheritance in which the property is divided (equally or not) among several heirs. Historically, this custom has been responsible for the gradual decline in power of families and states in the early Middle Ages. From the time of Holy Roman Emperor Charlemagne (who ruled a vast empire which included nearly all of France, most of Germany, Belgium, Holland, Switzerland, and

EDWARD HILARY DAVIS

half of Italy), lands had been divided amongst a series of male heirs and sets of brothers. This effectively divided the empire into kingdoms, then princely states, and from there into smaller duchies, counties and fiefdoms. As for William the Conqueror, he had three surviving sons – Robert, William Rufus, and Henry. We cannot be certain of the birth order of these brothers, although most agree on the aforementioned order, and for good or ill, William divided his lands between them.

Rivalry Between Sons

It is not difficult to imagine what the young sons of a bloodthirsty conqueror might have been like – perhaps similar to their father: competitive and quick to rage. Robert is even said to have led an insurrection against his father in response to a nasty prank played upon him by his two brothers. Reportedly, the other two brothers poured the contents of a chamber pot over Robert's head as a joke – which he was less than enthused about. This led to a brawl, for which Robert was reprimanded by his father, while his brothers were not. Upset at that indignity, he gathered some followers and laid siege to one of his father's Norman castles. This failed, and Robert fled in fear of his father's rage. He went into exile in Flanders, where he continued to be a nuisance to his father – although his mother Queen Matilda continued to send him money. Father and son even met in battle in 1079, and Robert actually unhorsed his father in combat. William is said to have cursed his son from that day. The following year, they were reconciled. However, after the death of Matilda, they parted company, and Robert proceeded to travel and have many illegitimate sons. He searched to find a rich heiress but failed.

It is therefore unsurprising that upon his deathbed, William I wanted to disinherit his eldest son. Instead, he was persuaded to adhere to convention and divide his lands among all three of his sons. Robert was to be given Normandy and be its duke, William Rufus was to be King of England, and Henry was to be given a large amount of money (perhaps five thousand pounds) so as to buy or conquer lands of his own.

He was also supposed to be left the small estates held by their mother in Buckinghamshire and Gloucestershire.

Naturally, no one was happy with their slice of the cake. Hoping to be given both Normandy and England, Robert was horrified to find that William Rufus had already raced across the Channel and been crowned William II. Robert consolidated his position in Normandy and prepared to invade England. Henry also stayed in Normandy, which led to William Rufus seizing his land in England.

Henry became a landless prince, but he did have a lot of cash. Robert, struggling in his plans to march on England – armies are expensive – asked his little brother for some financial help. In return, Robert gave Henry land and title in the west of Normandy. However, neither brother trusted the other. Henry was at one point imprisoned by Robert, and William Rufus took the war to Normandy and rescued Henry. From that point, Henry all but threw in his lot with William Rufus's court in England – they even campaigned together in France. The years following their father's death were full of plotting, violence and distrust.

In 1095, Pope Urban II called for the First Crusade. Being some-what gung-ho, Robert hoped to go capture Jerusalem for Christianity, but once again, he did not have the funds. This time it was from William Rufus that he sought help and, perhaps out of religious con-viction, mortgaged the Duchy of Normandy to him. William Rufus was quietly confident that this would mean he would eventually acquire Normandy, but he was also forced to levy very high taxes upon the disgruntled people of England in order to finance Robert's cru-sade endeavor. Meanwhile, as Robert went off to fight for Jerusalem, William Rufus ruled Normandy as regent.

The Convenient Death of William Rufus

It is possible that because of one carefully fired arrow, the succession to the English throne was changed. This was the arrow to King Harold's eye at Hastings (shown in the Bayeux Tapestry). In a twist of fate, another arrow was also destined to forever alter the history of the English throne. In 1100, William Rufus was out hunting in the New Forest with a small party where an 'accident' befell him. According to the Anglo-Saxon Chronicle, he was accidentally shot with an arrow, supposedly by one of his own men Walter Tyrell/Thurold, who seems to have mysteriously fled to France immediately afterwards.

In the context of William Rufus's unpopularity with many of his subjects and the political tensions between the brothers, many have suspected this death to have been an assassination. Certainly, the chroniclers did not miss him. Suspiciously, Henry was amongst the hunting party that day. He and reportedly all the nobles present abandoned William Rufus's body where it fell and dashed to Winchester where the royal treasury was. From there, they made for London, where Henry was hastily crowned just days after the 'accident'. He did not even wait for the archbishops of Canterbury or York to attend.

King Henry I may well have been waiting in the wings for his brothers to fight it out, looking for an opportunity to strike. In the New Forest, William Rufus had been isolated and vulnerable. Robert was away on his travels. The opportunity may have been irresistible. The exact truth of the events around the hunting 'accident' will probably never be known.

It was unfortunate for Robert that he returned to Normandy from the Crusade a month after the incident. By now he had married a wealthy heiress and so managed to raise a force to take on his brother and claim the throne of England for himself – but he did not prevail. After the Battle of Tinchebray in 1106, Robert was captured by Henry and held prisoner in Devizes Castle and later Cardiff Castle until his death in 1134, when he was about eighty-three, just a year before Henry.

HENRY I

King Henry I truly had won the crown from his brothers and earned the right to carry on the Norman dynasty – so many hoped. Reigning from 1100-1135, he had dynastic ideas and ambitions on his mind from the outset. Greatly aware that the Normans were still an alien race enforcing their rule upon the Anglo-Saxons, on becoming king, he decided to marry into the old native aristocracy, like so many Norman barons. He married Matilda of Scotland (formerly christened Edith), who was a member of the old royal family – both English and Scottish. Her parents were King Malcom III of Scotland and (Saint) Margaret of Wessex. She was therefore great-granddaughter of King Edmund Ironside, niece of King Edward the Confessor, and niece of Edgar the Ætheling (the last Saxon proclaimed king during 1066). This was a political marriage. Henry was securing his claim to the throne by aligning his blood with the more ancient and royal blood of the House of Wessex. His hope was that members of his future dynasty and all subsequent Kings of England would be descended both from King Alfred the Great and William the Conqueror (and, bar one, they have been).

The House of Normandy came to an abrupt end due to an accident and an unresolved debate about female rulers. Henry I's son and heir, William Adelin, died in 1120 in the White Ship incident. On a journey from Normandy to England, the ship carrying Prince William, his half sister, and other members of the court and royal family hit a rock and capsized in the English Channel off Barfleur. Prince William, reportedly attempting to save the life of his half-sister, drowned along with nearly all of the other passengers. He was just seventeen and had been married only a year but had no issue. The dynastic hopes of Henry I and the House of Normandy sank to the bottom of the Channel.

There followed a succession crisis. Henry had only one other legitimate child and was unlikely to father another. The trouble was that this child was a woman – Empress Matilda. She was known as the

Empress because her late husband had been the Holy Roman Emperor (Henry V) – though there was no issue. Henry tried to force the barons to accept her as his heir or as regent until she had a son who came of age. The barons were reluctant at best. A woman had never inherited the crown of England before, and her marriage in 1128 to Geoffrey of Anjou, whom the barons rather disliked, did nothing to improve the situation.

Upon the death of Henry I in 1135, the throne of England was once again exposed to a contest. Stephen of Blois, Henry's nephew and a cousin of Empress Matilda's, usurped the crown.

STEPHEN, MATILDA, AND THE ANARCHY

With the support of the church and the people of London (who claimed a loose right to effectively 'elect' the king by popular acclaim), Stephen of Blois became King Stephen. Technically he was not of the House of Normandy. His mother, Adela, was the daughter of William the Conqueror. She had married Count Stephen of Blois; the couple named their third son Stephen. King Stephen was therefore of the House of Blois – a French/Frankish family often more widely associated with being of the County of Champagne and Kingdom of Navarre in France.

Though he was successful, not all the barons and magnates of the kingdom supported King Stephen. Some favoured (formerly Empress) Matilda and her young son Henry. From 1138 there followed a long civil war known as The Anarchy – partly because it caused widespread disorder and a breakdown of law and governance across England. After years of battles and sieges (including a daring escape by Matilda), the war came to an end with the Treaty of Wallingford. Effectively, Stephen could remain as king, but his agreed successor would be Matilda's son, Henry – the next generation.

The House of Normandy disappeared almost as quickly as it appeared. Technically, as a ruling English dynasty, it lasted just two generations. This is not surprising given the family's tendency for violence.

A group of brothers tried to murder each other, and cousins fought long civil wars against each other. With Matilda's son (Henry I's grandson) taking the throne as Henry II in 1154, it must have felt like a victory for the House of Normandy.

Unfortunately, as we know, traditionally one's house (and surname) come from one's father. Henry was from the House of Anjou – but we know it as the House of Plantagenet. That said, he and his successors were to also bear the combined blood of Normandy and that of Wessex.

Henry II, 1154-1189

Richard I, 1189-1199
John, 1199-1216
Henry III, 1216-1272
Edward I, 1272-1307
Edward II, 1307-1327

Edward III, 1327-1377

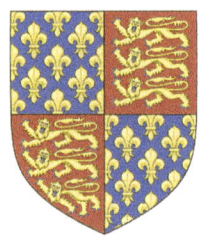

Richard II, 1377-1399

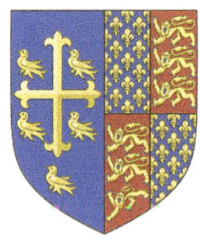

Henry IV, 1399-1413
Henry V, 1413-1422
Henry VI, 1422-1461
Edward IV, 1461-1470
Henry VI, (2nd reign), 1470-1471
Edward IV, (2nd reign), 1471-1483
Edward V, 1483
Richard III, 1483-1485

1c – A Great and Bloody Family

The House of Plantagenet

THE NAME PLANTAGENET evokes a mixture of ideas in the minds of the average Englishman/woman. The Middle Ages, feudalism, battles, cathedrals, Black Death, tournaments, murder, monks, conquest, crusades, castles, chivalry and sheer barbarism – all these are worthy word associations with the family name. Put quite simply, they are the most famous and longest-reigning dynasty to rule England. From 1154 to 1485, the Plantagenets, a family originally from France, governed their newly acquired country and shaped the way it was administered, widened its borders and transformed the monarchy. Many English institutions today were forged or developed in the fulcrum of the Plantagenet premiership.

Despite their French origins, the Plantagenets are also famous for making war and conquests in France – beginning a rivalry between England and its nearest continental neighbour, which arguably lasts to this day. From the Magna Carta to Bosworth Field, the Plantagenet family witnessed four centuries worth of English development, which ultimately ended with the destruction of their house and name in the Wars of the Roses. But where did this name Plantagenet come from, and who are they, and how do they tie in with English history?

ORIGINS OF THE PLANTAGENETS

Most books on the English or British monarchy will tell you that the Plantagenet dynasty was 'founded' by Geoffrey, Count of Anjou (1113-1151), husband of Matilda and father of King Henry II. However, that far back in European history, surnames were not yet used in a way that we would recognise, and furthermore, Plantagenet was not his real name but a nickname or epithet. Reportedly, Geoffrey often wore a sprig of common broom blossom in his hat. The Latin name for broom shrub is *planta genista* and is *plante genêt* in French – sometimes written: *plantegenet*. From here, the nickname Plantagenet is thought to have been coined. It is doubtful that he ever thought that the dynasty he was founding would be known by this name for centuries to come.

Geoffrey was the eldest son of King Fulk of Jerusalem, who had been the Count of Anjou, a prosperous county in France. In a typically dynastic marriage, Fulk had married Geoffrey's mother the heiress Ermengarde of Maine in 1110, which brought Maine into the control of Anjou. She later abandoned the family to run off with the King of France (Philip I), whom she bigamously married. Ermengarde died in 1126. The following year, Fulk received an embassy from King Baldwin II of Jerusalem. Jerusalem had been captured for Christianity in the First Crusade earlier in 1099. Since then, the Western European Christians (Franks) had set up a series of small states in the Holy Land with the Kingdom of Jerusalem being the most important. Baldwin had no male heirs and was concerned for the succession of his daughter Melisende. He wanted her to marry a powerful lord to solidify her succession. Fulk was an already experienced crusader warrior and successful leader and governor – a perfect candidate for the job. Such an opportunity was too great for Fulk to pass up. It was agreed that Fulk would reign as king alongside Melisende – not as just as a consort. The couple were wed on 2 June 1129, and Fulk became King of Jerusalem. He resigned his French title and lands as Count of Anjou and passed these to his son Geoffrey.

Arguably, the House of Plantagenet is actually the House of Anjou. The House of Anjou itself was a branch of another Frankish family known as Anjou-Châteaudun. Geoffrey Plantagenet's fifth great-grandfather was Gauzfred I, Viscount of Châteaudun (who died after 986). This house branched into several collateral noble French houses and

Kings of Jerusalem, but the longest-lasting and most prominent of these was the House of Plantagenet.

GEOFFREY AND JERUSALEM

Geoffrey (Plantagenet), Count of Anjou, like his father King Fulk, was given a stifling marriage opportunity. King Henry I of England (also Duke of Normandy) was in a constant power struggle with King Louis VI of France. Although Fulk initially supported his French king and overlord, he eventually sided with Henry. To cement their new alliance, King Henry arranged for his son and heir, William Adelin, to marry Fulk's daughter, Matilda – by then already a widowed Empress. However, Prince William's death in the White Ship tragedy in 1120 resulted in years of turmoil around the English succession, which came to be known as The Anarchy.

The treaty between England and the House of Anjou seemed broken. King Henry I no longer had any male heirs. The future of England looked uncertain. Like King Baldwin, Henry did not want his line to end. He wanted his daughter Empress Matilda to inherit the throne and rule, but for that she needed a strong and powerful husband as an ally and protector. Once again, the House of Anjou was ready to oblige. Their lands south of Normandy would shore up the borders of Henry's domains in France.

Geoffrey – son of Fulk, (then) Count of Anjou – was tall, strong, redheaded and handsome. However, Matilda was reportedly unimpressed. She was the widow of the Holy Roman Emperor and liked to go by her title of Empress; marrying the son of a count seemed a great demotion. Also, she was twenty-five, and he was thirteen. Nonetheless she agreed to the engagement, and the pair were married on 17 June 1128 in Le Mans. A year later Geoffrey's father left to become king in Jerusalem, which meant Geoffrey inherited the country, and Matilda was no doubt more satisfied with being married to a son of a king!

A Disputed Succession

Henry I had previously made his barons swear an oath to support his daughter's claim to the English throne and those of her legitimate heirs. However, promises are often broken. Matilda's cousin, Stephen of Blois – another grandchild of William the Conqueror – steadily positioned himself and members of his side of the family to take the crown following the king's death. Matilda gave birth to a son, which she named after her father. He would be the first English king from the House of Anjou (Plantagenet) – she hoped. All did not go to plan though. When King Henry I died in 1135, Stephen travelled quickly to London where he was proclaimed king and recognised as the Duke of Normandy. (The people/crowds of London at that time had a widely held, though misguided, belief that they had the right to 'elect' the King of England. In point of fact, English kings were and have been made by proclamation.) In this case, it was likely an easy choice as far as some barons were concerned: a young mother and her babe of two years or Stephen – a man in his prime with title and estates and a decent claim to the throne.

Stephen was the son of Stephen-Henry, Count of Blois, and his wife was Adela of Normandy, daughter of William the Conqueror. As the fourth son, he was not likely to inherit the bulk of his father's lands, but he was resourceful enough to acquire lands of his own via marriage, but this marriage may have had a dual purpose. He married Matilda (yet another one) of Boulogne in 1125. She was a great heiress – her father was Eustace, Count of Boulogne. She and Stephen would go on to jointly rule the county of Boulogne. However, she also possessed Anglo-Saxon royal blood which was equally valuable to Stephen.

Since the conquest, Norman warriors and barons had on many occasions married women from the pre-existing local Anglo-Saxon elite families in order to give their own presence in England some legitimacy and perhaps to curry favour and consent from the local population. King Henry I had even done this when he married Matilda of Scotland just months after clearing his way through his brothers to become King of

England in 1100. Matilda was the daughter of Margaret of Wessex, who was of the house and line of Wessex; niece to Edgar the Ætheling, arguably the last Anglo-Saxon monarch; and thus a descendant of Alfred the Great, King of the Anglo-Saxons. As the Anglo-Saxon monarchy was fairly recently defunct, this union with Matilda was a useful tool in cementing Henry's position as King of England. Similar unions were formed by many lesser Normans in their own English lands. Stephen, likely seeing a possible opportunity for himself in the impending succession crisis, followed suit. His wife (Matilda of Boulogne) was Matilda of Scotland's niece and a descendant of the Anglo-Saxon kings Edmund Ironside and Alfred the Great.

In the wars of succession following the death of Henry I, Stephen's forces battled Empress Matilda's supporting armies up and down the country from Lincoln to Arundel and more besides. The Anarchy (as the Victorians called it) lasted from 1138-1153, and there are libraries full of books on this dangerous time, which we will not expand on here. Hostilities were only terminated when Stephen conceded and designated Geoffrey and Matilda's son Henry as his heir in the Treaty of Wallingford. The following year Stephen died, and Henry Plantagenet succeeded as King of England – Henry II.

How right it was that the new royal dynasty was born out of war between cousins. It would end that way too.

HENRY II, FIRST PLANTAGENET KING

The new man at the helm of governance in the realm was not really known by the name Plantagenet. He went by a variety of other names before being Henry II. He was also called Henry Curtmantle (short-cloak) – probably because he was quite tall, which meant many cloaks would look short on him; Henry FitzEmpress – after his mother's title; and to a lesser degree, Henry of Anjou – as Count of Anjou and Maine.

Keeping the family tradition of advantageous marriages alive for a third generation, Henry married Eleanor of Aquitaine, one of Europe's greatest heiresses. At the height of Henry's power, combining her lands with his, he ruled (or laid claim over) all England and about half of France (viz: the Duchies of Aquitaine, Normandy and Brittany along with the counties of Maine, Touraine and Anjou). From the Pyrenees to the Scottish Borders, Henry ruled an empire which was not called the Plantagenet Empire but the Angevin Empire, named after his house – the House of Anjou. Later historians renamed the dynasty.

Henry II established the dynasty at the height of its territory. For several generations after him, future Plantagenet rulers sought to keep or acquire these lands in France by war or by ancestral claim. Not all were successful.

A Tradition of Dividing Empires

At this point in Western European culture, the concept of absolute male preference primogeniture had not yet taken hold. Since the time of Charlemagne, empires had been built up by one generation and then divided amongst the next through partible inheritance. Henry, long before his death, proclaimed he would follow tradition and divide his empire between his four sons: Henry, Richard, Geoffrey, and John.

His eldest son would receive the prime cut of England, Normandy and Anjou. Richard would be Duke of Aquitaine, and Geoffrey would be Duke of Brittany. There was no land yet for his infant son, John, (but Henry had aspirations of conquering Ireland for him). These promises may have been a mistake.

The impatient princes, hungry for more than what each had been promised, used force to battle each other and their father for dominion over the Angevin Empire. Son(s) fought father in open battle. Finally, in 1189 Henry II was defeated in battle by his son Richard, who was allied to the King of France. He retired to Chinon Castle in Anjou, enraged by the betrayal of all of his sons. He died later that year, having been predeceased by his eldest son, 'the Young King Henry'.

Richard the Lionheart and His Crusades

Henry II was succeeded by second son, Richard I 'the Lionheart' or 'Cœur de Lion'. Richard is famous as a crusader and warrior, not as a particularly effective King of England. During his ten-year reign (1189-1199), he spent perhaps as little as six months on English soil. For Richard, England was the means to fund his crusades, make a name for himself as a great Christian warrior, and perhaps retake the Holy Land.

The Kingdom of Jerusalem had lasted less than a century as the Holy Land had been lost to the Ayyubid Sultan, Saladin, in 1187. Its capture prompted the Third Crusade led by Richard and King Philip Augustus of France. Richard taxed and tithed England heavily to pay for Jerusalem's recapture.

When war, violence, and massacre failed him, Richard tried diplomacy in order to retake the Holy Land. He even attempted to get his sister Joan or his niece Eleanor to marry Saladin's brother Al-Adil as part of the negotiations. The Plantagenet line mingling with the line of Mohamed would certainly have been interesting, but of course it was inconceivable. Ultimately, though Richard had won many battles, he could not retake the prize, Jerusalem, and he journeyed back through Europe.

On his way to his French lands, Richard was captured by Leopold, Duke of Austria. Richard had offended him at Acre by casting down Leopold's banner into the moat as he had been flying it alongside the banners of the Kings of England and France – like and equal! Leopold never forgot it.

The captive Richard was later handed over to the Holy Roman Emperor, who demanded a huge ransom from England – two or three times the Crown's annual income. Under Richard's mother, Eleanor of Aquitaine, England was then taxed even more to pay the ransom. After his release, Richard continued to spend large sums of English money on castles defending his lands in France. Then, while laying siege to the Castle of Châlus-Chabrol in Limousin, he was shot with a crossbow by a mere boy, who had until then been defending the ramparts using a frying pan as his shield. Having forgiven the boy (whose name is uncertain), Richard died of his wound, which went gangrenous.

Though he did marry, Richard had no children. Historians of the late 20th century have speculated that he may have been homosexual, which seems unlikely given his militant faith. In actuality, Richard probably had at least one illegitimate son, Philip of Cognac.

Given that Richard was an absent King of England and mostly used the country's people to fund holy wars and defend his French lands, it is not surprising that he is the only Angevin/Plantagenet king not to be known by his English regnal number but by his epithet. The only other such English kings are the Anglo-Saxons and William the Conqueror. However, one of Richard's lasting contributions to the Plantagenet dynasty and to England was the royal coat of arms. We are all familiar with the three gold lions passant guardant on a red field. These first appear in use as the royal arms on Richard's second Great Seal (1198). (His previous seal had two lions facing each other or just one lion.)

Heraldry was in its infancy at this time and was quickly developing customs which would later become laws of arms and badges of the nobility and knightly classes. It is thought that Richard may well have designed these arms himself, perhaps modifying a previous design used by his father. One later interpretation was that two lions had oft been the symbol for the Dukes of Normandy and that Richard had added another lion representing the Duchy of Aquitaine. More simply, it could just be three as a reflection of his crusader faith – three for the Trinity. Nevertheless, the three lions have been the primary royal arms of England ever since and remain in the monarch's coat of arms to this day. The royal arms have inspired national sports kits as well as a chart-topping football anthem.

KING JOHN

Richard was succeeded by his last surviving brother, John, in 1199. It was the only time a Plantagenet brother would succeed to the throne. (Richard III being a debatable exception centuries later.) John is known as one of the worst or least successful Kings of England; perhaps that is why there has never been a John II. Popular culture has long cast him as the villain in various Robin Hood stories. John was not a warrior like his brother but was a meticulous, even petty, administrator, but he – like Richard – taxed England heavily, this time to pay for wars with the French king.

The royal house of France had grown in strength and was beginning to take back much of the lands of the Angevin Empire on the battle-field. It had recently acquired Normandy and Anjou – the ancestral lands of the House of Plantagenet.

John, like his father, fell out with the church over church property and the appointment of bishops. This led to his excommunication and an interdiction on the whole of the kingdom: Mass would not be said; baptisms, weddings and funeral rights would not take place. Naturally this made John unpopular with the barons and the people alike. Militant resistance to his rule was inevitable. Subsequently, at Runnymede near Windsor, John was effectively forced to sign the Magna Carta, which addressed the complaints of the barons but also focused on the rights of free men and put limits on the king's power. (John's legacy endures in this way: parts of the document are regarded in the modern era as one of the founding cornerstones of intentionally recognised human rights.) However, despite the document, war between John and the barons con-tinued. It is doubtful that he took the Magna Carta seriously or that the barons were seriously able to implement it, despite its ambitions.

Prince Louis Makes a Bid for the Throne

In their struggle to be rid of John, the barons considered replacing the Plantagenet line altogether. While John was marching north against Alexander II of Scotland (who had allied himself to the rebels), the bar-ons invited Prince Louis, son of King Philip II of France, to invade and take the English throne with their support. This was not as bizarre as one might think. Louis's wife – Blanche of Castile – was a granddaughter of

Henry II and Eleanor of Aquitaine. The barons were merely switching between cousins (in-law). That said, this would mean the end of the ruling House of Plantagenet/Anjou and the beginning of the reign of the House of Capet in England (as well as France).

Louis landed with an army on the Isle of Thanet, Kent, unopposed on 21 May 1216. He marched to London where he was proclaimed king at St Paul's amid celebrating crowds. The English barons paid homage to him. A month later, after capturing key cities such as Winchester, Louis controlled over half of the kingdom. It seemed that the writing was on the wall for the Plantagenets.

However, John fortuitously died later that year, saving his dynasty. With John out of the way and his nine-year-old son, Henry, set to inherit the kingdom, there suddenly seemed no need for Louis; many barons deserted him in favour of the Plantagenet boy who was under the protection and control of William the Marshal – one of England's greatest knights. Louis was eventually defeated on land at Lincoln and at sea near Sandwich in 1217. In the Treaty of Lambeth (1217), Louis was paid off in return for a promise never to attack England again. The House of Plantagenet/Anjou survived by a whisker in the form of John's young son – Henry III. Louis returned to France where he succeeded as King Louis VIII upon the death of his father in 1223.

HENRY III AND EDWARD I

From Henry III onwards, succession to the English throne would pass from father to son (or grandson) through the next five generations of Plantagenets. Though there was rebellion under Henry III in the guise of Simon de Montfort and the Provisions of Oxford, replacing the ruling English dynasty with an alternative one was not an idea that materialised.

Henry III passed his crown reasonably seamlessly to his son and heir, Edward I, who at that time was on crusade in the Holy Land. It is a testament to the integrity of the monarchy and the strength of the House of Plantagenet that, despite being a world away, the succession of Edward I was not challenged or contested. The new King Edward I was a proven warrior. As a prince, he had survived battles and defeated rebels at home. Abroad, he had narrowly avoided assassination by killing the would-be assassin himself. Edward I's reign was marked by the conquest of Wales, the expulsion of the Jews from England, and the near conquest of Scotland. Known as Edward Longshanks for his height, his real epithet became the Hammer of the Scots: *'Malleus Scotorum'* – which is engraved as the only decoration on his tomb.

During his 'dealings' with Scotland, Edward captured the ancient Stone of Scone or 'Stone of Destiny' – allegedly the stone upon which all Kings of Scots had been crowned. Taking it back to Westminster, he commissioned a special chair to house the stone. He named the chair after his namesake and the then patron saint of England, St Edward the Confessor. From then on, all Kings of England would be crowned sitting above the stone. The stone has been kept at Edinburgh Castle since 1996 on the proviso that it is returned for future coronations.

Edward I died in 1307, rather characteristically, during a march north to deal with Scottish rebels.

Edward II

Edward's son and heir shared his name but evidently none of his leadership or warrior qualities. Edward II continued the wars in Scotland but eventually failed in the face of King Robert the Bruce. The hope of conquering Scotland was subsequently put to bed, and the defeat at Bannockburn was followed by a great famine throughout the kingdom.

Wars with France had been starting and ending constantly for decades. In an effort to put an end to this, a year after becoming king, Edward married Isabella, daughter of King Philip IV of France. This marriage would later come to have great consequences for the House of Plantagenet.

At court, the young King Edward II had favourites, most notably Piers Gaveston and later Hugh Despencer the Younger. Authors and historians from then to the present have speculated that Edward and Gaveston were lovers. In a military society, such a relationship made Edward very unpopular with his courtiers who detested his rank favouritism and alleged flirtations. Eventually the resentment spilled over into internal war in England.

Edward's wife, Isabella of France, couldn't tolerate Despencer and, during a diplomatic mission to her homeland, allied herself instead with Roger, Lord Mortimer – with whom she may have been having an affair. Mortimer and Isabella returned to England with an army in 1326. Edward's allies and barons deserted him, and he was captured.

With her husband imprisoned, Isabella made herself regent. Since she had given the king two sons, Edward was forced to relinquish his crown in 1327 in favour of their eldest son, who was fourteen. Isabella would reign as regent until he came of age. Edward II was then moved to Berkeley Castle to be kept under guard by Mortimer's son-in-law, Thomas de Berkeley. For the new regime, however, it was dangerous to keep Edward alive. Then, a few months later he was dead (or at least gone). Some accounts state that not only was he murdered, but that a funnel was put into his fundament and a red-hot poker inserted into his anus. This may or may not be true, and the story may well be a response to his possible homosexuality. There is other evidence (from a letter to his son) that indicates that Edward actually escaped and became a hermit on the continent. Whatever the actual truth, as with all popular tales, the bloodiest story has long been the accepted version of events.

EDWARD III

The wheel came full circle in 1330. As he reached 18 years old, the new young king Edward III reclaimed control of the kingdom for the House of Plantagenet. At a gathering of Parliament at Nottingham Castle, the young Edward and his companions seized Mortimer and Isabella. Mortimer was tried and executed for treason at Tyburn, and Isabella was imprisoned (for a couple of years). The new monarch would become one of the most celebrated Plantagenet rulers, reviving and popularising one of England's favourite past times – annoying the French!

Because of the way feudalism (or feudal tenure) works, the young Edward III had previously paid homage to King Philip VI for the vast lands he held there as Duke of Aquitaine. Though this was relatively humbling, Edward was happy to do it – for now. The wine trade through Bordeaux from English-held Aquitaine and Gascony was highly profitable to the English Crown – indeed the Gascons preferred their association with the King of England rather than the King of France, who would only meddle in their trade. However, as the years went on, King Philip harassed the English possessions in south-west France and began to align himself with local lords in anticipation of war with England. Philip eventually attempted to confiscate Edwards's lands in Gascony – which did lead to war. Gascony is a long way from England; the Plantagenet forces would have to invade from the north and hope that the garrisons in the south could hold out against the royal French forces. But Edward had a trump card in his back pocket, which he now played.

Claim to the French Throne

Philip VI had only succeeded to the French throne because the male line of his uncle, King Philip IV, had died out over twelve years His sons Louis X, Philip V and Charles IV had died one after another, with none of the brothers leaving surviving sons of their own (that lived to adulthood). However, their sister was Isabella, Edward III's mother. According to English law/custom, that would make Edward III the rightful successor to the dead brothers. (The precedent for such a thing was set with Matilda and her son Henry II following The Anarchy.) At the time, however, such a notion was inconceivable in France, who followed a form of Salic law – no woman could inherit – which would disqualify Isabella and subsequently Edward from inheriting the crown. Also, politically speaking, it was impossible that Edward should inherit France.

However, as Shakespeare pointed out in his play Henry V, Salic law was a grey area as it referred to a land that no longer existed and whose borders were not widely comprehended. Laid down around 500 AD by Clovis, King of the Franks and founder of the Merovingian dynasty, the law was an ancient Frankish civil law code, which dictated the succession to the Frankish and later French throne. It effectively forbade any female succession whatsoever – which actually strongly contrasted with most other European monarchies at that time. Shakespeare's argument was that the land Salic was actually now part of Germany, so the male-only succession law didn't apply to France. This is erroneous, as the Salian Franks settled on the western banks of the Rhine and later the Scheldt in what can today be described as the Flemish region, which was at this point under the power of France. (That said, the Salian Franks did probably originate from further east – but that was centuries before Salic law was drafted). However, when Philip VI succeeded to the throne in 1328, Salic law had widely been forgotten and was not specifically mentioned. It was Edward who resurrected it for his own political purposes.

Needless to say, this legal grey area, and the fact that Edward III was a grandson of the King of France (Philip IV) and married to Philip VI's niece, put the English king in a strong position to claim and challenge the French succession. Which he did in 1340, declaring himself both King of England and rightful King of France. At the outset of Edward III's reign, he had not troubled himself with the French succession, originally accepting it. However, it was arguably Philip VI of France's attempt to confiscate the long-held English possession of Gascony that then made Edward press his claim to the French throne.

Some have argued that this claim was merely a political weapon used against Philip and that the main serious objective was to get Gascony back as well as some other former English possessions in France. Nevertheless, if it were not a serious claim, so much effort would not have been taken to perpetuate it. Aside from the military and economic wars that came as a consequence, subsequent English kings would keep and use the title of King of France (amongst their many other titles) and quarter the arms of France (many fleurs-de-lys) with those of England (the three lions of Plantagenet). In future centuries, despite the changes of ruling dynasties in England (viz: Plantagenet, Tudor, Stuart, Orange, Stuart, Hanover), English monarchs continued to claim to be titular King of France until the reign of George III in 1801. By that time, France had become a republic. George III dropped both the title and the use of the fleurs-de-lys, and Britain formally recognised the French Republic in the Treaty of Amiens in 1802.

Edward's claim to the French throne was the beginning of what became known in later centuries as the Hundred Years War. The name is incorrect for three reasons. Firstly, it did not last 100 years – it was over 116 years. Secondly, it can be argued that it continued as far as 1801-02 (when the Kings of England finally gave up their claim to also being Kings of France). Thirdly, not all medieval battles and campaigns are easily connected. There were several and complicated reasons for them – economic and political, not just dynastic. There were also many pauses and peace treaties between periods of hostilities. Most of the time it was impossible to conceive of how the English would win or what a complete English victory would look like. Total dominion over France? A difficult thing to achieve.

Broadly speaking, our collective English knowledge of the Hundred Years War is punctuated by gloriously bloody battles such as Crecy, Poitiers, and Agincourt, but these are just a few of many battles. We seem to only remember the victories, forgetting the defeats – and the fact that England eventually lost the war completely, losing all its possessions in France by the mid-sixteenth century. It would be easy to digress here into the many stories and battles of the Hundred Years War, but we must only concern ourselves with the dynastic succession of the Plantagenets.

THE BLACK PRINCE

Edward III had proved during his long reign that he was an excellent tactician and commander on the battlefield. As luck would have it, and contrary to Plantagenet tradition so far, so was his son and heir. His son, also Edward, Prince of Wales, was known as the Black Prince. This was likely because of the black armour or shield he took to battle and to jousts but perhaps also because he was devilish in combat or on the field of battle. His time is often thought of as the peak or height of chivalry or the chivalric code.

The English succession had never been so strong or so promising. For not only did Edward III have many able sons, but the Black Prince was a natural-born leader and commander. His greatest victory in the war against the French was at Poitiers (1356), where he captured the French King John II (son and successor to Philip VI) and took him back to England, where he was held as a prisoner. The eventual ransom arranged was three million crowns to be paid to England, and France would cede Edward III a third of western France. Not since Henry II had a King of England looked so powerful. (Ten years prior to Poitiers, King David II of Scotland had also been defeated and taken prisoner in England for eleven years. His ransom was far less, and he struggled to pay it all, even offering his kingdom to Edward instead.)

Edward the Black Prince did not marry a foreign princess but instead married his half-first-cousin once removed, Joan, Countess of Kent. She was also a Plantagenet. Her father, Edmund of Woodstock, was a younger son of King Edward I but by his second wife Margaret of France (daughter of Philip III of France) – making Joan and the Black Prince also related through their French families. They were technically within the prohibited degrees of consanguinity accepted by custom at that time, but a special dispensation was granted by Pope Innocent VI, owing to their close relationship, which allowed the two to eventually marry in 1361. The couple spent the next decade ruling their English Principality of Aquitaine. Their firstborn, another Edward (of

Angouleme), died at age five in 1370. Their second son, born in 1367, was named Richard after the Lion Heart.

Edward the Black Prince was one of the great 'what-ifs' of English history. Had he not contracted dysentery and died what can be assumed to have been a fairly unpleasant death, much might have been different. As many have stated, he was perhaps the best medieval monarch we never had. Like his father, Edward III, and his grandfather, Edward I, he was a born leader, a natural military commander and exceptional tactician. He was everything the royal family, nobility and people of England would want in a monarch. Strong, warlike, wise, devout and generous. His reign was arguably the pinnacle of chivalry in England (and also France). He was aware for some time that he was dying and so gave generously to churches, good causes and his servants. Edward the Black Prince of Wales died in 1376 at Westminster at age forty-five – only one year before his father the King.

KING RICHARD II

Upon the death of King Edward III, the hopes of the House of Plantagenet came to rest on his very young grandson, Richard II. Richard's reign was highlighted by ostentatiousness, revolution, rebellion, harsh suppression and his eventual capture and usurpation by a cousin.

King Richard II succeeded his grandfather, Edward III, in 1377 who had died aged sixty-four. Richard was only ten years old, so naturally he was helped by his several uncles. Initially, regency roles were performed by John of Gaunt (Duke of Lancaster) and Thomas of Woodstock (Duke of Gloucester); however, owing to a heady cocktail of the Black Death, a population decrease and a shortage of labourers together with the continuation of the wars in France and the taxes to pay for them, the Peasants' Revolt was the first major event of Richard's reign. In the face of the carnage and murder of officials in East Anglia, in London and elsewhere, the boy King Richard showed great bravery and promise as he rode to meet the rebel peasant army at Smithfield.

A famous scuffle took place between Watt Tyler and the Mayor of London, William Walworth, during which the rude and bawdy Tyler was slain. The outraged rebels may have been preparing to charge, but the young Richard II rode out alone before the rebel army to calm them, declaring himself to be their captain now! They were awestruck at the brave and youthful king. They were submissive, and Richard peacefully led them from the fields and granted them clemency (though many were slaughtered later).

Witnessing his own power at Smithfield at such a young age, must have confirmed in Richard's mind his divine right to rule over his people and the right of the royal prerogative – the near absolute power of the Crown. Unlike his grandfather, he was not warlike and preferred to restrain the power of the nobles. He focused his court's attention on art and culture, which elevated him to almost godlike ceremonial status. It is during this time that Geoffrey Chaucer came of note, Westminster Hall's impressive hammer beam roof was constructed, and the handkerchief invented. Richard is credited with its creation. His grandfather is famous for the Battle of Crecy, his father – the Battle of Poitiers; but Richard had the dainty handkerchief. We can't all be like our fathers!

Power and Royal Favorites

Richard II's reign depended on a small number of retainers and particular favourites, such as Robert De Vere, 9th Earl of Oxford. Richard and his favourites became unpopular, and soon the government was taken over by the Lords Appellant – effectively an angry group of nobles. Richard did regain control but ruled rather tyrannically afterwards.

In rash retribution for the takeover, in 1399 Richard disinherited and exiled his cousin Henry Bolingbroke – John of Gaunt's son – to France. In return, Henry invaded England with his own force, determined to reclaim his birthright, namely, the lucrative Duchy of Lancaster. Few were prepared to defend Richard, and Henry met little opposition. Henry captured the childless Richard and had him imprisoned. Eventually, having re-established himself as the Duke of Lancaster, it was all too easy for Henry, who had the support of much of the nobility, to simply depose Richard and have himself crowned king at Westminster, which he did in October 1399. (Incidentally, it may have been the first time since 1066 that the monarch made an address in English.)

Richard is presumed to have been starved to death in captivity at Pontefract Castle in Yorkshire. His body was displayed in London to prove he was indeed dead. Henry ordained that his Duchy of Lancaster would never again be parted from the Crown – as is the case to this day. The monarch of England is also the Duke of Lancaster.

The Wars of the Roses

Henry's succession as Henry IV is one of the causes of the Wars of the Roses – the term often used to denote the war between the Houses of York and Lancaster. York and Lancaster, in this case, do not refer to those cities of England but only to the principal titles of these two branches of the royal family and their subsequent descendants (Duke of York and Duke of Lancaster). Both these branches are descendants of Edward III. In their own time, these wars were just known as the civil wars. Historians began to rename them around 1727 – with Bevil Higgons and David Hume recounting a 'quarrel between roses'. As any English eleven-year-old should be able to tell you, the roses refer to the different heraldic badges used by the York and Lancaster families – white and red respectively. During these wars, the English crown switched a handful of times between the opposing sides.

It is difficult, in a single chapter, to convey all the complexities of the Wars of the Roses, which was effectively a dynastic war between generations of cousins. Nonetheless, in the interest of showing the chronology of the passage of the crown, we must try, albeit in a succinct way, to give an overview.

The Plantagenet cousins' battle royal did not begin immediately following Henry's usurpation of Richard's throne. During his reign,

Henry IV sought to make amends for the indulgent and tyrannical reign of Richard II. However, this was met with rebellions: first from nobles and relatives seeking to reinstate Richard, then from Owain Glyndŵr in Wales, and later from Henry 'Hotspur' Percy in the north. Henry succeeded in putting these rebellions down. Interestingly, Glyndŵr had received aid during his revolt from a certain Anglesey-based family – called Tudur/Tudor. More on them later. Needless to say, much, if not most, of this first Lancastrian king's reign was spent putting out fires of rebellion in many parts of the land. Henry IV died a feared king (not a loved one) in 1413 in the Jerusalem chamber of the Abbot's House at Westminster after a long illness. His crown passed to his eldest son, Henry of Monmouth – Henry V (of Agincourt fame).

Roger and Edmund Mortimer

Henry IV's rule was cause for some dissatisfaction because, regardless of his usurpation and probable murder of his cousin Richard II, he was not in fact the next in line for the throne. True, Richard II had no children, but he had several uncles, all of whom were sons of Edward III. Henry's father had been John of Gaunt, who was only the third son of Edward III. The second son was Lionel, Duke of Clarence. Lionel had only a daughter, Philippa. She had a son, Roger Mortimer. During King Richard's reign, Roger was the heir presumptive by dint of the English custom of male preference primogeniture. This meant that, if one followed the logic of the Plantagenet claim to the throne of France, and the succession of Henry through his mother (Empress) Matilda, Roger had the primary claim to the English throne after Richard's death.

Roger spent much of his time in Ireland. He inherited the Earldom of March from his father and the Earldom of Ulster (in Ireland) from his mother. He cemented his connection to the royal family by marrying King Richard's half-niece, Eleanor Holland. Roger died in 1398, two years before Richard II and only a year before his downfall. Roger's son, Edmund Mortimer (5th Earl of March, 7th Earl of Ulster), was barely eight when Richard was overthrown. He was also, conveniently for Henry IV, over the water in Ireland. Any claim Edmund had on the English crown was quietly disregarded for a short time – though it was not altogether unnoticed. Besides, Edmund was merely a Mortimer; Henry, although a usurper, was at least a Plantagenet.

Edmund's claim was eventually used in 1402 by his uncle and namesake, *Sir* Edmund Mortimer in 1402. Sir Edmund, fighting on the king's side against Owain Glyndŵr, was captured at the Battle of Bryn Glas. Henry, perhaps smelling a chance to get rid of a potential dynastic rival, refused to send ransom money. He accused Sir Edmund of deserting and confiscated his lands. In retaliation, Sir Edmund married Glyndŵr's daughter and proclaimed his nephew, Edmund, the true heir of Richard II.

To add to the plight of Henry IV, Sir Edmund's sister was married to Henry 'Hotspur' Percy – who stirred up rebellion in the north but was defeated and slain at the Battle of Shrewsbury in 1403.

King Henry VI had secured young Edmund at Windsor Castle. His uncle and Glyndŵr attempted to rescue Edmund and initially succeeded in retrieving the boy, but he was recaptured. Also implicated in this plot was Edward, 2nd Duke of York – who was son of Edmund of Langley, the fourth son of King Edward III. His wife, the Duchess of York was briefly imprisoned for her part in the plot. This was not the first time the Yorks would attempt to meddle with the Mortimers. After this failed attempt at rescue, Edmund and his little brother were moved to Pevensey Castle and kept under close guard where they remained for the rest of King Henry's reign.

Henry V succeeded his father Henry IV in 1413. Perhaps out of Christian charity, he set Edmund Mortimer at liberty. Surprisingly, despite having a genuinely senior claim on the crown, Edmund seems to have been loyal to Henry throughout his career. So much so that, during the king's preparations for an invasion of France as part of the

Agincourt campaign, Edmund exposed a plot, which would have actually been to his own advantage. Richard, Earl of Cambridge (son of Edmund of Langley and husband to Edmund Mortimer's sister, Anne), had plotted with fellow relations, Lord Scrope of Masham and Sir Thomas Grey, to take Edmund Mortimer (Earl of March) to Wales and declare him king. This plan backfired when Edmund was made aware of the plan and informed the king. The three conspirators were executed in Southampton.

Edmund Mortimer then loyally went to France with Henry's army, as did Edward, 2nd Duke of York – brother of the executed Cambridge. Conveniently for Henry, Edward of York was killed during the Battle of Agincourt in 1415, thinning out the rival bloodstock.

Victory in France

Henry V's victory at Agincourt was monumental. Against fearful odds, which Shakespeare ambitiously described as five to one, a small English force, mainly consisting of archers, stood victorious against the full might of the French noble and knightly mounted cavalry. Such a victory was seen by both sides as a favour from God and would have political consequences. By warring with the old enemy, France, instead of with rival family factions, he had united much support behind him and as well secured the greatest gain of all, succession to the French throne. This silenced rival claims in England for a time.

At the treaty of Troyes in 1420, it was agreed that Henry would marry the daughter of the mad King Charles VI of France (Catherine of Valois) and that Henry and his heirs would succeed him. England and France were to be one kingdom united. Henry had achieved what his great-grandfather, Edward III, could only have dreamed of. The dynastic question of succession to the throne of France seemed to be settled. There was hope that the Hundred Years War was now won and that the civil wars (Wars of the Roses) were also over. It was not to be.

The Hundred Years War Continues

Sadly for the English, Henry didn't live long enough to inherit his French crown. He died in August 1422, just two months before the mad Charles VI. His death therefore resulted in a succession crisis in France. From the treaties (and the English perspective), the lawful heir to both kingdoms was Henry and Catherine's son, Henry VI – who was an infant. French factions of course favoured the mad king's son who was also called Charles (VII). Young King Henry VI had succeeded as King of England at age nine months and as King of France at only eleven months. Charles was a man of nearly twenty.

To cut a very complex period of history short, there was a struggle for control of France. English occupation was limited to the northern parts of France, while much of the south was disputed. Major third parties, such as the Dukes of Burgundy, often tipped the scales in favour of the English – whose claim on France was often enforced through military occupation. It was during this time that the mysterious Joan of Arc made her appearance as a saintly mascot for the French army. With Charles's blessing, she led his armies to lift the siege at Orleans and accomplish other strategic objectives along the Loire River, especially at the Battle of Patay in 1429.

The French managed to secure the town of Rheims (which was the traditional place Kings of France had been crowned) and held a coronation for Charles VII later that year. The English had planned to wait for Henry VI to be older before he was crowned but, in response to the French, he was crowned at Notre-Dame de Paris in 1431 at the age of ten. He was the only King of England to also be physically crowned King of France. It is often thought that this was the last time an English monarch made an official visit to Paris until Queen Victoria's state visit in 1855.

There were two kings in France, power politics were at play in the region, and young King Henry had several men ruling in his place during his minority. Most of the power lay with his uncles: John, Duke of

Bedford, and Humphrey, Duke of Gloucester. They oversaw the governing of France (the occupied territories) and England on the boy's behalf.

However, the succession crisis in France deepened – only the English, the Burgundians, and the allied-controlled lands north of the Loire accepted Henry as king. The English only maintained control through their network of allies, and when the most important of these, Philip, Duke of Burgundy, effectively switched sides and recognised Charles VII as the rightful King of France, it became clear that this was a struggle that the English were unlikely to win in the long term. Following a series of French victories in 1453, the dual monarchy effectively came to an end. The English lost all their territories in France including the town of Bordeaux (which had been a possession of the English Crown since Eleanor of Aquitaine). The only land that remained part of England was Calais. Charles VII became the de facto King of France. Thereafter, each successive King of England would declare himself King of France, but without ever coming close to achieving this title in reality. As for Calais, it remained part of England for just over a century until 1558.

Instability Back in England

The many hardened English soldiers returning from France came home to find instability in their own country. Henry, perhaps because he had been surrounded by sycophants and ambitious advisors from infancy, had grown up but proved to be ineffective and relatively unfit to rule. This being the case, real power was being exercised by the nobility – who were fractious at best. Powerful regional magnates accrued large private armies and retainers, which began to fight each other and weaken the government.

Henry's wife, Margaret of Anjou (Charles VII's niece), was the true power behind the throne. She gathered around herself and Henry a clique of advisors and favourites, with whom she attempted to govern

England, while possibly overspending on court and the building of institutions such as Eton College and King's College Cambridge. However, with the military disasters in France and political and financial unrest in England, these extravagant projects became unpopular. Also, around 1453, Henry began to have a series of mental health breakdowns, probably after receiving news of the English army being routed by the French at Castillon. He became withdrawn, weak and completely unresponsive to things around him, including the birth of his son Edward of Westminster. It is likely that he inherited the 'madness' or psychiatric condition of King Charles VI of France through his mother, Catherine.

From 1454, Richard, Duke of York, was made Lord Protector of the Realm while the king was incapacitated. He was a leading critic of Margaret and had a very strong claim to the throne himself. He spent much of his time as regent reorganising the finances of the government and formed a close link and alliance with a leading nonroyal magnate in the land Richard Neville, 16th Earl of Warwick. At the end of 1454, when King Henry seemed to have recovered and once more tried to take up the reins of state, the nobles who were dissatisfied with him began to take matters into their own hands. They rallied around the Duke of York, pointing out his stronger claim and descent from King Edward III (via two of his sons: Lionel, Duke of Clarence, and Edmund of Langley, Duke of York).

Peace was almost maintained in the Act of Accord; Richard, Duke of York, laid his hand on the empty throne and forced Henry to agree to name him as his heir (despite being older), excluding Henry's own son. (Technically, in the same parliament, York was made Prince of Wales too.) However, distrust and arguing soon broke out into open war – what we would understand as the Wars of the Roses. Nobles stood either with the House of Lancaster and the king or the House of York and Richard (the Duke of York).

King Henry was captured by rival Yorkist forces at the Battle of Northampton on 10 July 1460 – though they would not kill an anointed sovereign. Queen Margaret fled to Scotland to raise some support there. She returned in December with an army and met Richard's army at the Battle of Wakefield. Richard was killed in battle. Margaret then went on to face the Earl of Warwick at the (second) Battle of St Albans the following February and not only won but liberated her husband who by now was reportedly quite mad. Henry and Margaret were de facto king and queen again, but this was short lived. In March 1461, around six weeks after St Albans, Richard's son, Edward, the new Duke of York, won an impressive victory at the Battle of Towton amid a snowstorm. Margaret took her son and fled to Scotland again. Henry VI was on the run in England, sheltered by loyal supporters until the Yorkists found and captured him. He was imprisoned in the Tower of London. There was no point in killing him as he had a young son who would then become the centre of Lancastrian support.

THE HOUSE OF YORK

Edward, the Duke of York, having been victorious on the battlefield (and in the eventual captor of his cousin Henry VI), was at last able to do what his father was unable to accomplish – successfully claim the throne for himself. He was crowned at Westminster on 28 June 1461. His reign was heavily dependent on the powerful Neville family, especially Richard Neville, the Earl of Warwick (known as 'Warwick the Kingmaker'). However, Warwick and the king fell out over Edward's marriage. Warwick had planned for a dynastic marriage with France or Savoy, but Edward secretly married Elizabeth Woodville in 1464. This indicated to Warwick and the world that the king was not under Warwick's control. Elizabeth was not of the high nobility; her father was a provincial knight. Many advised against the marriage, which today most consider to have been an impulsive decision or indeed a genuine love match. Warwick had no choice but to go along with it.

Queen Elizabeth Woodville had many sisters who then entered the courtly marriage market and began making extremely advantageous matches – which only caused more resentment among some of the upper nobility towards King Edward and Queen Elizabeth. Edward sacked Warwick's brother, the Archbishop of York, as Lord Chancellor, which led to Warwick forming an alliance with Edward's younger brother, George, the Duke of Clarence. George married Warwick's daughter Isabel in a ceremony conducted by the Archbishop of York in Calais. George returned to England with Warwick's family, and they eventually rose in open rebellion. They captured Edward and executed his Woodville father-in-law. Warwick and George's revolt could not last; eventually Edward was released, and an uneasy peace existed between them.

Warwick's plotting continued, and in 1470 he fled to France, where he effectively switched sides completely. He met with Margaret of Anjou and pledged to return her husband, Henry VI – who was still a captive of the Yorkists – to the throne. The Yorkist regime under Edward IV was dwindling in popularity by now. With French support, Warwick landed back in England later that year, and Edward IV fled to Bruges. It seemed that Henry VI had been restored as King of England. Indeed the throne seemed to be going back and forth like a shuttlecock – and the game was not over yet.

Edward regrouped himself in Bruges. He was accompanied by his youngest brother, Richard, Duke of Gloucester. In England, the restored Lancastrians under Henry VI were beset with the same problems they had faced before. To make matters worse, Henry's bouts of madness may have increased. Popularity and support waned yet again. Eventually, Edward, backed by Flemish merchants, returned to England (Hull) in 1471. His meddlesome brother, George, Duke of Clarence, returned to the family fold, and Edward marched unopposed into London, taking Henry VI captive yet again. Edward's forces eventually caught up with the Earl of Warwick at the Battle of Barnet in April 1471. Warwick was slain. The following month Edward of Westminster (Henry VI's son and heir) was killed at the battle of Tewksbury, which seemed to be the final nail in the coffin of the Lancastrian line. King Henry VI, held captive in the Tower of London, was now without an heir but would always be a threat to the Yorkist regime. He 'died' the same month. It is likely that he was killed on the orders of Edward IV. Although it could have been one of his brothers, it could have been, as reported at the time, that the king died of melancholia!

The Three Suns of York

Despite the House of York becoming the unrivalled power in the land, the divide between Edward, George, and Richard deepened. Shakespeare and others used the pun: the 'sun of York' or even 'three suns of York' to describe the York brothers. This was not just because they were all sons of the Duke of York but because of events at the battle of Mortimer's Cross (2 February 1461). At dawn on 2 February 1461, as the Yorkist forces prepared for battle, they saw what appeared to be three suns in the sky. This phenomenon, known as a parhelion or sun dog, is caused by the refraction of sunlight through ice crystals in the atmosphere and appears as a bright spot on one or both sides of the sun. Edward took it as a good omen and was proved right when he won the battle. The *Sun in Splendour* was adopted as one of his badges and one of the main Yorkist badges. Now that the three brothers were truly victorious and seemed to have put to bed any future Lancastrian claims, they began to fall out and plot against each other – which ultimately disabled Edward's reign. Despite being the strongest force in the land, Edward, George and Richard as good as destroyed the House of York by themselves.

George and Richard married the two daughters of their former-patron-turned-enemy, the Earl of Warwick. His lands were among the richest in England, and his daughters were set to receive a considerable inheritance from their mother (Anne Beauchamp) too. Unsurprisingly, there were some disputes as to which brother would control which share of this inheritance and who would effectively inherit the Earldom of Warwick. When George's wife died, shortly after giving birth to a short-lived son, he went into a rage and claimed they had been poisoned. He had a woman and a man hanged for murder in a hastily devised court. King Edward had them posthumously pardoned, but George continued to suspect that his brothers were somehow involved.

George railed against his brother in several ways, which led to some of his closest retainers being arrested; some of them actually confessed to potential treason. George himself was eventually reprimanded by King Edward and held in the Tower of London on charges of treason. Edward appears to have been merciless to his brother.

Some have said that George may have been reviving old rumours about Edward's possible illegitimacy – a conspiracy theory which exists to this day. Edward's parents are proven to have been a hundred miles away from each other during the five-week period around the time of Edward's conception – but that is assuming a typical nine-month pregnancy. Ultimately, Edward's parentage is impossible to prove without digging up a lot of bodies for DNA testing.

George may also have been questioning the legality of Edward's marriage to Elizabeth Woodville, seeing as he had previously been betrothed to someone else (Lady Eleanor Talbot).

Whatever the truth of the offence, in short, Edward had his own brother put to death on 18 February 1478. Reportedly, George was permitted to choose the method of execution. He was drowned in a butt of Malmsey wine.

Richard III

Edward died somewhat prematurely five years later in 1483 at age forty. His son and heir, Edward V, was only twelve; therefore, in his will, he appointed his brother, Richard, Duke of Gloucester, to be Lord Protector until the boy came of age. Richard rushed to get safe custody of the young king, Edward V, as well as his little brother Richard of Shrewsbury, who was nine. As many will know, Richard housed the two princes in the Tower of London, claiming it was usual for the king to reside there in preparation for coronation. Edward's coronation, of course, did not happen.

Shortly after the princes were taken by Richard, a sermon was preached from Old St Paul's Cathedral, claiming that Edward IV's marriage had indeed been illegal and so his sons (Edward V and Richard of Shrewsbury) were illegitimate with no right to succeed to the throne. That right therefore passed to the Lord Protector, Richard, Duke of Gloucester – Richard III. Richard was crowned on 6 July 1483.

The Princes in the Tower (as they have come to be known) were not seen again. Their death or disappearance is famous and practically legendary and the subject of much debate. Long was it said that Richard III ordered their deaths, but the Duke of Buckingham and King Henry VII are also suspects. The truth will likely never be uncovered. Regardless, Richard clearly deprived his two nephews of their inheritance and right to succeed their father.

Richard had bypassed the sons of both of his older brothers when he took the throne. It seemed that the Yorkist squabbles were over and that the House of Plantagenet and its future was safe in the line of Richard III, although there was a setback when his wife and son died prematurely. However, trouble was brewing. It would come from a very obscure corner of the family and from an unlikely place – Wales!

King Richard III was defeated at the Battle of Bosworth Field in 1485 by a Welshman and very distant cousin, Henry Tudor, who was shortly after proclaimed King Henry VII. The result of the battle was partly down to bad luck and partly down to last-minute betrayal – though to some it would have been seen as God's will. Richard's downfall marked the end of the Plantagenet dynasty and its occupation of the English throne, whose power and might it had helped forge. It is ironic that, after successive Plantagenet wars and the brutal occupation of Wales, their successor dynasty should come out of that land.

Henry VII, 1485–1509
Henry VIII, 1509–1547
Edward VI, 1547–1553

Mary I and Philip, 1553 and 1554–1558

Elizabeth I, 1558–1603

O F COURSE, THE FURTHER we go into English royal history, the more difficult it can be to succinctly summarise its story. This is partly because we know more about what happened as more writings and evidence survive but also because there are so many books (both history and historical fiction), motion pictures, and plays about these times. Therefore, many people have their own ideas about what is important and what isn't.

Perhaps no time in British royal history is as well known as the Tudor century. This means that everyone, however well or ill informed, has an opinion on the Tudors and the politics and religion of their day. We will attempt to navigate this without 'ruffling too many feathers', as Dr David Starkey CBE would say. For the uninitiated in Tudor history (who are likely few in number as the Tudors are so often dramatised in film and television), we start in Wales – land of dragons, sheep and unpronounceable words.

How did a dynasty from the Welsh mountains with no strong blood connection to the Plantagenets end up acquiring the throne of England? You might well ask. The Tudors give their name to a century of English history (the sixteenth century) which is perhaps one of the most 'over-done' centuries in popular media and historical fiction. This was the century of Holbein, Hilliard and other portrait painters. It is the first time in English monarchical history when 'convincing' images of the characters of court are well represented. (Arguably this is a contributing factor in our fascination with the Tudor Age.) Near-complete Tudor dwellings are dotted throughout the countryside and market towns of England, from country houses to humble high-street shops. Great strides were made in the development of music too, and much of the music of the time can be accurately recreated today thanks to surviving manuscripts. Therefore, we can actually touch, see and hear the Tudor times in a slightly higher definition than previous centuries. Art, music and architectural history aside, it was, truth be told, an age of constant dynastic worry and frustration, of huge changes in English law, politics, culture, religion and foreign policy. From the Reformation to the Spanish Armada, the Tudors saw some of the most troublesome times in English History – knife edge moments that, should they have turned out differently, would have made England look very different today.

For readers who have not taken advantage of any of the range of feature films or television dramas and documentaries (many of dubious accuracy) available or who did not get a run-through during their school days, here is as brief an overview of the Tudors as one can muster. That said, we will of course mostly concern ourselves with the passage of the crown and the family links that 'justify' it.

Why the change from Richard (III) Plantagenet to Henry (VII) Tudor? The answer could easily consist of a mixture of divine intervention, battle, luck or lack of it! To understand the answer, we need to look back a few generations.

In hindsight, much of the fate of the Tudor dynasty pivoted on the decisions or relationships of key women. This is not solely because of Anne Boleyn, Bloody Mary or Elizabeth I. But how one might ask, do the Tudors even have a claim on the English throne?

A Queen and a Knight

Catherine of Valois (1401-1437), widow to the great Henry V of England (he of Agincourt), was still young and of childbearing age at the death of her husband. As the daughter of the late King of France and mother to England's (and France's) new infant king, Henry VI, she was a mighty prize to any man who could marry her. Her influence and dynastic connections were worth more than mere gold. It is therefore surprising that the lucky chap in question was a mere knight from Wales, Sir Owen Tudor – or in Welsh: *Owain ap Maredudd ap Tudur*. ('*ap*' meaning 'son of'). Put simply, the widow of the English king married a Welsh knight, and their grandson would one day be the first Tudor King of England.

Little is known for certain about the history of Owen's family. They may originally have come from the Isle of Anglesey. Owen's father and uncles had been prominent magnates in support of Owain Glyndŵr's revolt against English rule (1403-1406). Owen's own early life is mysterious to say the least – which only highlights his lowly state as a mere Welsh gentleman, if that. Rumours of his origins include that he was actually the illegitimate son of an innkeeper; that his father was an outlaw and murderer; that he may have been a soldier at Agincourt;

and that he may have been the keeper of Queen Catherine's wardrobe or at least in her service. Other rumours regarding how Owen and Catherine met include her becoming enamoured of him when she accidentally saw him swimming or bathing and Owen falling into her lap at a dance. Many of these tales were likely invented following the Tudor monarchy's rise. That said, it is recorded that some Welshmen, including a man named Owen, joined the service of the steward of the king's household following Agincourt. It may or may not be the same Owen. Regardless, this only illustrates that, comparatively speaking, Owen Tudor was practically a nobody compared to the Dowager Queen of England. Exactly how a meeting or affair came about between Catherine and Owen is in truth uncertain, and their marriage did not actually take place until about six years after her first husband had died. Regardless, due to that marriage, his lineage was to sit on the throne of England.

After Henry V died, Queen Catherine had lived with her infant kingly son and his court. During those years, rumours persisted that she was having a 'relationship' with her late husband's cousin, Edmund Beaufort, Count of Mortain (future 2nd Duke of Somerset). The Beauforts were a legitimised line from John of Gaunt, younger son of Edward III and grandfather to Henry V. The relationship was disturbing to the king's closest councillors and guardians because little King Henry's claim to France came through Catherine. A union between Catherine and the Beaufort family would doubtless pose a threat to the young King Henry in future generations. Whether the rumours of that relationship with Beaufort are to be believed or not, Parliament soon passed a bill (1427-28) that, if a dowager queen remarried without the king's consent, the husband would forfeit all his land, money and titles. The king, in this case, was still a child of about six. The rumoured couple would have to wait many years before he came of age to legally consent — assuming he would. If Catherine had intended to marry Edmund Beaufort, she would no longer.

Very shortly after this bill, Catherine seems to have married a rank outsider. Owen Tudor and Catherine were wed sometime in 1429. Though there remains little evidence of the marriage, there do not appear to have been any contemporary objections to its validity either. Yet, for the queen to move her affections from a powerful princely duke to a mere servant immediately after the passing of such a bill in Parliament could be seen as suspicious! It does not help steer the mind away from conspiracy, especially when one learns that Catherine's firstborn of her new marriage (in c. 1430) was named Edmund! With that in mind, it is easily imaginable that he may have been a Beaufort and not a Tudor.

Believe what you will. After Edmund's birth, Catherine and Owen Tudor went on to have three further children together: Jasper, Edward and Margaret. Owen himself was granted by Parliament the rights of an Englishman in 1432 – as there were certain laws in existence then which limited the rights of the Welsh. (In certain places, such as Gonville and Caius College, Cambridge, such limitations technically remain – though they are not necessarily observed.)

Owen and Catharine's relationship was kept largely private. Shortly after Catherine's death in 1437, the true extent of their union became known. The marriage contravened a special Act of Parliament (of 1427-28) which specifically banned any man of any rank from marrying the Dowager Queen. Owen was subsequently imprisoned at Newgate. He escaped only to be recaptured and taken to Windsor. In 1438 Owen was pardoned and received various pensions and grants of land from his former stepson, Henry VI.

THE LANCASTRIAN PEDIGREE

Owen's sons, Edmund and Jasper, were given prominent earldoms by Henry VI: Richmond and Pembroke, respectively. As members of the extended Lancastrian royal family in the earlier Wars of the Roses, Edmund and Jasper were particularly active in the Wars of the Roses in support of Henry VI.

Edmund Tudor, Earl of Richmond, married within the Lancastrian clan. In November 1455, at Bletsoe Castle, he married Lady Margaret Beaufort, only daughter of John, Duke of Somerset. She was the niece of Edmund Beaufort, a strong link back to the throne via John of Gaunt. She was the most desirable heiress in England at that time, not only owing to her wealth but because she was also of the blood royal. Even at the time, it was thought that, with the couple's family connections, any son of theirs would be well placed to become king one day, should Henry VI falter.

Even though she was deemed underage, Edmund Tudor wasted no time in consummating the marriage. (Margaret was about 12; he was about 25.) Husband took wife deep into Wales, specifically to Pembroke Castle, to live together in peculiar matrimony. (Edmund's brother, Jasper Tudor, was the Earl of Pembroke.) However, in 1456, only a year after their marriage, Edmund was captured by Yorkist forces under William Herbert during a minor Welsh skirmish. He died (probably) of plague while in captivity at Carmarthen... Margaret was still around seven months pregnant with Edmund's first son – Henry Tudor.

Margaret gave birth to Henry Tudor at Pembroke Castle on 28 January 1457 under the watchful care of her brother-in-law, Jasper Tudor. Owing to her age at barely 13, she was underdeveloped, and it was a difficult birth, but miraculously mother and son pulled through. (However, the difficulty may explain why she had no further children despite having two more marriages.) Baby Henry was entrusted to his Uncle Jasper.

Margaret, meanwhile, made yet another political marriage, presumably with the priority of protecting her son, Henry. In 1458, she married secondly Sir Henry Stafford, second son of the 1st Duke of Buckingham and younger brother of the 2nd Duke of Buckingham. The Stafford Buckinghams were also strongly connected to the blood royal via their ancestor Edward III. So they were in fact all cousins, and all with an ambition to cement their ties to the throne and potential succession.

EDWARD HILARY DAVIS

The Tudors in the Wars of the Roses

The crown changed hands twice – which nearly ended things for Henry Tudor and his mother. The Yorkist King Edward IV, was betrayed by his onetime friend, the Earl of Warwick, and was forced to flee London for his life in 1470, taking refuge in Flanders. Warwick restored his one-time enemy and captive, Henry VI, to the throne. Once again, Henry Tudor's uncle sat the throne, and things were looking up for the Tudor family. Young Henry was presented at court to the king – who may or may not have recognised Henry's potential for future greatness. The king was, after all, considerably mad at this time.

The Lancastrian restoration was very short-lived, however. The following year, in 1471, Edward IV returned to England and landed in Yorkshire at the head of an army of Flemish mercenaries. He quickly gained local support. He killed the Earl of Warwick at the Battle of Barnet and Henry VI's son and heir, Edward of Westminster, at the Battle of Tewksbury. He entered London unopposed and recaptured Henry VI – who, possibly on Edward's orders, was conveniently dead a few days later. It seemed that the Lancastrian cause had been well and truly vanquished as all direct claimants had been killed and their allies slain or defeated. All but one that is.

After the return of Edward IV, Henry Tudor had fled for his life across the Channel to the Duchy of Brittany under the protection of the duke there. He was too closely associated with the Lancastrian cause and had a marginal claim to the throne. That said, it is interesting to ponder how seriously his claim was considered at this time. He was not a Plantagenet, so not a direct male descendant; Edward IV was and so were his two brothers. There was no comparison really. Nevertheless, for his safety, Henry Tudor remained in Brittany for the next fourteen years or so.

Margaret's husband, Sir Henry Stafford, died at the Battle of Barnet in 1471. Their marriage was childless. She needed a way back to court to potentially promote the interests of her son so that one day he might return. To do this, she married Thomas Stanley, 2nd Baron Stanley, in 1472. Stanley was from a rising family at court who had been steadily gaining titles and influence. In 1405, King Henry IV had given the Stanleys suzerainty of the Isle of Mann with the wonderful title of King of Mann. This marriage to a powerful upcoming ally was to prove the making of Margaret's son, Henry Tudor.

Division in the House of York

Following military campaigns in France and Scotland, Edward IV became gravely ill in spring of 1483. He was able in his last days to will that his brother, Richard, be Lord Protector while his twelve year old son was too young to reign alone. He died on 9 April. The cause of Edward IV's death is not entirely clear. Poison is sometimes suggested, as are pneumonia, malaria or apoplexy. Regardless, he was automatically succeeded by his young son, Edward V.

As we have already seen, Richard, Duke of Gloucester, moved quickly to declare that his nephews, Edward V and Edward's younger brother Richard of Shrewsbury Duke of York, were actually illegitimate. Richard had them detained in the Tower of London, and he was made King Richard III. The boys were never seen again and were most likely murdered. They were about twelve and nine, respectively.

Richard's actions in becoming the king divided the once-mighty House of York. He was not popular with everyone, and some sought an alternative ruler. Edward, Earl of Warwick (son of George, Duke of Clarence), was not considered mostly because he was a small child at this time but also because his father's attainder for treason technically barred him from succession. It was clear that any contender would need to be backed by powerful allies and a great army to wrestle the crown from Richard III. Lady Margaret Beaufort knew this was the time to secretly promote her son, Henry Tudor.

Revival of the Lancastrian Cause

The mother of the 'missing' Princes in the Tower, Queen Dowager Elizabeth Woodville, and Lady Margaret formed an alliance which in former years would have been unthinkable. Elizabeth's daughter by Edward IV, known as Elizabeth of York, would marry Henry Tudor and thus unite the Houses of York and Lancaster – potentially. Still in Brittany, Henry swore an oath on Christmas Day 1483 promising to do this. Richard III got wind of the plot. He executed a co-conspirator and Tudor ally in England, Henry, 2nd Duke of Buckingham.

In 1484, Henry Tudor landed in Wales near his old home of Pembroke with a small force of French soldiers. Owing to his Welsh ancestry, he gained enthusiastic local support across the principality, and men flocked to his adopted dragon banner – a wise choice of device and a clear example of just how important heraldry and symbols were in the medieval world. With the dragon flying proudly, Henry amassed an army of around five to six thousand men.

Richard III gathered his own forces, and on 22 August 1485 the two sides met at Bosworth Field for one of the few battles which changed the course of English history with just the stroke of a blade. We will not dwell on the details of this battle, but needless to say it was bloody and hard fought. In summary, the battle hinged on which way Lord Stanley, Henry Tudor's stepfather, would fight. He was publicly a Yorkist man and had declared for King Richard. In the battle, however, he waited for an opportunity to strike Richard. The battle was dwindling and Richard had seen an opportunity to end the Lancastrian rebellion forever. He made a brave do-or-die charge at Henry's position. As he rushed forward, Richard got close enough to cut down and kill Henry's standard bearer, Sir William Brandon. Henry quickly dismounted and hid himself among his French mercenaries and English pikemen. This slowed Richard's advance and slightly separated him from the main Yorkist forces. It was at this point that Stanley made his move. His forces, who until now had merely spectated, betrayed the Yorkist cause and charged on Richard who, as we now know from the recent 'King in the Car Park' discovery, was brutally hacked to pieces. Richard, the last Plantagenet king, was dead. On the battlefield, Henry Tudor was proclaimed king, possibly over Richard's very dead body.

A Slight Claim to the Throne

Henry Tudor and his supporters knew that his claim to the throne was tentative at best and was only through a legitimised maternal line – through his mother – back to Edward III around a century earlier. It helped, of course, that he was also descended from Henry V's wife, Catherine of Valois, so he could at least keep up the pretence of some sort of kingly claim to France – which had been the tradition for English kings. In point of fact, his whole claim by descent was undermined by the fact that Henry Bolingbroke (Henry IV) had barred his legitimated Beaufort relatives from the succession in a special decree in 1406 – which by extension included the Tudors. However, in the face of seemingly divinely ordained military success of Henry Tudor, this was politely ignored by many. To the victor the history!

Perhaps more than by birthright, Henry Tudor could claim his kingship by right of conquest – which no one could argue with. He had invaded England (through Wales), and he had killed the king in open battle. In those days, such events indicated a kind of divine approval – as God was thought to decide the fate of battles, at least in the common mindset. In other words, Bosworth had been a trial by combat; God supported the victor.

Richard III's body was hastily discarded (in what became a car park), and Henry Tudor rode triumphantly into London. It took him a while to make good on his promise, but Henry VII did indeed marry his (distant) cousin, Elizabeth of York (daughter of Edward IV), in 1486, thus (mostly) uniting the Houses of York and Lancaster. As part of his public relations campaign to convince all his subjects that the decades of civil war were indeed over, he adopted the new royal badge:

EDWARD HILARY DAVIS

the Tudor Rose. This combined the red Lancastrian rose with the white rose of York. The Plantagenet dynasty had effectively ripped itself asunder and was succeeded via marriage and luck in battle by a rank outsider dynasty: the Tudors.

Securing the Dynasty

With Henry VII's marriage to Elizabeth, the new Tudor dynasty seemed secure. The two produced seven children including two sons, Arthur and Henry (VIII). Their third son, Edmund, only lived a year. Since, as we know, women were crucial to the history of the Tudor family, the surviving daughters Margaret and Mary should not be forgotten.

Other Plantagenet cousins and potential descendants were eventually eliminated or exiled. Edward, Earl of Warwick (Elizabeth's nephew), was executed in 1499. Perkin Warbeck, an imposter from the Low Countries posing as the missing Richard, Duke of York (one of the Princes in the Tower), was executed in 1499 too. Another pretender, Lambert Simnel and 'his' rebellion were put down and Lambert imprisoned or executed. The de la Pole family (cousins with a better family claim to the old Plantagenet line) continued to be a dynastic threat, and various members were questioned, imprisoned, exiled or executed during the next few decades.

With his own claim to the English throne being won by arms and not necessarily descent, Henry VII looked to secure his future dynasty by marriage. He was swift to broker marriages for his children to strong foreign powers – for the safety of his kingdom and his family. Prince Arthur, the heir, was wed in 1501 to Catherine of Aragon, daughter of the joint monarchs of Spain, Ferdinand and Isabella; Princess Margaret was wed to King James IV of Scotland in 1503; and in 1514, after Henry's death, Princess Mary married King Louis XII of France – who was thirty years her senior and the first and only French sovereign to marry an English princess.

As most will know from their education, reading or Netflix watching, Arthur Tudor, Prince of Wales, died prematurely of sweating sickness (or tuberculosis) at age fifteen, just months after his wedding to Catherine of Aragon. Both Henry VII and the Spanish in-laws were keen to hold their plans together and stand by an alliance of marriage. So it was agreed that Catherine would wed Arthur's younger brother, the new heir apparent – Henry, Duke of York, now Prince of Wales, the future Henry VIII. Prince Henry was no longer the spare, but the heir. He inherited his brother's titles and committed to marrying his brother's widow for state reasons. Had Arthur lived, so much about British history might have been very different.

Henry VIII

King Henry VII died at Richmond Palace a few years later in April 1509. The new, young King Henry VIII was a breath of fresh air to the English court. He hastily married Catherine in June 1509, after a special dispensation from the pope had been granted. (It was against canon law for a man to marry his brother's widow. In order to get the dispensation, Catherine had to testify that her marriage to Arthur had never been consummated.) They were crowned a few weeks later at Westminster.

Henry's early reign was marked with military campaigns abroad in France and in Scotland. While away in France, Henry appointed his wife regent of England in his absence. It was under her regency that, despite being pregnant, she was able to order troops in the north of the kingdom against the Scots and direct them towards Flodden Field in 1513. The Battle of Flodden (commanded by Thomas Howard, Duke of Norfolk) was a significant victory for the English. King James IV of Scotland (Henry's brother-in-law) was killed, as were four of his major battle commander earls. Catherine sent James's bloodied coat to Henry in France as a souvenir. What wife could do more?!

The Search for an Heir

Henry and Catherine were happily married for several years. However, she had several miscarriages and stillbirths. A son (also Henry) born 1 January 1515 lived just a little over a month. Their fifth child together was the only one to survive past infancy – Princess Mary, born 15 April 1516 – but this was not the son and heir Henry needed to continue the Tudor dynasty. After yet another stillborn child in 1518, Henry began to lose interest in his wife and to wonder as to the cause of their inability to create a healthy son.

In 1519, Henry VIII proved to his satisfaction that the problem did not lie with him. He sired an illegitimate son on a mistress, Bessie Blount, in 1519. Named Henry Fitzroy, he was actually conceived during Queen Catherine's last confinement. He was paraded at court by his father and showered in titles, honours and high offices. At various times during his life, he may well have been considered as a potential heir to the throne. There were even suggestions of a papal dispensation for him to marry his half-sister, Mary, to secure the dynasty. Fortunately, sense prevailed, and this did not happen. He is another 'what-if' of English history. He died of consumption (or tuberculosis) in 1536 at only seventeen, predeceasing his father.

As you have doubtlessly been anticipating, Anne Boleyn emerged on the scene in King Henry's life around 1525. Henry's wife was older than him, and it was clear that she was no longer able to bear children. In contrast, Anne was possibly seventeen years his junior, young, vivacious and charming. Naturally, he began pursuing her (despite having previously had an affair with Anne's sister). It is during this time that Henry began to question the validity of his marriage to Catherine. He had found a verse from Leviticus which declared that men who marry their brother's widows shall be childless. For 'childless,' Henry read 'without sons'. Such was the case in his marriage. He then questioned if the pope had been right to give his special dispensation for the marriage to take place.

However, this is a book following royal dynasties and the passage of the English crown, so we shall not get too bogged down in the complications of the divorce, the break with Rome, the Reformation and the many famous statesmen that played a role in this part of our history. Anne's rise from a knight's daughter to mistress, to wife and queen cost the careers and lives of many famous men from Thomas Wolsey to Thomas Moore and others. Her relationship with Henry also changed England forever in that it resulted in the formation of the Church of England (with the king, not the pope, being supreme head of the church) and in a gradual but swift move towards Protestantism across the kingdom. Pushing these vast political and religious themes aside, Henry essentially gambled all on getting a son and heir via Anne Boleyn.

Having failed to do so on the first attempt (only producing a daughter, Elizabeth), Anne's position became perilous. As Henry was now supreme head of his own church, swapping Anne out for a new wife was not going to be hard for Henry the second time. In fact, Henry went much further. Anne was charged with treason, adultery, and even incest with her brother and was executed in 1536 by sword at the Tower. Most agree that it is unlikely that all, if any, of the accusations against her were true.

It should be noted that Anne herself possessed some royal blood. Through her maternal grandfather, Thomas Howard, 2nd Duke of Norfolk, she was descended from Thomas of Brotherton, eldest son of King Edward I by his second marriage. Consequently, she was also descended from Philip III of France. Her father too, via the Earls of Ormond, descended from Edward I. These were significant facts that did not escape the attention of the court. In the sixteenth century, much of the English nobility were already related to each other to varying degrees. Henry VIII and Anne Boleyn were distant cousins. In fact, it can be demonstrated that all six of Henry's wives were related to him and to each other. Catherine of Aragon, Jane Seymour and Catherine

Parr were all descended from Edward III. Anne Boleyn, Anne of Cleves and Katherine Howard were descended from Edward I. But I'm getting ahead of myself.

The Anticipated Heir

Having cleared the way for wife number three, Henry wasted no time in remarrying one of Anne's former ladies-in-waiting, Jane Seymour. They were formally betrothed the very next day after Anne's execution. Henry evidently required even less time than a teenage boy to get over the death of his ex! Just ten days later, on 30 May 1536, Jane and Henry were married at Whitehall. She is known to have been a compassionate and kind person, popular with courtiers and commoners alike. Unlike her predecessor, she did not meddle in Henry's affairs. It was hoped by some senior churchmen and nobles that she might bring Henry back round to the Roman Catholic Church. However, the one time she did voice an opinion to Henry, he quickly reminded her of Anne's fate. "Know thy place" was the order of the day for Jane. That said, she did much to bring about a reconciliation between Henry and his eldest daughter, Mary.

During her pregnancy, like many soon-to-be mothers, Jane had some rather niche cravings. One such craving was for quail meat. Henry keenly and diligently ordered bountiful amounts of quail from his lands around Calais, and the birds were shipped directly to the palace. Jane gave birth to the much-awaited son and heir, Edward, on 12 October 1537 at Hampton Court Palace. He was christened there in a lavish ceremony just three days later. Queen Jane was left to recover in her chambers. The labour had been difficult, lasting about two days owing to bad baby positioning. She died on 24 October probably of some sort of infection relating to the pregnancy.

Though Henry was grief-stricken, he now had his heart's desire – a son and heir. He even had two spares in the form of his daughters, whom he restored to the succession after Prince Edward. If Edward were to die childless, the heir would be his eldest sister Princess Mary, and in the event of her death without issue, Princess Elizabeth. Jane's family had and would benefit from their solid connection to the throne. Her brother, Edward Seymour, was made Duke of Somerset – a title which formerly belonged to Henry VIII's mother's family. The present Duke of Somerset is Edward Seymour's direct descendant.

The Final Three Wives

Famously, another three wives followed. Anne of Cleaves (married January 1540) was deemed by Henry to be too ugly, and he divorced her almost as quickly as he married her. Catherine Howard (married July 1540) – another niece of the Duke of Norfolk – was caught in adultery with one of Henry's Gentlemen of the Privy Chamber (Thomas Culpepper, her distant cousin) and she had 'known other men' before the king. She was stripped of the title of Queen in 1541 – the same year Henry had established the Kingdom of Ireland with himself as king. The following year he had Catherine executed. The sixth wife, Catherine Parr (married 1543), already twice a widow, outlived King Henry, as all good school children can tell you. After his death the dowager queen married one of Queen Jane's brothers, Thomas, Lord Seymour of Sudeley. The two of them became guardians to Princess Elizabeth following Henry VIII's death.

Henry VIII died on 28 January 1547 at Whitehall Palace. He was succeeded by his son, Edward VI, who was just nine. A Lord Protector was appointed in the form of the boy-king's uncle, Edward Seymour, Duke of Somerset. During Edward's reign, Protestant reforms continued at pace. These policies further dissolving the monasteries widened the gap between the Roman Church and the Anglican Church. When the Duke of Somerset was executed for treason in 1549, he was replaced as Lord Protector by John Dudley, Duke of Northumberland.

Edward VI

Edward VI was a sickly child. In 1553, when he was fifteen he fell gravely ill. The illness is thought to have been tuberculosis or at least lung related. As it was thought to be terminal, he decided to put his affairs in order. Neither Edward nor Dudley wanted a resurgence of Catholicism in England. However, Edward's father's will clearly stated that Mary was to come after Edward in the line of succession, and Mary was a devout Catholic. So, naturally, Edward did the only thing he could do; he changed the line of succession. He debarred his older sisters (particularly Mary) from the succession and appointed as his heir his cousin Lady Jane Grey and her heirs. Jane was the same age as Edward and had been similarly schooled in the Protestant faith. She was also the granddaughter of Henry VIII's sister, Mary, Duchess of Suffolk (who had at earlier time been Queen of France). For reasons unknown, the succession bypassed Jane's mother, Lady Frances Brandon (Duchess of Suffolk), who was still living. Jane's 'claim' to the throne was curious because it was based on her descent through her mother and grand-mother back to Henry VII. For the common people, this would later be hard to understand bearing in mind that two of Henry VIII's daughters were living and surely had seniority.

It is often speculated that the Duke of Northumberland (the Lord Protector, John Dudley) was partially behind this sudden change to the succession and that he persuaded other councillors, peers and courtiers to support it. This idea stems from the fact that he himself was a Protestant and that his younger son had married Lady Jane Grey the same year that the king became seriously ill. (Lord Guildford Dudley married Jane on 25 May 1553.)

Perhaps sensing his oncoming death, King Edward VI named Jane as his successor probably in early June. By 21 June, the formal letters patent were issued declaring the king's new will regarding the succession and were signed by 102 high ranking officials. The king died on 6 July 1553.

JANE GREY

The Arms of Lady Jane Grey after her marriage to Lord Guildford Dudley

Dudley (Northumberland) was cautious, but he had to act fast. News of the king's death was suppressed for four days while he put plans in place for Jane's ascension to the throne. It was unfortunate that he did not have Princess Mary in his custody. She had the good sense to retreat to her estate at Kenninghall in Norfolk, an area abundant with Catholic sympathisers. Finally, after four days of silence, Northumberland announced the king's death and proclaimed Jane (his daughter-in-law) Queen of England on 10 July 1553. Jane had only been informed of her accession the day before. She later claimed that she accepted the crown reluctantly. As per tradition, she took up residence in the Tower of London pending her coronation. A proclamation was given before a confused crowd of Londoners near the Tower. Jane did not name her husband, Lord Guildford, as king, however much he tried to push himself forward, because that would require an act of Parliament.

Princess Mary, with her support in East Anglia growing, had declared herself queen on 12 July in response to Jane's claim. Mary gathered together an armed force from the surrounding countryside. Knowing he must quickly and decisively consolidate his position, Northumberland marched his own troops out of London in the hope of stopping her advance. In his absence, most of the Privy Council, who had initially supported him, flocked to Mary's side – as did most of the common people. Northumberland was captured, and Mary marched into London unopposed. On 19 July, Jane went from being hostess to prisoner in the Tower along with her husband Guildford. On 22 August, Mary had Northumberland executed. The following month Parliament declared that Mary was the true successor of Edward VI and that Jane's reign and proclamation were null and void and that of a usurper.

EDWARD HILARY DAVIS

Jane and Guildford were tried for high treason. Naturally, they were found guilty and condemned to execution; however, Jane's life was initially to be spared. She was after all Mary's cousin, and too many cousins had killed cousins in the Wars of the Roses only two generations ago. Guildford too was initially spared owing to being Jane's husband.

MARY I

Queen Mary I was crowned on 1 October 1553. It should not be overlooked that, despite her less-than-good reputation today, she was England's first regnant queen – our first queen in her own right. She initially enjoyed popular approval across the kingdom until she made it clear whom she intended to marry. She was hell-bent on marrying her cousin Prince Philip – soon to be King Philip II of Spain – a Habsburg and the Catholic Church's most ardent supporter. For some Englishmen, who naturally had a fear/resentment of foreigners, the idea of a Catholic king ruling over England as well as Spain was too much. Sir Thomas Wyatt led a rebellion against Mary in January 1554. The rebellion failed, and the ringleaders rounded up. Unfortunately for Jane Grey, her father and two uncles joined the rebellion. They too were taken to the Tower.

As a consequence of her family's involvement with the latest rebellion, the Privy Council decided to have Jane's death sentence carried out. Lady Jane and Lord Guildford were executed on Tower Hill on 12 February 1554. She was 16 or 17, and he, 18 or 19. The execution was in fact postponed a few days to give Jane a chance to convert to the Catholic faith. She did not. It is likely that, even if she did, Mary still would have had her executed – which is what happened to Archbishop Thomas Cranmer, Jane's father, who was executed a few weeks later on 23 February. Despite Parliament declaring her reign void, Jane is often described as England's 'nine-day queen'. If one were to count from the death of Edward VI, she was actually queen for eighteen days – which admittedly doesn't sound as good.

Mary I believed it was her duty and mission from God to restore England to the Catholic faith. She was aware that next in line was her younger half-sister, Elizabeth – a Protestant. In order to secure the continuation of Catholicism in England, Mary needed to produce an heir with a strong Catholic man.

Philip of Spain

Mary married Philip in Winchester Cathedral on 25 July 1554 with the eventual and reluctant approval of Parliament. The wedding was only two days after they had first met. There had been many negotiations leading up to this moment. There were legal considerations. Under English common law, all property of the wife became the property of her husband. Would Philip therefore be king both in England and eventually Spain? Mary's councillors were anxious that England should not become a mere part of the much larger Habsburg Empire – which was the largest in Europe and also controlled much of the Americas. The conditions brokered were that Philip could be named as king and they could rule England jointly whilst Mary lived; however, he could not appoint foreign councillors nor demand England fight his wars abroad. Laws in the English parliament would be made in the names of both Queen Mary and King Philip.

At the time of the wedding, of course, Philip was still just a Prince of Spain. In order to make him the equal of his wife, Philip's father (Emperor Charles V) ceded him the Kingdom of Naples and his claim to the Kingdom of Jerusalem. So, technically, on their wedding day, Mary was not just Queen of England but Queen of Naples and Jerusalem (and later Spain) – all very apt for such a Catholic monarch. She was thirty-eight, and he was twenty-seven.

This was not a marriage of love for Philip; it was a political opportunity to exploit. The Habsburg Empire had grown and would continue to grow thanks to rather advantageous marriages. For Philip, this was no exception. He and his father hoped that it would add England to their growing collection of kingdoms throughout Europe. Mary, on the other hand, was infatuated with Philip. It is safe to say that for her it was love or at least lust. Perhaps her age brought about an ardent urge for the match to work. Certainly, there was a lot of pressure. The purpose of the union depended on her ability to produce a Catholic Habsburg heir to the English throne. and this could have happened, but, perhaps thankfully, it did not. Of course, one can form one's own opinions there.

A Phantom Pregnancy

In late 1554, Mary began to swell with child. She had previously kept her sister under house arrest for fear of more Protestant plots. However Princess Elizabeth was released during the end of Mary's pregnancy in order to witness the birth.

Parliament had already appointed Philip regent in case the queen died in childbirth. Philip may even have been preparing to marry Elizabeth should Mary die. All did not go well however. There was a delay of some months, so much so that many began to gossip that the queen was not pregnant at all. In short, Mary is popularly believed to have experienced a phantom pregnancy or something similar; it has been speculated that the pregnancy was imagined by Mary owing to her overwhelming desire for a child or that it was a tumour of some kind. Worryingly, Mary believed that her inability to produce an heir was God's punishment on her for being too lenient on the heretical Protestants. It was also following the pregnancy that her age began to show. It seemed likely she may never bear children, and Philip grew colder and more distant.

An Awkward Succession

Philip of Spain was concerned about the English succession. After Mary might come her sister, Elizabeth, but after Elizabeth might come their cousin Mary, Queen of Scots, who was married to the Dauphin of France. That might potentially shift dominance in Europe away from the Habsburgs and into the hands of the French House of Valois who would gain both England and Scotland as new kingdoms. What a world that could have been: Scotland, France and England simultaneously united under one crown!

Whilst married to Mary, Philip could not formally propose marriage to Elizabeth, so he tried to arrange for Elizabeth to marry his cousin Emmanuel, Duke of Savoy. As Emmanuel was a Catholic, Mary liked the idea, but Elizabeth refused, and it was highly unlikely the English parliament would agree.

By May 1588, Mary was unwell, probably suffering from ovarian or womb cancer. She begrudgingly accepted that Elizabeth was her lawful heir and died in November that same year. Philip commented that he felt just a reasonable regret at her death. He married Princess Elisabeth of France just months later, having been turned down by Elizabeth of England. Queen Mary I had hoped to be buried next to her mother. Those wishes were ignored, and she was laid to rest at Westminster, later to be overshadowed by the grander more ornate tomb of her sister, Queen Elizabeth I.

Elizabeth I

Elizabeth I was the last (royal) Tudor remaining, the last of the dynasty. Her forty-four-year reign is considered to be one of the most glorious and important in English history. Despite being a woman in what was very much a man's world, she remained unmarried throughout. This is perhaps because whomever she married would have had power over her. Her road from princess, to bastard, to queen had been long and hard won, and power sharing with an ambitious man was probably repugnant to her. Many suitors from many different foreign realms, including France and Spain, tried for her hand as well as noble courtiers but all to no avail. She was known as the Virgin Queen owing to her assumed retained maidenhead – though there is considerable speculation about her early life and later affairs with her favourite, Robert Dudley, Earl of Leicester.

Elizabeth upheld the Reformation, the Protestant faith and the Church of England. Arguably this set a course for England and determined the way it has looked upon Europe and the world ever since. Catholic European powers, guided by the pope, sought to bring England back to Rome. If this could not be achieved by marrying Elizabeth to a Catholic prince or monarch, then it would be achieved by plots, intrigue, assassination or all-out war. All of these were attempted during Elizabeth's reign, and all of these failed. The pope even decreed that it was permissible for a good Catholic to murder the usurper bastard Elizabeth!

From attempts on her life to the Spanish Armada in 1588, Queen Elizabeth sailed through the turbulent times of her reign, seemingly untouched by the foreign forces opposing her.

At home in England, Catholicism was effectively forced underground. Illegal masses had to be heard in secret, the practice of which gave rise to the priest hole in certain country houses. Catholic priests in England were seen, at best, as highly suspicious or, at worst, as spies or assassins from the pope. Arguably it has taken centuries for that deeply rooted sentiment to die out – assuming it has!

Mary Stuart

It would be easy here to extend this chapter to include the details of the highs and lows of Elizabeth's reign. However, there are many far greater publications written for this purpose. We must concern ourselves with the succession through and ending of the Tudor dynasty. Queen Elizabeth I was unmarried and therefore unlikely to have a child. This meant that her hold on the throne could be ended with just a shot of the bow, a swing of the sword or even a passing illness. It was always known that her nearest heir was her cousin Mary Stuart, Queen of Scots. This always posed a slight looming threat to Elizabeth, particularly as Mary was a Catholic.

Mary Stuart was born on 8 December 1542, the only legitimate child of King James V of Scotland. He died just a few days later on 14 December, making Mary the Queen of Scots at just six days old. James V's mother had been Margaret Tudor, sister to Henry VIII – making Mary a great-granddaughter of Henry VII of England. Seeing as Henry VIII of England had three heirs in his son and daughters (plus there was also the Grey family), it originally seemed unlikely that Mary would stand any chance of inheriting the English crown. Fate however had other ideas.

Having avoided marrying Edward VI of England, in 1558 Mary married firstly the Dauphin of France, later King Francis II of France, making her both Queen of Scotland and France. However, Francis died just two years later, and Mary returned to Scotland. She had long asserted and reminded everyone of her claim to the English throne as her cousin Elizabeth's rightful heir. To push this claim still further, she took as her second husband yet another cousin, Henry Stuart, Lord Darnley – another descendant of Henry VII via Margaret Tudor. Mary and Darnley were first cousins. Although it was certainly not a happy marriage, they did produce a son and heir, James.

Mary may have been responsible for the assassination of her husband, who was not popular with the nobility in Scotland. However, she too was eventually dethroned by the Scottish people. She abdicated in favour of her son James VI and sought refuge in the kingdom of her cousin Elizabeth.

Mary's presence, indeed her very existence, posed a real threat to Elizabeth's rule. As a Catholic, Mary had the support of many dissolute Catholic nobles in England. Plots and conspiracies were made at home and abroad to assassinate Elizabeth and replace her with Mary and thus restore England to the Church of Rome. In short, Mary was kept under house arrest – usually far from London or Scotland but also as far from the sea as possible to prevent escape or rescue attempts.

Eventually, too many plots were uncovered. The last of these was the Babington Plot, in which Mary consented to an attempted assassination of Elizabeth in a letter to Anthony Babington. The letter was deciphered by Sir Tomas Walsingham, and Mary was arrested for treason. She was tried and sentenced to be executed at Fotheringhay Castle in 1587. Elizabeth tarried over the death warrant for several days. Like her sister before her, she struggled with the idea of doing away with a relative and heir to the throne. Also, she was concerned that Mary, like herself, was an anointed sovereign. It did not sit well with Elizabeth that such a person could or should be executed. Elizabeth signed the warrant on 1 February and entrusted it to one of her secretaries, William Davidson – ironically of Scottish descent. Reportedly, she asked that the act not be carried out and that the document be hidden away while she continued to consider the matter. However, two days later, the Privy Council met – without Elizabeth's knowledge – viewed the warrant which Davidson produced and decided to carry out the execution.

Sovereign Executes Sovereign

The execution in the Great Hall at Fotheringhay was famously a shambles. Firstly, Mary appeared in dark crimson – the colour of Catholic martyrs. Secondly, the executioner botched the job, cracking her skull with the first blow and not entirely severing her neck on the second. Thirdly, on picking up Mary's head it became apparent that she wore a wig, out of which her head fell onto the floor. William Cecil, the Lord Privy Seal, sent his nephew to make a report of what he saw. According to that report, Mary's lips continued to silently mutter for around fifteen minutes after execution, and her small pet dog – who presumably had gone unnoticed earlier – emerged from under her dress.

Elizabeth was incandescent with rage. She blamed Davidson for arranging the execution behind her back and had him sent to the Tower. This may have been a ruse to give Elizabeth plausible deniability; with Davidson's arrest, she could wash her hands of killing her cousin. Curiously, at the request of Cecil and Walsingham, Davidson was released just a year and a half later.

THE SPANISH ARMADA

In retaliation for Mary's execution, England's alliances with the Dutch, and England's privateers raiding Spanish treasure ships, Philip II of Spain declared war on England and launched the famously ill-fated Spanish Armada in 1588. This was a fast fleet of ships which carried with it an army with it, intent on invading England and taking it by force. Through seamanship, technology and lucky weather, the English saw off the Spanish fleet which never landed on English shores. Elizabeth remained supreme.

Queen Elizabeth I lived to the age of sixty-nine. In the last years of her reign, it was obvious that she would not produce a legitimate heir to the throne, owing to her age and lack of husband. The reality was that James VI, the only child of Mary, Queen of Scots, was arguably the nearest legitimate relative with a solid claim to the throne. Elizabeth, however, refused to name any successor, probably for her own safety lest she be shuffled off before her time so she could be replaced. In fact, there had been more than a handful of heirs considered – from the English and Scottish nobility to overseas royals and nobles, all with a claim via an English princely ancestor, some as far back as John of Gaunt (younger son of Edward III). There were also additional Suffolk claimants – members of Lady Jane Grey's family. However, from 1601 until Elizabeth's death in 1603, secret correspondence between King James VI of Scotland and Elizabeth's ministers went back and forth. During this time, it was eventually agreed that James would indeed succeed his cousin twice removed and be the first monarch of both England and Scotland. Elizabeth's personal opinion of the succession can only be guessed at, but it is likely that in her last years she became agreeable to a Stuart succession.

By late 1602, Elizabeth was really showing her age, and she entered a period of deep depression. By March 1603, she fell quite ill. She sat melancholic and motionless, staring into the distance for an alarming amount of hours. When told she must take to her bed, she uttered the immortal phrase: "'Must' is not a word used for princes!" Having eventually taken to her bed at Richmond Palace, she died on 24 March 1603. James VI of Scots was proclaimed as King James I of England. Elizabeth was laid to rest at Westminster Abbey alongside her half sister, Mary I. It should be noted that, having become king, James had the remains of his mother, Mary, Queen of Scots, moved from Peterborough Cathedral and placed in a tomb close to Elizabeth's.

The 'Tudor century' was over. The Tudors had effectively been a Welsh import. From now on however, Britain's royal houses would be imported from lands further outside the jurisdiction of England, beginning with the Stuarts of Scotland.

James I, 1603)–1625
Charles I, 1625–1649

*Interregnum, 1649-1660

Charles II, 1660–1685
James II, (1685–168

Mary II and William III, 1689–1694
William III (alone), 1694–1702

Anne, 1702–1714

EDWARD HILARY DAVIS

1e – One Land, One King

THE HOUSE OF STUART

JAMES STUART, KING OF SCOTS, succeeded Elizabeth I in 1603 as King of England.

Legend had told of a king who would – like the legendary King Arthur – once more unite the tribes of Britain as they had been under the Romans. It seemed that fate and succession had led to that man being James VI of Scotland – now also James I of England. He was the first man in history since the Romans (with the then-assumed exception of the legendary King Arthur) to rule all the lands and Kingdoms of Britain: from Land's End to John o'Groats, from St David's to Lowestoft; England, Wales and Scotland. One land, one king – or so he must have hoped.

ORIGINS OF THE HOUSE OF STUART

The name of the House of Stuart conjures up images of glens, mountains, castles, tartan, sheep's bladders and terrible weather. The name is so closely associated with the rich history of Scotland, it feels as old as time and just about the most Scottish family one can think of. The truth is very different. Like many an old British noble family, they were originally foreigners who came to this island as invaders for land and booty – or at the command of their lord. They certainly did not start off Scottish nor indeed was their name originally Stuart.

The house traces its foundation somewhat obscurely back to the years following the Norman Conquest of England. The probable and widely assumed founder of the dynasty was a man called Alan FitzFlaad (born c. 1078 and died sometime after 1121). He was a Breton knight or warrior from the north-west of France. He and his son were likely employed as mercenaries by King Henry I of England – the son of William the Conqueror. Alan and his son may have been known to Henry before he succeeded to the English throne, following the murder of his older brother, William II (Rufus). Following Henry's accession, Alan FitzFlaad and his son travelled to England. They may have been part of the entourage of Henry's wife – Matilda of Scotland – although it is also possible they may have been part of Henry's Breton forces in Normandy during the military struggle against his brothers.

In short, Alan FitzFlaad's progress and elevation in the court of Henry I was owing to his loyalty. He was the beneficiary of lands confiscated by Norman barons who rebelled against Henry. Alan received lands in Norfolk, estates around Arundel in Sussex and territory in Shropshire where he was appointed Sheriff. Coincidentally, some of his lands near Arundel (called Peppering) had been taken from another Norman noble, Rainald de Bailleul – the ancestor of the House of Balliol who also provided a King of Scots. (Today, the present Duke of Norfolk lives at Peppering Farm, overlooking Arundel Castle across the Arun Valley.)

Alan FitzFlaad married a Norman heiress, Avelina, who came with yet more land. Their two eldest sons cemented the family connections by marrying into two royal families. The eldest, William FitzAlan (son of Alan), married a niece of Henry I's bastard son, Robert, Earl of Gloucester, and became the Lord of Clun and Oswestry. He is seen as the founder of the FitzAlan family who eventually inherited (or were granted) the title of Earl of Arundel. The Earldom of Arundel is the oldest extant earldom in England and perhaps the oldest extant peerage, being first created in 1138.

The second son of Alan FitzFlaad was Walter FitzAlan (c.1106-1177). As a second son, he might not have been expected to have such a glittering career. As a young man, he held the lands of North Stoke near Arundel by gift of his brother. However, following Henry I's death in 1135, The Anarchy descended on England – the succession struggle between Henry's daughter, (Empress) Matilda, and Henry's nephew, Stephen of Blois. The FitzAlan brothers had been close to Henry I and occupied a prominent position at court. They needed to pick the winning side in the oncoming struggle. They chose the legitimist group in support of Matilda – after all, William FitzAlan was connected to Matilda's half-brother by marriage. William FitzAlan remained in England and fought revolts against King Stephen. The younger brother, Walter FitzAlan, journeyed to Scotland in 1136.

Walter offered his services to King David I of Scots, who supported the claims of Matilda as she was his niece. King David appointed Walter as High Steward of Scotland in c. 1150. As such, Walter became responsible for the day-to-day running of the king's household. Prior to this, members of Walter's family had also been stewards to the Breton lords of Dol – so he was well qualified for the role. Indeed this was a time when Scottish kings attempted to attract more Anglo-Norman knights and lords into their service with the promise of the gift of land and titles. The FitzAlans were one such family as was the family of de Brus (later known as 'de Bruce' or 'the Bruce'). Walter was granted lands in Renfrewshire. King David I's grandson and successor, Malcom VI, made Walter's position of steward a hereditary one. So it was that the High Stewardship of Scotland remained in the FitzAlan family for several generations and served many Scottish kings.

By September 1290, there was a succession crisis in Scotland. Margaret, the Maid of Norway, the last heir of her grandfather King Alexander III of Scots, died at Orkney en route from Norway to Scotland, at about the age of seven. She had been engaged to Edward of Caernarvon (future Edward II of England), which would have united the Kingdoms of Scotland and England centuries before James Stuart arrived on the scene – but alas not. Around thirteen families from Scotland, England and Flanders came forward with varying claims on the Scottish crown (including Robert the Bruce's grandfather). In order to avoid civil war, the Lords of Scotland asked Edward I of England to preside over the succession. Together with a Scottish commission, Edward and the Lords of Scotland chose John Balliol as King of Scots in 1292. However, following this, Edward treated Balliol as a puppet king and Scotland as his own vassal territory. The Lords of Scotland opposed John Balliol, who was now tainted by association, and set up a council to rule Scotland. Edward answered this challenge by invading. Balliol abdicated in 1296 and went into exile in France for the remainder of his life, and Scotland was left without a king for several years.

Robert the Bruce

Following many internal wars and much infighting between rival Anglo-Norman-Scots families for the Scottish throne as well as wars with England, Robert the Bruce emerged as the victorious successor to the throne of Scotland. He had politicked, murdered and fought battles and now emerged as the acknowledged King of Scots. The Battle of Bannockburn (1315), the Declaration of Arbroath (1320), the pope's recognition of the declaration (1324), and the eventual Treaty of Northampton with England (1328) recognised Robert I as King of Scots and Scotland as a separate kingdom from England.

At the time of Robert the Bruce's reign, the FitzAlan family were still High Stewards of Scotland. The family had also now assumed and adopted a 'sort of surname' based on their title: Stewart – sometimes and later more frequently spelled 'Stuart'. For most of Robert I's reign, it was Walter Stewart who was the 6th Lord High Steward. The family's close association with royalty reached another landmark when Walter Stewart married Marjorie Bruce, eldest daughter of the king. This was later to prove an important match. Walter and Marjorie had just one child together, a son, in 1316, but Marjorie died during the birth. Walter called his son and heir Robert in honour of the baby's grandfather the king. He went on to become High Steward of Scotland from 1327.

DAVID II OF SCOTLAND

King Robert the Bruce died in June 1329. He was succeeded by his only surviving legitimate son, King David II, who was only five years old. During David's minority, Scotland was governed by a series of lords until he came of age.

It was during this time that Edward III of England opportunistically exploited the weak situation in Scotland. He supported a potential invasion of Scotland led by another claimant to the throne: Edward Balliol – son of King John Balliol. This sparked another war with England, and following the Scottish defeat at the Battle of Halidon Hill in 1333, King David II and his court were forced to flee Scotland for France temporarily. David and his forces attempted to invade England, but David was captured at the Battle of Neville's Cross (near Durham) in 1346. He was held prisoner for around eleven years. Meanwhile, his nephew, Robert Stewart (High Steward of Scotland), governed Scotland reasonably well on his behalf. Quite the baptism of fire! This may well have created deep resentment between Robert and David.

With the Treaty of Berwick in 1357, David II was ransomed back to Scotland for 100,000 marks which would need to be paid in instalments. In order to get the money for these payments, David taxed his Scots subjects heavily, making him unpopular, and still he could not pay the ransom. Instead, he sought to have it cancelled in exchange for offering the succession to his throne to one of Edward III of England's sons – Lionel, Duke of Clarence. David himself was childless, having had no children by his wife, Princess Joan of England. However, in 1364 the Scottish parliament rejected the idea of an Englishman succeeding. David was determined to avoid his nephew, Robert Stewart, from succeeding him. In a bid to achieve this, he married his mistress, Margaret Drummond, in 1370 in the hope of producing an heir. When it seemed she could not provide him with one, he tried to divorce her. However, Margaret Drummond travelled to Avignon to petition the pope who decided in her favour. There was no divorce, and David died the following year in February. He was the last king of the House of de Brus/Bruce.

The Royal House of Stuart / Stewart

David's nephew Robert, the High Steward of Scotland, was crowned king, and the Royal House of Stuart (or Stewart) had begun. King Robert II (Stuart) owed his succession to a woman – his mother, Marjorie Bruce. Succession via women would be important for the Stuart dynasty. Technically, the Stuart dynasty would end with a woman too.

From Robert II, the House of Stuart continued to rule Scotland for the next several centuries. The crown was passed from father to son for the next six generations to King James V in 1513, who at the time was only seventeen months old. James V was the eldest surviving legitimate son of King James IV and Princess Margaret Tudor – daughter of Henry VII of England. Rather awkwardly, James IV was killed at the Battle of Flodden in 1513 at the hands of an English army – his in-laws! Despite this, his widow, Margaret Tudor, actually ruled Scotland as regent during their son James's minority.

James V

As part of an arranged marriage alliance, young James V married Princess Madeleine of France (daughter of Francis I) on New Year's Day 1537 in Notre Dame, Paris, in a bid to bolster the Auld Alliance between Scotland and France to spite the English. There were some French objections owing to Madeleine's frequent bouts of bad health, but having briefly 'honeymooned' at Chateau de la Roche-Guyon, the couple sailed for Scotland in May that year. Madeleine became unwell during the voyage. After taking up residence at Holyrood Palace, she died in July in the arms of King James.

Though this was a setback for Scotland and France, their courts wasted no time in finding a suitable replacement wife to continue to honour the Auld Alliance. Mary of Guise (1515-1560) was a young French noblewoman who had also been widowed the same year as James V. (Her first husband was Louis, Duke of Longueville, Grand Chamberlain of France.) King Francis I of France was content to arrange the marriage even though Mary and James both required persuasion.

The couple were married in St Andrews in 1538. Within two years they produced two sons – the cliché but desired 'heir and spare'. The line of the Stuarts seemed assured, at least until both of these infant sons died within a day of each other in April 1541. A year later (8 December 1542), James and Mary produced their only other child, also named Mary. However, as we have seen, James V died just a few days later on 14 December, making Mary the Queen of Scots at just six days old.

John Knox, the famous Scottish minister and theologian, recorded that King James, whilst on his deathbed, was informed of the birth of his daughter. The king, Knox recounts, was not best pleased but responded that what began with a woman would end with a woman. He was referring to the House of Stuart. In some ways he was right and in some ways wrong. The dynasty did not end with Mary, but its unchallenged control of the Scottish and English thrones ended centuries later in 1714 with another woman, Queen Anne (Stuart) .

Mary Queen of Scots

James V died in the same fashion as his father James IV, while being defeated in battle by the English. As his successor was female, it seemed like the end of centuries of rule for the House of Stuart in Scotland.

In 1453, the Treaty of Greenwich was signed between England and Scotland. It arranged for a marriage between Henry VIII's son, Edward, and the infant Mary, Queen of Scots. The marriage would not take place until she was ten. This would have united the crowns of the two kingdoms with the agreement that the countries themselves would remain separate.

However, owing to Catholic factions in the Scottish court, a Catholic match with France began to be favoured by many of Mary's ministers, and the Treaty of Greenwich was rejected by the Scottish parliament. There followed what is known as the 'Rough Wooing' (Eight Years' War) – during which Henry committed the English to raiding Scottish and French territories in an attempt to persuade them to honour their former agreement. Battles continued even after Henry VIII's death, and in 1547 the Scots were defeated at Pinkie in the last pitched battle between the two countries.

The young Mary was moved to Dumbarton Castle for her safety, and the Scots appealed to the French for help. A small French fleet arrived at Leith to help push back the English, and the Scottish parliament met in a nearby nunnery to agree to a new French marriage proposal: Mary would wed the son and heir of the King of France, the Dauphin Francis. She would not be Queen of England, but she would be Queen of France. The Auld Alliance would be cemented together by marriage and Catholicism. This was grave news indeed for the English – and yet another great 'what-if' of British History.

Young Mary grew up at the French court and married Francis in 1558. Through her paternal grandmother, Margaret Tudor, Mary was always conscious of her strong potential claim on the English throne too, especially as the succession of Elizabeth I was seen as void by many Roman Catholics, who considered her illegitimate. Mary deigned to use the royal arms of England alongside those of France as a personal flaunt of her claim. A year after the marriage, Francis became King Francis II of France, and therefore Mary was both Queen of Scotland and Queen of France. Francis too was recognised as King of Scots. Scotland and France were royally united. Similarly, England and Spain at the time were similarly united through the marriage of Philip II of Spain and Mary I (Tudor) of England. However, in both cases the union was short-lived. Francis II died in 1560 at age sixteen from an ear-related condition.

Politically, dynastically and emotionally, Francis's death was a huge setback for Mary. She had spent most of her life in the French court but now had to make the journey back to her other kingdom where she was the queen regnant. Hers was a fiery and chaotic reign, which has been covered in many books and films of dubious historical accuracy. Nonetheless, her personal life is full of murder, assassinations and executions – so worthy of a biopic or two! We shall not, therefore, delve into the details of her complicated reign but merely summarise.

Marriage to Lord Darnley

It is almost needless to say that Mary, having lived in France from the age of five, had little understanding of Scotland, its people or the complicated politics and religion of the day. The Reformation and Protestantism were on the rise in her kingdom, and she was outwardly Catholic. For the sake of stability, it seemed prudent for her to find another husband. The successful candidate was none other than a first cousin, Henry Stuart, Lord Darnley. He too was a grandchild of Margaret Tudor, but he was also of a cadet branch of the House of Stewart (the Earls of Lennox). He was a direct male descent from Alexander Stewart, 4th High Steward of Scotland. Lord Darnley was also a more recent descendant of a daughter of James II of Scots. Mary and Darnley were married at Holyrood Palace in 1565.

Darnley did not settle into the marriage. He behaved erratically and irritated many of the Lords of Scotland with his arrogance. Not content with being the king consort, he wanted to be recognised as co-sovereign with his wife with the right to keep the crown for himself should Mary die, but Mary and her court refused. Add to this the possibility of him being a homosexual, and his reputation amongst the great of Scotland was on a knife edge. After he was found complicit in the lynching and murder of Mary's close companion and advisor David Rizzio – who was stabbed to death in front of her while she was pregnant – Mary never trusted Darnley again.

A year after they were wed, Mary gave birth to her only child, James, at Edinburgh Castle. There was once again a Stuart heir for the Scottish throne.

Eight months after James's birth, Darnley was murdered on 10 February 1567. Barrels of gunpowder had been placed under his sleeping quarters in Edinburgh. After the explosion, his body was found nearby with his throat slit. There was an outcry for the murderer(s) to be brought to justice. The first witness on the scene, Captain William Blackadder, was later arrested, hung, drawn and quartered. However, most in Scotland and abroad felt that Mary must have at least been aware of the plot. In fact, she was widely believed to be complicit in the murder of her husband together with one of her lords, the Earl of Bothwell. In April, only two months after Darnley's death, Lord Bothwell abducted her (though she may have gone willingly), took her to Dunbar Castle and raped her (though again this may have been consensual). The next month they went to Edinburgh to be married in the Protestant church. Lord Bothwell had divorced his wife not twelve days earlier.

A Queen in Exile

Naturally, the lords and people of Scotland were furious that the queen should marry the man who was suspected of helping her murder her late husband. The Confederate Lords took Mary into custody the following June. Many subjects denounced her as a murderer, adulterer and heretic. In July, she suffered a miscarriage (presumably of Darnley's child). Days later, she was forced to abdicate the throne in favour of her one-year-old son, James VI. Bothwell went into exile in Denmark where died in prison in 1578. Mary eventually escaped to England. She had the strange audacity to expect her cousin, Elizabeth I of England, to help her regain her throne in Scotland – after she had spent a lifetime claiming that she alone was the rightful Queen of England. Queen Elizabeth was cautious and even made enquiries as to the conduct of the Confederate Lords in Scotland, their deposition of Mary and whether Mary was truly guilty of Darnley's murder. Eventually, Elizabeth took the decision to have Mary 'housed' far from London, Scotland and the sea. While imprisoned, Mary continued to plot against Queen Elizabeth. She was finally tried for treason and executed in 1587.

JAMES I

After Mary's abdication in 1567, Scotland had a new Stuart king, James VI. As we have seen, owing to plans made during the last years of the childless Elizabeth I, James was able to peacefully succeed to the English throne on 24 March 1603, uniting the Kingdoms of Scotland and England, if only in the person of the king.

James I had been raised a Protestant, as much of Scotland had by now become so. As a young man, James is famous for having preferred the company of men or boys to women, and it now seems quite probable that he was a homosexual. Nevertheless, the man did his duty and duly married a foreign princess to secure a Stuart succession and to ensure Scotland had an ally in Europe.

Of particular note for this book, the princess in question was Anne of Denmark who married James on 20 August 1589 – whilst James was only king in Scotland, not England yet. Her father was King Frederick II of Denmark (who was incidentally the man responsible for the imprisonment and eventual death of James's 'stepfather,' the Earl of Bothwell.) Frederick II and indeed his daughter Anne were both of the House of Oldenburg who had ruled Denmark for around three centuries since the time of Christian I. James could have had no idea that his bride's family would one day occupy his thrones of England and Scotland in place of his own line – as is the case with the present King Charles III who is descended in the male line from the Oldenburg family.

The couple took up their place in London as King James I and Queen Anne of England in 1603 following the death of Elizabeth I. By then, they had produced the three children who would live to see adulthood. Their eldest son, Henry (born in 1594), later became Prince of Wales but sadly died of typhoid fever at age eighteen in 1612. Their only surviving daughter, Elizabeth (1596-1662), was married off abroad to the

Elector Palatine of the Rhine, Frederick V of the House of Wittelsbach (Palatinate-Simmern), who was briefly King of Bohemia. It could not be known then, but this would be an important marriage in the history of the British Crown. More on that later. James and Anne's second son, the spare, was called Charles (1600-1649). Following his older brother's death, he became heir to two kingdoms at around the age of twelve. As the only surviving son, it was upon Charles that the hopes of the Stuart dynasty were therefore placed.

Assassination Attempt

We should of course give a brief honourable mention to the fact that most of James's reign as King of England nearly became a 'what-if' of British history. Some dissident Roman Catholic gentlemen led by Robert Catesby attempted to assassinate the king along with most of his family and court by blowing up the House of Lords during the State Opening of Parliament on 5 November 1605. This is famously known as the Gunpowder Plot and involved some barrels and a certain Guido/Guy Fawkes. The rebels plan was, having blown up the king and Parliament, to start a revolt, abduct the king's daughter, Elizabeth, who was only nine at the time, and install her as a Catholic queen. However, the Roman Catholic plotters were foiled, probably by the Cecil family and their network of spies. James could have been blown up like his father had been but was saved by the loyalty of certain Protestant subjects. To this day, towns and villages throughout the kingdom mark the anniversary by burning an effigy of Guy Fawkes (or in some extreme cases the pope). This is most spectacular in and around Lewes in East Sussex.

CHARLES I AND CIVIL WARS

James I's reign, which we do not have to delve into the details of, passed peacefully, and his crown was passed to his son and heir, King Charles I. As any good school child will tell you and as Monty Python famously relates, the most important thing about Charles's reign was that he was a lot shorter at the end of it than he had been at the beginning! Charles is the king who lost his head, after which followed the strangest of things in the UK – a republic. Once again, we must rush through an important and complex part of British history, the English Civil War (1642-1651). At school, many of us will have defined it merely as Cavaliers versus Roundheads.

The Civil War was fought on the basic principle that the king should not tax his people at will or on a whim and could only levy taxes with the consent of Parliament. In short, this became a struggle to correct the (im)balance of power between the king and Parliament. It led to open war and divided the kingdom into two opposing groups of thought: those who upheld the belief that the king had a God-given right to reign as he wills and those who believed that the king only had power by consent of Parliament and should rule with it. Many bloody battles and sieges were fought in nearly every region of England and later in Scotland and Ireland too. There were three distinct civil wars; arguably they should be called the British Civil Wars – though they were fought for different reasons in different kingdoms. There were religious grievances too. Many were anxious that the monarch remain a supporter of the Protestant faith as head of the Church of England, yet Charles I seemed to be sliding in the direction of the Roman Catholic faith via his wife Henrietta-Maria of France, sister to Louis XIII, and his belief in his divine right to rule as he saw fit.

For our own brief purposes, we only need to concern ourselves with the fact that the Royalists lost several battles towards the end of the Civil War. Following Charles's defeat at the Battle of Naseby in 1645, Royalist forces began losing battles up and down the kingdom – in part thanks to Parliament's New Model Army led by Thomas Fairfax and Oliver Cromwell. At the siege of Oxford in 1646, King Charles was even forced to disguise himself as a servant in order to escape.

Charles fled and placed himself in the hands of a Scottish army. However, after months of negotiations between the Scottish parliament and the English parliament, the Scots effectively sold the king to the English (Parliamentarian) forces for £100,000 or so in January 1647. Charles became a captive in his own land. He was moved from house to house (or palace to palace) until he was confined at Hampton Court. From there he managed to escape to Southampton hoping to get to France. However, Charles was caught and incarcerated at Carisbrooke Castle on the Isle of Wight in the English Channel – to ensure little chance of rescue or escape.

From his castle prison on the Isle of Wight, he contracted secret agreements and treaties with the Scots which involved them invading England and helping to restore him in exchange for establishing Presbyterianism in England. The Scots invaded and a second civil war began, but the Scots were defeated by Parliamentarians at Preston in 1648. The Royalists' hopes were dashed. Charles had no choice but to try to negotiate with his captors.

A King Tried for Treason

Parliament had difficulty deciding what to do. There were many factions and disagreements. Most wanted to continue negotiating with the king, but Oliver Cromwell together with representatives from the army and Puritans in the House of Commons wanted to hold Charles to account and believed that they had done all that they could through negotiations. In what was effectively a military coup, they purged Parliament of members unsympathetic to their cause and formed the Rump Parliament which aimed to put King Charles I on trial for treason. They created an ad hoc tribunal known as the High Court of Justice and tried the king in January 1649 in Westminster Hall. He was found guilty of being a tyrant, traitor, murderer and public enemy to the good people of this nation and was sentenced to death by beheading.

The execution took place on a specially constructed platform on the side of the Whitehall Banqueting House in London on 30 January 1649. Before walking from St James's Palace where he was being held,

Charles elected to wear an extra shirt as it was chilly and he did not wish to shiver and look as though he were afraid.

Charles I's death came as a shock to many both in the British Isles and abroad. After all, he was tried and executed over a century before the French got the idea.

The Commonwealth of England

The Rump Parliament ruled England only for a short time before Oliver Cromwell was eventually named as Lord Protector – with all the powers, courtesies and abilities of a king. Indeed, he was king in all but name. (Parliament offered him the title of King, but he refused. There were a variety of reasons, not least of which was that it would undermine the Parliamentarian cause.) Nominally, England was now a republic.

The Arms of the Williams alias Cromwell family *The Arms of Oliver Cromwell as Lord Protector*

It is easy to cast Cromwell as a common country character, and Hollywood has and does just that. He was a country gentleman without an aristocratic title, yes, but his ancestry is of note.

Oliver Cromwell was descended from Morgan ap William, a Welsh brewer from Glamorgan. Morgan moved to Putney where he married Katherine Cromwell, sister of the famous Thomas Cromwell, who eventually became chief minister to King Henry VIII and was briefly Earl of Essex and Knight of the Garter.

Morgan and Katherine's son, Richard Williams, decided to take on the name of his then-successful uncle, becoming Sir Richard Williams alias Cromwell (sometimes just Cromwell). Sir Richard benefited from his uncle's patronage and the dissolution of the monasteries and his gains were passed down the generations. Sir Richard's cousin, Gregory, 1st Baron Cromwell, was married to Elizabeth Seymour, sister of Jane Seymour, Queen of England – making the Cromwells (briefly) brother-in-law and cousin-in-law to King Henry VIII and uncle to Edward VI. Sir Richard Cromwell's son (Oliver Cromwell's grandfather), Sir Henry Cromwell, was one of the richest men in Huntingdonshire. However, he had many children, and this wealth was not altogether passed to Oliver's father, Robert. Therefore, though they were of the landed gentry, Oliver's family were not rich but not poor either.

Oliver Cromwell was himself also descended from Alexander Stewart, 4th High Steward of Scotland – mutual ancestor of Charles I. Cromwell and the King were very distant kin.

Royalists Revived

The days of the English Republic (aka the Commonwealth or the Protectorate) are often referred to as simply the Interregnum, literally, the period between reigns. However, this could be considered a misnomer as one could argue that there was, in fact, a king during this time. The Royalists believed that succession to the throne was automatic. Thus, when Charles I was executed, the title of king immediately passed to his eldest son, Charles II. (Charles II was strategically in exile in The Hague, seeking support for the Royalist cause, when his father was tried and killed.)

The following month the Scottish parliament declared him to be King Charles II of Great Britain and Ireland – although they refused to let him enter Scotland unless he agreed to establish Presbyterianism as the state religion in all three kingdoms. Eventually he agreed to this and arrived in Scotland in June 1650. This made him popular with the Scots but unpopular with the English. Undeterred, he was crowned King of Scotland at Scone in June the following year, and war soon broke out between the two countries.

EDWARD HILARY DAVIS

Charles II marched with a Scottish army south into England but did not attract many English Royalist supporters. He met Oliver Cromwell's forces at the Battle of Worcester on 3 September 1651 and was soundly defeated. Fleeing for his life and hunted by Cromwell's Roundheads, at one point he very narrowly avoided capture by famously hiding up an oak tree on the grounds of Boscobel House. The tree has long been referred to as the Royal Oak, a name afterwards adopted by many a pub as well.

Charles made a difficult escape from safe house to safe house on a convoluted journey from Worcester to Shoreham on the Sussex coast. (This route is now a footpath called The Monarch's Way.) There was a thousand-pound reward on his head, yet no one turned him in, even though they might be put to death for harbouring him. From Shoreham, Charles went into exile in Normandy and later the Southern Netherlands.

An Invitation To Be King

Oliver Cromwell died in 1658. Rather like a king, he was buried with much pomp at Westminster Abbey and was succeeded as Lord Protector by his son Richard Cromwell. It soon became obvious that Richard was inexperienced and lacked the ability to govern. The Rump Parliament was recalled, and he resigned the Office of Lord Protector. In the uncertainty that followed, General George Monck, a Parliamentarian commander, was keen to avoid the nation descending into anarchy. In April 1660, he marched his army to London to keep the peace. As popular opinion was turning towards the idea of restoring the monarchy, Monck made overtures to the exiled Charles II about the possibility of return.

Following new elections, Parliament invited Charles II to return as king. Charles left Scheveningen, the Netherlands, in 1660 and arrived in England on 29 May, his thirtieth birthday.

England rejoiced in its new king. Amnesties were offered to all those who had supported Cromwell, with the exception of the regicides who signed the death warrant of Charles's father – some of them were executed. Along with some of his comrades, Oliver Cromwell was exhumed and posthumously beheaded.

Charles II, the Merry Monarch

The reign of Charles II was punctuated by unfortunate disasters such as the return of the plague, repeated naval defeats at the hands of the Dutch and the 1666 Great Fire of London which destroyed much of the Old City including St Paul's Cathedral. That said, there were also great advances in science, art, music, architecture and astronomy, in part thanks to Charles's vibrant and merry court and his own interests. He was known as the Merry Monarch, and not for nothing. Despite being married to a Portuguese princess, Catharine of Braganza – which gave the English Tangier into the bargain – Charles fathered no legitimate children with her. Instead, he had a stream of mistresses and a dozen illegitimate children, many of whom were given titles such as the Duke of Monmouth, Duke of Grafton, Duke of Northumberland, Duke of St Albans, Duke of Richmond and Earl of Plymouth. None of these children could inherit the throne however. Throughout his entire reign, Charles's lawful heir was his younger brother James, Duke of York.

A Dangerously Catholic Influence

As Charles was going on his merry way, James had stealthily married Anne Hyde in 1660 – perhaps because she was already visibly pregnant by him. Anne was the daughter of Charles's closest adviser, Edward Hyde, who shortly after the marriage was made Earl of Clarendon. The couple had four sons and four daughters together. However, only two of the children survived childhood: Mary and Anne. The eldest, Mary, at the age of fifteen, married her first cousin, William of Orange, to help make peace with the Dutch in 1677. Anne married Prince George of Denmark (son of King Frederick III) in 1683. The Stuart succession seemed relatively secure in James, Duke of York, and his daughters should he not produce yet another son. Parliament was content in the knowledge that at least all those near in the line of succession were Protestant.

The waters were somewhat muddied, however, when James converted to Roman Catholicism in 1668 or 1669. He kept his conversion relatively secret until the Test Act of 1673, a new English law effectively banning Roman Catholics from holding high office. Furthermore, holders of such offices had to take an oath that confirmed they did not believe in transubstantiation and were therefore not Roman Catholic. Instead of doing this, James resigned his office as Lord High Admiral, which made his conversion public knowledge. On the face of it, King Charles II opposed his brother's conversion, but he likely had very Catholic leanings himself, which were kept secret until right before his death. Parliament and the public were disappointed with James but became down right suspicious when, after his wife Anne died, he took a new Italian Catholic wife (Princess Mary of Modena) in 1673. He was forty, and she was fifteen, only four years older than his eldest daughter. Most of the British public believed she was a plant or a spy for the papacy.

The succession was now cause for great concern in Parliament, and the perceived threat of a Catholic invasion or conspiracy was cause for outright public hysteria. A failed Anglican clergyman named Titus Oates talked up an imagined Popish Plot to kill Charles and put his Catholic brother on the throne. Some members of Parliament proposed excluding James from the throne in favour of the King's eldest bastard son, James Scott, Duke of Monmouth – a Protestant. King Charles II repeatedly had to dissolve Parliament in order to stop a Bill of Exclusion from being passed. For a time, James was encouraged to live abroad and then in Scotland. Monmouth himself was found to be involved in a plot to kill his own father, and he went into exile.

James had returned to favour by 1684, though his succession had divided Parliament between those who were comfortable with him becoming king (Tories) and those who were not (Whigs). James was put on the Privy Council in 1684, a year before his brother died. Charles II supposedly had a deathbed conversion to Catholicism.

James II

Though there were misgivings about his religion, James did succeed his brother as James II and VII to popular rejoicing and relief at the smoothness of the succession and the avoidance of another civil war. He initially ruled with success and support from both Parliament and the public, taking more of an active interest in state affairs than his brother had. However, his religious inclinations, about which so many had harboured doubts, soon came to the fore. He appointed Catholic friends to prominent positions wherever he could; he allowed the pope's envoy back into the kingdom (for the first time since the reign of Mary I); and he issued the Declaration of Indulgence.

On paper, the Declaration showed more tolerance to all Christian sects, but it was seen as a thinly veiled attempt to open the door for a full return of Catholicism throughout the land. James even went so far as to influence the appointment of the lord-lieutenants and the election of Masters of Oxbridge Colleges and Livery Companies. He ordered that the Declaration of Indulgence should be read from every pulpit alienating the bishops and clergy. He began to fill Parliament with his Catholic friends, planning to establish a Catholic majority to repeal anti-Catholic acts – alienating many MPs. James was unknowingly creating a ticking time bomb of common Anglican dislike for his rule. It would not take much to spark an explosion.

James inadvertently lit the fuse a year after issuing the 1687 Declaration of Indulgence. In 1688, he re-issued the Declaration, and seven of his bishops formally protested. In response, James decided to have them arrested to much public outcry. To make matters worse for the largely Protestant population, in June that year, James's second wife, Mary of Modena, gave birth to a Catholic son and heir, James Francis Edward. It was feared that there would be no end to the re-Catholicisation of the kingdom. Several disgruntled peers and MPs (as well as a bishop) issued an invitation (drafted by Henry Sydney) to the king's son-in-law, William of Orange, inviting him to invade England and become joint monarch with his wife, Mary. William accepted the invitation and so began what is now known as the Glorious Revolution.

THE GLORIOUS REVOLUTION

William landed at Brixham in Devon on 5 November (an auspicious date for Stuart kings) with roughly half the Dutch army (around fifteen thousand men). As William's army progressed, it gathered not just the support of the public but also of many of the wealthy and powerful magnates of King James's court – including John Churchill, Duke of Marlborough, and both of James's own daughters.

James gathered his own forces near Salisbury, but he could not trust the loyalty of many of his commanders nor stop men defecting. His tactical withdrawal was effectively an admission of defeat. Fearing for his life, he fled rather than fight for his crown, which many saw as an act of cowardice. He was eventually captured at Faversham and brought to Rochester, where William of Orange allowed him to quietly escape to France during the night on 23 December 1688. Before leaving England, James tossed the Great Seal into the Thames as a final act of spite, vainly hoping that without it Parliament could not be recalled.

WILLIAM AND MARY

Soon afterward, both parliaments deemed that James had, by his flight, effectively abdicated and so proclaimed that, by right, his daughter, Princess Mary Stuart, and her husband/cousin Prince William of Orange would rule jointly as co-monarchs. Their joint coronation was held at Westminster Abbey on 11 April 1689, and soon new legislation was passed to bar Catholics from the succession in the future. The new King William III and Queen Mary II cemented their hold over the kingdoms.

Meanwhile, James was received in exile in France by his cousin Louis XIV – the arch nemesis of William of Orange and an ardent Catholic who persecuted Protestants (Huguenots) in his own country. Louis supplied James with an army to invade Ireland, where James had a fair degree of support from the large Catholic population there. For their part, the Irish parliament remained loyal to James and even passed a bill of attainder against James's usurpers in England.

However, William III personally took his own army to Ireland to dispute the matter, and James was ultimately defeated at the Battle of the Boyne on 1 July 1690. Once again, having faced a military setback, James feared for his own life and hastily fled back into exile, abandoning his loyal Irish followers to their fate and potential reprisals. For this, James is sometimes in Irish writings called *Séamus an Chaca* – James the Sh*t!

James, the Catholic Stuarts and their supporters (known as Jacobites) went into exile in Catholic France. His cousin King Louis kindly housed the Roi d'Angleterre (French for 'King of England') at the château of Saint-Germain-en-Laye west of Paris. After 1690, James's chances of reclaiming his throne(s) began to diminish. He still had pockets of support in Britain, and there were assassination attempts made on William III. However, once these plots were unveiled, they did nothing but harm to James's cause.

Six years into his exile, an exciting opportunity fell into James's lap. Louis XIV had influence over the election of the new King of Poland. Louis suggested putting James forward for the Crown of Poland; however, James declined, feeling that accepting the crown of Poland would mean he and his heirs could never return as Kings of England because Parliament would disqualify them. As it turned out, it made little difference. James II and VII remained a penitent Catholic in France. He died at Saint-Germain-en-Laye in 1701. His daughter, Mary II, had died seven years earlier. King William III died the following year.

William III and Mary II ruled together until her death in 1694; then William reigned alone until his own death in 1702. His story is further told in the next chapter. With the death of Mary and the imminent death of her husband, it was obvious that their successor should be the only other Protestant child of King James II by his first marriage: Anne.

Queen Anne

Anne was crowned on St George's Day 1702. For nearly all of her life, Anne had been weak and sickly. She did not even attend the wedding of her elder sister because she was in isolation with smallpox.

In 1680, during the reign of her uncle, Charles II, Anne's second cousin, George of Hanover (the future George I and Anne's successor), made a visit to England, which may have sparked rumours of an engagement between them. The Hanovers, however, had other plans for George, and King Charles had other plans for Anne. The king surveyed the royal marriage markets for a suitable partner for his granddaughter looking for someone who would keep his Protestant subjects happy and also aggravate his Catholic ally and cousin, Louis XIV of France. The wisest option, as it has repeatedly been for many royal families over the centuries, was to marry someone from the Danish royal house. The Danes were allied with France but were, conveniently, Protestant. A Danish match for Anne was agreeable to the courts on both sides of the Channel. Prince George of Denmark was the younger brother of King Christian V, making him Anne's second cousin once removed via James I's marriage to Anne of Denmark (Anne's great-grandmother and namesake). Anne's father consented to the match, and the two were wed at St James's Palace in July 1863.

Prince George was of the Danish Royal House of Oldenburg – which, as we will later see, is very apt. Oldenburg, which is today a city, is located in Lower Saxony. Founded around 1100, the Counts of Oldenburg eventually became the Kings of Denmark through profitable marriage and ancient lineages. Christian, Count of Oldenburg, became Christian I of Denmark in 1448. Anne's husband, Prince George of Denmark, was a direct male-line descendant of Christian I. A few years after his marriage to Princess Anne of England, the joint monarchs William and Mary gave George the title Duke of Cumberland in 1689.

A Prince of Denmark

George of Denmark was quiet and unambitious. He knew that he had a job to do in providing spare Protestant heirs for the throne. He quickly obliged. Anne was pregnant within months of their marriage; however, the pregnancy ended in miscarriage. More pregnancies followed and produced two daughters. However, in 1687, father and daughters suffered from smallpox. George survived, but both infant daughters died. Anne then suffered further miscarriages in January and October that year then again in 1688. The couple went on to have a further eleven children, all of which were either miscarriages, stillborn or dead within a year.

George diligently served as Anne's consort when she succeeded her brother-in-law as monarch. By then however, it had already become clear that they would not have any living children. For fear of her father James or half-brother James Francis Edward returning and claiming the throne, in 1701 (the year before Anne became queen), Parliament drew up the Act of Settlement. It confirmed two things: Anne's succession and the barring of all Catholics from succeeding the English/British throne. Therefore, after Anne, the crown would bypass all the other Stuarts (James II and his descendants) and pass to her cousin once removed, Princess Sophia of the Palatinate. Sophia was a Protestant and a granddaughter of King James I and King James VI. She was also married to the Elector of Hanover.

Thus, there was to be no House of Oldenburg dynasty reigning over England. Like the childless William and Mary, Anne and George are considerable 'what-ifs' of British history, both families ruling the kingdom for but a single generation. George died at Kensington Palace in 1708. Anne would continue in her reign until her own death in 1714. Although they tragically did not have children to found a new house or dynasty, in 1946 one of George's kinsmen, another member of the House of Oldenburg, would marry another female British monarch and be her consort – Prince Philip of Greece and Denmark. On that occasion, the marriage did produce healthy children, the eldest of

EDWARD HILARY DAVIS

whom succeeded to the British throne in 2022 – Charles III. The plan to put a member of the Oldenburg family on the British throne, which was hatched in the late seventeenth century, has finally come to fruition. But let's not get ahead of ourselves.

Great Britain

It is worth noting that, from 1707, Anne was Queen of Great Britain. The new Kingdom of Great Britain, finally uniting the Kingdoms of England (which already included Wales) and Scotland, was formed by the 1707 Acts of Union passed by both parliaments. From the first day of May 1707, the new single indivisible kingdom was governed by one central parliament as well as one monarch.

Anne's reign of this newly united kingdom was short-lived. By 1713, the queen was suffering from declining health – possibly brought on by her diet and also her workload. In fact, she had become so fat that she was unable to walk. She suffered a stroke in 1714 and died a few days later on 1 August. Due to Princess Sophia's death only two months prior, the crown passed to Sophia's son, George, now Elector of Hanover.

Jacobites: End of the Line

The Stuarts would never sit on the throne of Britain again, though not for lack of trying. Over the proceeding decades, several attempts were made to re-establish the reign of the House of Stewart through invasion and rebellion. Perhaps the most famous example of this took place from 1745 to 1746 in Scotland under the leadership of Prince Charles Edward Stuart, grandson of James II (Bonnie Prince Charlie).

The uprising of Bonnie Prince Charlie initially had some success, with the Jacobites winning battles in Scotland and Prince Charles taking Edinburgh. Charles and his followers were even able to invade England, getting as far south as Derby. The Jacobite cause was all but destroyed, however, at the Battle of Culloden (16 April 1746). After the battle, Prince Charles returned to exile in France. He died in 1788.

On the death in 1807 of Prince Charles's younger brother, Henry Benedict Stuart, Cardinal Duke of York, the legitimate male line of the Stuarts died out, and the Jacobite cause died with it. There are, however, some hard-line Catholic societies today who support the legitimacy of a Jacobite succession to this day through various female lines. At the time of this writing, the present heir would be Franz, Duke of Bavaria (born 1933). His own heir is his younger brother, Prince Max (born 1937). The line thereafter passes to Max's daughter, Princess Sophie (born 1967), and then to her son, Prince Joseph Wenzel of Liechtenstein, heir apparent to the throne of Liechtenstein (born 1995).

It is possible that one day this Catholic Jacobite line might merge with the reigning house in Britain – via a royal marriage. However, this would likely involve one party dispensing with their religion and converting to the other's.

1 f – A Brief New Colour

The House of Orange

William III (1689-1702)

WILLIAM III is known as William of Orange. We generally think of the House of Orange as Dutch. Prince of Orange is a title still used today by the Dutch royal family. At one time, this princely Protestant family stood in the way of France and Louis XIV's total influence over the Netherlands. It is therefore interesting that the House of Orange should itself be a French house in origin. When we think of French families ruling England, we usually think of the Normans and the Plantagenets. The Oranges were technically the last French house to do so.

While technically French in origin, the House of Orange was essentially a Dutch family. The House of Orange is a convenient shortening of its proper name: the House of Orange-Nassau. This was effectively a cadet branch of the House of Nassau, which was founded around the same time as the building of a castle of the same name (in modern-day Rhineland-Palatinate in Germany) by Dudo of Laurinburg at the turn of the twelfth century. He is considered the founder of the House of Nassau since his descendant successors styled themselves the Counts of Nassau. In the Germanic tradition, the family lands were divided between brothers. Two brother descendants of Dudo, Walram and Otto, made such a division. Walram's descendants became the Dukes of Nassau and, in the late nineteenth century, the Grand Dukes of Luxembourg. Indeed, the present Grand Duke, Henri, is a direct descendant of Walram.

Otto's descendants eventually inherited the County of Nassau, which was a state within the Holy Roman Empire. Generations of the Ottonian line also accumulated estates in the Kingdom of France. Intermarriage with Dutch, Germanic and French nobility propelled the fortunes and estates of the Nassau family upwards. They became close at times to the Kings of France and later the Habsburg Emperors and the Dukes of Burgundy. In 1515, Emperor Charles V appointed Count Henry III of Nassau-Breda stadtholder (steward) of Holland. Henry married Claudia de Chalon that same year. This was a fortuitous pairing, as their son René inherited his mother's brother's title of Prince of Orange in 1530. But what is Orange?!

Prince of Orange as a title today sounds like it could be a new brand of orange-flavoured fizzy drink. However, in the sixteenth century, it referred to the Principality of Orange north of Avignon in modern-day Provence in the south of France. (Interestingly, the etymology of Orange – the place – is not linked with the fruit. It is derived from a Gaulish word with the same spelling but a different pronunciation.) Orange was a feudal state, so its title was that of a sovereign prince. The principality was created by none other than Emperor Frederick I Barbarossa, when he elevated it from a county in 1163 – making it a sovereign principality within the Holy Roman Empire.

ORIGINS OF ORANGE

In 1544, the title of Prince of Orange passed to René's cousin in the Spanish Netherlands, William 'the Silent' of Nassau, later known as (the first but lesser-known) William of Orange (1533-1584). From him, the family was known as the House of Orange-Nassau. This William led successful Dutch revolts against the Spanish, eventually leading to the formation of a decentralised republic. It was William the Silent's great-grandson who would eventually become stadtholder of Holland, Prince of Orange, King of England (from 1689), and the William of Orange in school history books. He was, however, the last of his house to actively rule the Principality of Orange.

EDWARD HILARY DAVIS

The Principality of Orange was effectively dragged into the post-Reformation wars of religion on the side of Protestantism. The region is far from the Netherlands and further still from England, but during the wars, it became a safe destination for (Protestant) Huguenots fleeing the persecution of Louis XIV of France – a fact of which the French king was not unaware. The principality was captured by the French twice, but William did not give up his claim of sovereignty over the small state.

Following William III's death without issue in 1702, there were a few claimants to the title of Prince of Orange. For strategic reasons, the French entered their own claimant. The matter of Orange was not resolved until the 1713 Treaty of Utrecht. Effectively, the principality was ceded to France, but the title of Prince of Orange was not renounced and therefore has stayed in use in the Orange-Nassau family ever since.

Furthermore, since the forming of the Kingdom of the Netherlands in 1815 under King William I of Orange-Nassau, the title of Prince of Orange has traditionally been the title given to the heir apparent to the throne. Since 1983, this title may be passed by absolute primogeniture, meaning the eldest child (not eldest son) may inherit. Today, the title is held by Princess Catharina-Amalia (born 2003), daughter of King Willem-Alexander of the Netherlands.

Whilst the Orange title is more exotic than that of Nassau, it is worth noting that Nassau is the senior male line of the House of Orange-Nassau. Orange was acquired from a female line. It is perhaps for this reason, and in the interest of simplification, that William III of England, on his royal arms, used only the arms of Nassau as an escutcheon and not those of Orange.

GLORIOUS REVOLUTION AND DUTCH COURAGE

As we have seen, William of Orange was invited to take the throne of England owing to his birth, his marriage and, perhaps just as crucially, his religion. It was hoped that he and Queen Mary would be able to forge a new Protestant dynasty – conceivably called Orange-Stuart or similar! It was not to be.

Following Queen Mary's death in 1694 from smallpox at just thirty-two, William III ruled alone. He had been a popular co-monarch sharing the crown with his wife following the Glorious Revolution, but after Mary's death ,William's popularity with the people gradually diminished. It is likely this was caused by the realisation that he would not form a new Protestant dynasty to rival the Stewarts/Jacobites. Also, he was often pushing the interests of some of his Dutch favourites at court such as Hans Wilhelm Bentinck and Arnold Joost van Keppel. This has led to speculation of his homosexuality – but only speculation.

During his own reign, William III managed to establish an uneasy peace with France for a time. To this day, he is recognised as one of the great military nemeses of King Louis XIV. However, in William's later reign, his chief concern was the succession. Now that it was obvious that he would not found a Dutch royal dynasty in Britain and with his aging sister-in-law Anne having produced no surviving heirs either, plans for the succession needed to be made.

Protestant Princes Only

As we have seen, there was some fear that the Catholics would return in the form of the Jacobites and plunge the Kingdoms into more civil wars or wars of religion. Parliament drew up the Act of Settlement which was passed in 1701 – during William III's reign. It effectively stipulated that following the succession of Anne, should she fail to produce any heirs, the throne would pass to her cousin Sophie, Electress of Hanover – and then to her heirs in turn. (At this time her son, George, was already forty-one.) This bypassed many Jacobite, Catholic family members, but the objective was to achieve some stability and to keep the kingdom Protestant by retaining an actively Protestant monarch.

William III died on 8 March 1702 at Kensington Palace, at only fifty-two, following a fall from his horse which broke his collarbone

EDWARD HILARY DAVIS

and later led to pneumonia. The succession passed to his sister-in-law, Anne. He was the first and last of his house to rule England. Following the defeat of Napoleon, in part thanks to the British, the Kingdom of the Netherlands was established under Wilhelm I, Prince of Orange, in March 1815. The House of Orange-Nassau remains the ruling house in the Netherlands today.

On William III's death, the succession passed to his sister-in-law, Anne, in 1702. She reigned alone as sovereign. Having tragically failed to produce any heirs, upon her death, the crown passed to her Protestant second cousin, George of Hanover (Sophie's son) in 1714. (The Catholic members of the Stuart dynasty, the Jacobites, were barred from the succession by the aforementioned 1701 Act of Settlement.)

George I, 1714-1727
George II, 1727-1760
George III , 760-1801

George III, 1801-1816
(after renouncing claim to the Kingdom of
France)

George III, 1816-1820
(after Hanover is elevated from an
electorate to a kingdom)

George IV, 1820-1830

William IV, 1830-1837

Victoria, 1837-1901

1g – The Germans are Coming

THE HOUSE OF HANOVER

THE HOUSE OF HANOVER is the first of two (or arguably three) German dynasties that by fate and fortune found themselves ruling Britain. It is because of that fact that there have been jokes for several centuries about the British always importing their monarchs from Germany. With the Hanovers, however, it is almost true. Because of the 1701 Act of Settlement, the British had looked abroad to the Germanic states to find another safe (Protestant) pair of hands to take up the British crown. King George I was in fact quite reluctant to leave his native Hanover and take up the crown of an island he had never been to and whose language he could not speak.

Origins of the House of Hanover

Who, one might ask, are these Germans anyway? It is certainly confusing that such a family should replace a native Scottish ruling family in Britain. The Hanovers unsurprisingly came from a town called Hanover in central Germany – now the capital of the state of Lower Saxony. As we have seen, a name of a house is usually derived from the territorial lands that family holds – in this case the Electorate of Hanover within the Holy Roman Empire. The House of Hanover was itself a cadet branch of the House of Welf (later known as Guelph, founded in the eleventh century), which in turn was a branch of the even-older House of Este. In the eighteenth century, some historians suggested that the Este family was originally part of the plebeian Attii family of ancient Rome who moved to Este to defend it from Germanic tribal invasions.

There is little surviving evidence for this however, but it is certain that the House of Hanover, a very recognisable German family, through the Welfs and Estes, had Italian origins.

Alberto Azzo II, Margrave of Milan (996-1097), chose a location near Padua for a castle – Este, after which his dynasty was named. Two of his sons founded their own dynasties. The elder son, named Welf IV (c.1035-1101), became Duke of Bavaria, founding the Elder House of Welf (or Guelph). In the early and mid-Middle Ages, the Welfs held possession of huge swathes of Germany, including the Duchies of Saxony in the north and Bavaria in the south as well as other lands. Like similar powerful families of the day, the House of Welf struggled and fought to keep these lands. In the twelfth century, these lands were held in part by Henry the Lion of the House of Welf, Duke of Saxony and of Bavaria (c.1129-1195). He founded a series of cities in his duchies and counties, including Lüneburg and Brunswick. The city of Brunswick became his capital, and he had a bronze statue of a lion erected there, probably in 1166. Henry the Lion took as his second wife Matilda (the last Matilda we will include in this particular history), daughter of Henry II of England. One of his sons, William of Winchester, was born in 1184 (during a brief spell of exile) and became Lord of Lüneburg. Henry the Lion's brother-in-law, Richard I of England, later earned the similar epithet of 'the Lion-hearted'. One can imagine that perhaps this was because 'the Lion' was already taken!

Following both ups and downs in the family's fortunes, Henry the Lion's grandson, Otto (c.1204-1252), inherited the Duchy of Saxony and the newly created Duchy of Brunswick-Lüneburg. Through the Middle Ages and beyond, the Hanover lands were divided amongst different branches of the family but always within the House of Welf. The lands were sometimes separated into smaller principalities or fiefdoms – usually named after the principal residence and/or the head of that branch, such as Brunswick-Wolfenbüttel, thus named when the rulers of the Principality of Brunswick physically moved to Wolfenbüttel castle. That said, most male-line members of the family were known as Dukes of Brunswick-Lüneburg by courtesy – which can certainly make things confusing.

From some of the Brunswick-Wolfenbüttel lands, the Principality of Calenburg was formed in 1432 under William the Victorious (c.1392-1482), Duke of Brunswick-Lüneburg and one-time reigning Prince of Lüneburg. The new principality was named after William's residence, Calenburg Castle. William the Victorious himself gained his illustrious epithet because he managed to regain control of the Brunswick-Wolfenbüttel lands as well as those of Brunswick-Göttingen – another Welf principality. In fact, he successfully consolidated these Welf principalities and passed them to his two sons. Incidentally, William the Victorious was also made a Knight of the Garter in 1450 by Henry VI of England.

Expanding Hanover

Centuries later, William the Victorious' descendant and successor Frederick Ulrich (1591-1634) died childless. The Principality of Calenburg (which included Göttingen) was passed to his distant cousin, George (1582-1641), whose family had built and resided at Celle Castle on the banks of the River Aller in Lower Saxony. George chose to make his new home and residence in Hanover – which began to give his branch of the family the name the House of Hanover. George was the first of three rather fortunate generations of his family.

George's fourth and youngest son was Ernest Augustus (1629-1698). As a fourth son, he could not hope to inherit much of his father's titles or estates, so he knew he needed a marriage that would provide important allies. He married a woman who was initially meant for one of his elder brothers – Sophia of the Palatinate, daughter of Frederick V, Elector Palatine and King of Bohemia. After this, Ernest seems to have had a streak of exceptionally good fortune.

Following the Peace of Westphalia in 1648, Ernest was appointed Prince-Bishop of Osnabruck in 1662. Three years later, in 1665, his eldest brother, the ruler of Lüneburg, died childless. His second-eldest brother had earlier ceded his right to Lüneburg; thus Ernest inherited as Duke of Brunswick-Lüneburg. Then, in 1679, Ernest's third-eldest brother died leaving only daughters, so Ernest also inherited the Principality of Calenburg. This was an impressive array of titles and accumulation of power for a youngest son who was not expected to inherit, and there was more to come.

Ernest had, against the odds, been fortunate in bringing together many of the Welf estates. However, with six sons himself, he knew it would soon be divided up again as had been the case in countless previous generations. It was the Germanic custom. He decided to institute (male preference) primogeniture – so that the territories would not be broken up or lost again. This may have been a precondition for acquiring yet another more coveted title.

After Ernest took part in the Great Turkish Wars for the Holy Roman Empire, Emperor Leopold I elevated Ernest to the status of prince-elector in 1692 (although this did not officially become effective until 1708). This granted Ernest membership in the electoral college which elected the Emperors of the Holy Roman Empire, which was usually hereditary and limited to the senior-most families (and churchmen) in the Germanic territories. Having raised and established the position of his family and house, Ernest died in 1698 in Hanover.

FROM ELECTOR TO KING

The third fortunate generation was headed by Ernest's eldest son, George Ludwig, though today he is better known as George I of Great Britain (1660-1727). But how, one might ask, did this seemingly distant, though well-connected, German family end up on the throne of England?

As we have seen, George's mother, Sophia, was born the youngest child of Frederick V, Elector of the Palatinate, in 1630 and married Ernest of Hanover in 1658. Meanwhile in England, following the Civil

War, the Glorious Revolution, the anticipated death of the childless William III of Orange, and the potential childless death of his cousin/ sister-in-law, Anne, the 1701 Act of Settlement effectively barred any Catholic (or anyone married to a Catholic) from succeeding to the English throne.

The nearest Protestant heir after Anne was her first cousin-once-removed, Sophia. (Sophia's claim came through her mother, Princess Elizabeth Stuart, daughter of James I.) All of Sophia's older siblings were Catholic and were therefore bypassed. Sophia, for her part, had married into an established Protestant family, the Hanovers, and had already produced a son (the future George I) and a grandson (the future George II), further solidifying the succession. Sophia's official recognition as heir-presumptive not only bypassed some of her own family but more importantly bypassed the Stuart/Jacobite succession. Parliament was eager to avoid the descendants of King James II returning to power. With arguably a stronger dynastic claim upon the thrones of England and Scotland (by birth – in the male line – as opposed to by right of Parliament), the exiled Stuarts were both haunting ghosts and at times a real threat to Hanoverian rule in Britain.

When the Act of Settlement took effect in 1701, all Sophia could do was wait in Hanover for her cousins William III and then Queen Anne to die. If Anne were to have any children, they would succeed as king or queen; however, by the time Anne became queen in 1702, it was already apparent that this was highly improbable. Sophia, therefore, waited patiently as heir presumptive. Although older than Anne, Sophia enjoyed better health and certainly had no problems in producing children – seven of them. Yet, in May 1714, Princess Sophia was caught in a rainstorm in the gardens of Herrenhausen Palace in Hanover. She fell quite ill and died soon after at age 83. Queen Anne died only months later in August at the age of forty-nine. How different things would have been if Queen Sophia I of Great Britain had reigned over Britain we shall not know. At such an advanced age for that era, it is unlikely it would have been a long reign, but she would have been the oldest person to ever ascend the throne.

After the death of Anne, the heir presumptive was Sophia's eldest son George, who travelled to London in September 1714 as king. He was crowned the following month.

Arguably, from here on, the path of succession to the crown in Britain was happily straightforward – in part thanks to the procreative powers of the new Germans who then made up the royal family. King George I passed his throne seamlessly to his eldest son, George II, in 1727 – who already came as a package deal: a Protestant king with a Protestant wife (Caroline of Ansbach) and a sizable brood of Protestant heirs, the eldest being Frederick, Prince of Wales. Yet all was not as assured as it seemed for the House of Hanover on its new British throne. Across the water, the Royal House of Stuart plotted their return.

JACOBITES

Since the Glorious Revolution of 1688 and the fleeing of King James II, the Stuarts had largely been in exile in France, the domain of their Catholic cousins, the House of Bourbon, Kings of France.

In Scotland and England, some Catholic families made secret toasts to the 'king across the water' – usually by clinking glasses above a bowl of water. As the crown passed from William and Mary and eventually to the House of Hanover and then down through the Hanoverian succession, those who believed in the absolute divine right of kings continued to support the Stuart dynasty in exile, despite various Acts of Parliament. This included support for the exiled King James II as well as his son, James Francis Edward Stuart (known as the Old Pretender), and his grandson, Charles Edward Stuart (known as the Young Pretender or Bonnie Prince Charlie). It was Bonnie Prince Charlie who led the most notable rebellion against the Hanoverian crown – the Jacobite Rising of 1745.

Having landed in Scotland with the support of his cousin the King of France, Bonnie Prince Charlie initially had several military successes.

EDWARD HILARY DAVIS

He marched unopposed into Edinburgh, where his father was proclaimed king. The Jacobites then took the war to the English, invading south as far as Derby. However, the rebellion lost momentum and was eventually defeated at the Battle of Culloden the following year in 1746.

Bonnie Prince Charlie abandoned his Scottish supporters and returned into exile, and the Stuarts never again seriously attempted to reclaim England or Scotland. Had the Bonnie Prince been successful in his reconquest of Britain, he would have been King Charles III. By the 1750s, the Jacobite cause, both real and imagined, began to diminish and became less of a serious worry for the Royal House of Hanover and the British Government.

GEORGE II AND PRINCE FREDERICK

In the royal family of George II, there was a division at court. George II and his son and heir, Frederick, Prince of Wales, did not see eye to eye. Indeed, they formed practically separate courts. The Prince of Wales, who resented his father, filled his court with politicians of the opposition. The prince was a keen musician and an avid gambler, and he took a great interest in the arts and sciences. Perhaps to annoy his father, but also to anglicise himself (being Hanover born), he involved himself heavily in the most popular team sport of the day, cricket. In those days, there was considerable gambling around the game, and Frederick soon became involved through that route. However, he also became a very accomplished player, effectively playing at county level.

In 1736, Frederick took his wife, Princess Augusta of Saxe-Gotha-Altenburg, and, like many Hanoverian men, began to have children – many of them. In the end, he had nine with Augusta and at least two or three illegitimate children as well. But that end came early. In March 1751, at only forty-four, the Prince of Wales died in London; he may have been wounded by a cricket ball, but more likely his death was the result of a blocked artery in his lung. His is yet another name on the list 'what-ifs' in the annals of the British monarchy.

Foreign Wars and Rebellion

While Prince Frederick was gambling, playing cricket, and siring children, his father, George II, was fighting – not just at home with the Jacobites but also on the continent in the wars of Austrian Succession (1740-1748), in which Britain sided with the Habsburg monarchy against France, Spain and Prussia. It was during these wars, at the Battle of Dettingen, that George II became the last British monarch to lead troops into battle. The battle was fought on 27 June 1743 in Germany against the might of the French force. Whilst it is considered a victory, it did not significantly alter the wider context of the war. The historian William Lecky famously described it as being more of a happy escape than a grand victory.

Having ruled over a kingdom with a growing economy and empire (in America, India and elsewhere) and seen rebellions at home and wars abroad, King George II still lived longer than most men of his time. By the end, he was even blind in one eye. He died at the age of 76 at Kensington Palace in 1760. At that time, he was the oldest monarch in British history. He was succeeded by his twenty-two-year-old grandson – yet another George.

King George III was the eldest son and heir of the late Frederick, Prince of Wales. The crown had skipped a generation. It was the first time this occurrence had taken place since Edward III was succeeded by his grandson.

George III

George III was a mere twenty-two when he became king in 1760. Unlike his two predecessors, he was seen as being British and not German. He had been born in London and brought up speaking English as his first language. Indeed, he prided himself on being British, was notoriously low-key in his dealing with the public, and took an active interest in native agriculture, earning him the affectionate title of 'Farmer George'.

After his accession, it was time for George to marry. He had been in love with an Englishwoman: Lady Sarah Lennox, daughter of the 3rd

Duke of Richmond. From a dynastic point of view, that marriage would have been interesting, as it would have united the Houses of Hanover and Stuart (albeit in an illegitimate line) since Lady Sarah and her father were descended from King Charles II. However, Lord Bute, (the eventual Prime Minister) strongly advised against the match. We shall, therefore, have to wait until the reign of Prince William (the present Prince of Wales) for a descendant of Charles II to sit on the throne.

Instead, George took to wife Princess Charlotte of Mecklenburg-Strelitz in 1761. It became a long love match, or at least one would think so, as the couple managed to have fifteen children together, thirteen of which lived into adulthood.

EMPIRES AND REVOLUTIONS

George III's reign was a time of change for Britain, witnessing the indefatigable rise of the British Empire to become the world's first super-power and ruler of the waves. Britain's dominance on the world stage arguably began with the defeat of the French in the Napoleonic Wars at sea (Trafalgar, 1805) and on land (Waterloo, 1815). A few years prior, another Act of Union had taken place in 1801, bringing Ireland into the fold, making all four countries – England, Wales, Scotland, and Ireland – one combined nation: The United Kingdom of Britain and Ireland.

As the Seven Years War drew to a close in 1763, Britain was dominant in North America, much of India and the Caribbean. That said, it was following this war that taxes were levied on the English colonists in America, as it was for them that the war had been fought.

The colonists and settlers rose up to begin the American Revolutionary War, which led Britain to recognise the independence of the United States in 1782 and 1783. In the wake of this humiliating defeat, King George considered abdicating the throne.

It is also important to note that, during George III's reign, the anti-slavery movement in Britain gained more and more strength and popularity, led by men such as William Wilberforce and Olaudah

Equiano. Much of British trade depended on the international slave trade, and abolition would no doubt cost the realm and the empire greatly. However, it was felt that slavery had no moral place in enlightened society. Therefore, in 1807, George III signed into law the Act for the Abolition of the Slave Trade.

The French Revolution

Another monumental world event during George III's reign was the French Revolution, which was arguably caused, at least in part, by the spread of ideas of freedom from America. The revolution in France led to the trial and eventual execution of their king, Louis XVI, in 1793, over one hundred years after the English had executed Charles I in similar fashion.

The revolution plunged France into turmoil. A revolutionary republican government was established, and mass executions of aristocrats, politicians, officers and priests were carried out during what is known as the Reign of Terror. The other crowned heads of Europe were understandably appalled and concerned. It was inevitable that many neighbouring nations declared war on France.

In the aftermath of the revolution, George III allowed the surviving exiled family of the Bourbon monarchy to reside in England. As an example, the future Louis XVIII lived at Hartwell House in Buckinghamshire.

THE NAPOLEONIC WARS

In the political chaos of the revolution, it was not long before a political strong man came to the fore to take control and restore order in France. That man was General Napoleon Bonaparte – a man who had already been twice defeated by the Royal Navy. To summarise hugely, Napoleon began a campaign to make France great again! In Europe, the Napoleonic Wars caused death and destruction from Lisbon to Moscow from c. 1803 to 1815, and all over the world, Britain and France were again archrivals from the Caribbean to the Mediterranean, from Africa to India.

EDWARD HILARY DAVIS

It may be surprising to learn that the French Revolution brought about a change that has affected all British monarchs since. Because there was no longer a King of France and because the British government was supporting the potential restoration of the Bourbon monarchy, King George III was to lose one of his titles. Ever since 1340 and King Edward III (whose mother was a French princess), the Kings of England had claimed the title King of France as well. It had even appeared in their arms as a quartering for nearly five centuries. Now, in the Treaty of Amiens (1802), King George recognised the Republic of France and dropped the title King of France. The fleur-de-lys was then removed from the British royal coat of arms, and the title has never been used since. Perhaps a future king may choose to revive it!

Following Great Britain's union with Ireland, it was proposed that George III be declared Emperor of the British Isles – but he dismissed the idea. Napoleon, on the other hand, had declared himself Emperor of the French in 1804 with the blessing of the French senate and the pope.

Following Napoleon's and France's initial defeat in the wars that followed, in 1814, the German states, duchies, counties and territories were reorganised by the Congress of Vienna. Hanover was upgraded from an electorate to a kingdom in its own right – which made sense as there was no longer a Holy Roman Emperor to elect. George III of Great Britain and Ireland was recognised as the King of Hanover in 1814. The British royal coat of arms had to change once again to incorporate the new kingdom.

The Napoleonic Wars finally ended with the British and Prussian victory at the Battle of Waterloo and the eventual capture of Napoleon in 1815. Napoleon, trying to escape to the USA, was cut off by a Royal Navy blockade. He surrendered himself to the British onboard HMS *Bellerophon* and was then taken prisoner to Plymouth Sound to await whatever fate the British government had organised for him. He had hoped to live in exile as an English country gentleman. Instead, he was exiled to the far-off British-held island of St Helena in the South Atlantic. He never saw Europe again.

The Regency

Throughout the middle and latter parts of his reign, King George III was beset with bouts of madness. Doctors of the day were at a loss and could not completely diagnose the king's illness with their limited scientific understanding. For decades, historians and doctors thought that the king suffered from porphyria, possibly inherited from his ancestor Charles VI of France or his relative Henry VI of England, both of whom were 'mad'. More recently, however, porphyria has been dismissed, and it is thought that George may have suffered from bipolar disorder. There are many stories of dubious truth surrounding the king's mental illness: in one, the king is said to have spoken to a tree for hours believing it to be the King of Prussia; in another George supposedly insisted that he could see Hanover through his telescope in Windsor.

Owing to increased concerns about the king's illness, a Bill of Regency was introduced to the House of Commons in 1789 in favour of his son, the Prince of Wales, but the king made a recovery before the bill was enacted. However, after the death of his daughter Amelia in 1810, George III seemed to regress to his bouts of madness, and another act was passed in 1811, making his son, George, the Prince of Wales, prince regent and acting head of state. Prince George was regent until he succeeded his father upon his death. This period is therefore referred to as the Regency Period. George III died on 29 January 1820 at Windsor Castle at the age of eighty-one. He reigned for just under sixty years, making him the longest reigning king in Britain – still only surpassed by Victoria and Elizabeth II.

GEORGE IV

After having been regent for nine years, George IV succeeded his father at the age of fifty-seven. He had waited impatiently his whole life for this moment. By the time it arrived, he was overweight and may have had a laudanum addiction.

Through his youth as Prince of Wales and while serving as prince regent, George had been something of a bounder. He went through money and mistresses like water. He fell in love with a commoner, Maria Fitzherbert, and foolishly married her in secret in 1785. This contravened both the Royal Marriages Act of 1772, which required that permission from the sovereign be obtained in order for a prince to marry, and the Act of Settlement of 1701 because Maria was Roman Catholic. Word of this scandalous union dripped into the press, and Parliament was forced to deny the marriage's existence. The king was furious and refused to help the prince financially. Prince George had to rely on a reluctant Parliament for funds. At one point, he was forced to abandon his London townhouse and live at Maria's home until he had more funds. Because of the Royal Marriages Act of 1772, the marriage was not considered legal as the king had not given his consent. Furthermore, if the king had consented (and legalised the marriage), Prince George would have been (legally) married to a Catholic and therefore barred from the succession according to the Act of Settlement of 1701.

Prince George spent frivolously on gambling, entertaining, and also on buildings such as his pleasure palace, Brighton Pavilion. Still, the king bailed out the wayward prince, paying his debts for him time and time again. Finally, his father the King reached his limit; he refused to pay unless George renounced Maria Fitzherbert in favour of marrying his cousin Princess Caroline of Brunswick. Keen to remain in the lifestyle he was accustomed to and no doubt anxious to be king one day, Prince George abandoned Mrs Fitzherbert and married Princess Caroline in April 1795.

George and Caroline had a famously unhappy marriage. She was not one of the great beauties of the day, and George resented being lumbered with her in order to pay his way out of debt. Nonetheless, their union did produce a single daughter – Princess Charlotte of Wales.

Once regent, however, Prince George restricted Caroline's access to their daughter and effectively left her in social isolation. The couple became entirely estranged. Eventually she agreed to go into exile in exchange for a generous allowance. Rumours later swirled about her Italian servant who was thought to be her lover.

When George became king in early 1820, Caroline hoped to return to Britain as queen consort; however, George had other ideas. He tried to divorce her. Meanwhile, the government of the day did not wish to risk the scandal of a public divorce trial and so offered Caroline even more money to stay abroad. She refused and returned to England to assert her claim. George accused her of adultery and had her tried in the House of Lords. During the trial, George's ministers tried to prove Caroline's adultery, but owing to her popularity amongst the population, the accusations were withdrawn.

On the day of George's coronation, 19 July 1821, Caroline tried to gain entry to Westminster Abbey but was turned away at the doors. After bayonets had been pointed at her chin by the guards on duty, who had received strict orders not to let her in, she stormed off fuming. She died the next month – possibly of cancer – at Brandenburg House in Hammersmith. She had been queen for only a year.

Princess Charlotte

Despite Caroline's death, the succession was secure in Princess Charlotte. Charlotte had been born in 1796, the year after George and Caroline were married, and it became not long after that she would be their only child. She was heir to the throne of Great Britain and Ireland and therefore would be the first queen regnant since Queen Anne. Naturally, as soon as she neared maturity, plans were made for a royal match. The prince regent favoured Prince William of Orange.

By 1813, it became clear that the Napoleonic Wars would eventually come to an end with Britain and her many European allies victorious. Plans were made to carve up Napoleon's captured territories and reform

Europe. Strong and well governed states were needed between France and the Germanic territories. One such nation was to be the Kingdom of the Netherlands, and the young William Prince of Orange was to be its first king. (This was in place of the Kingdom of Holland, a puppet state which Napoleon had set up; he put his younger brother on the throne there only later to absorb it into his empire.)

From a dynastic point of view, a match between Orange and Hanover was exciting. It would rewind the clock back to the Glorious Revolution and put an Anglo-Dutch dynasty in place as had been the plan with William III and Mary II. The British government supported the match, although it did not wish the Crowns of Britain and the Netherlands to be united. To that end, Parliament proposed that if Charlotte and William were to wed, their eldest son would be King of Britain and their second son would be King of the Netherlands. However, these plans were scuppered when Charlotte actually met William at her father's birthday party and found him objectionable, at least in part because he got rather drunk and behaved poorly. Not for nothing did he acquire the nickname of Silly Billy.

Charlotte played for time while she considered her future. At one point, her preference may have been for another Prince William, the Duke of Gloucester – her father's cousin. This certainly would have kept the crown 'in the family' and avoided any distressing foreign matches. The prince regent, however, found this William objectionable.

Other cousins may have also caught her fancy along the way. She was reportedly besotted with George FitzClarence (later Earl of Munster), the eldest son of her uncle, the Duke of Clarence (later William IV). Young George was hurried away to his regiment to avoid such a match. Another (probable) cousin was Lieutenant George Hesse, who was reputedly the illegitimate son of another of her uncles, the Duke of York. There were many letters and clandestine meetings between the couple, and it is certain that they were in love. This relationship was encouraged by Charlotte's mother Caroline, but Hesse was eventually sent off to fight in the Napoleonic Wars in Spain and Portugal (the Peninsular Wars) and in southern France. He was ordered to return Charlotte's letters and portrait, which he reluctantly did. Several years later, in 1832, while duelling with the illegitimate son of Napoleon, Charles Leon, Hesse received a shot to the chest and died.

Meanwhile, the prince regent pressured his daughter into meeting with Prince William of Orange again. The experience this time being more convivial, Princess Charlotte relented and agreed to the marriage contract in June 1814. Shortly afterwards, Charlotte went to a party at a London hotel, where she met a senior officer of the Russian Cavalry, Prince Leopold of Saxe-Coburg-Saalfeld – a German. To summarise hugely, Charlotte eventually settled on Prince Leopold as the husband of her choice.

Charlotte broke things off with William of Orange by stipulating conditions that she knew he would reject such as insisting her mother would live with them. The prince regent was furious and isolated her from the court, effectively putting her under house arrest. However, the prince regent mellowed when William of Orange became engaged to a Russian princess – and was therefore beyond hope of return.

After persisting in her course, Charlotte won her father over. She and Leopold were married in 1816 at Carlton House. He was a penniless German duke, but he had proven himself a good officer during the Napoleonic Wars and an honest and loyal man at Charlotte's side. Charlotte is reported to have giggled during the vows when Leopold declared he would endow her with all his worldly goods! All joking aside, it was clear that the royal house of Britain was one day to be Saxe-Coburg – not Hanover.

The following year, tragedy struck. After a previous miscarriage, Charlotte gave birth to a large stillborn boy on 5 November 1817. Later that evening she died. The nation went into a frenzy of mourning the likes of which was not seen again until the death of Dianna Princess of Wales in 1997. Charlotte was only twenty-one. It was lamentable. The prince regent was not popular, but Charlotte was the beloved hope of the nation.

Now that Charlotte was no more, the future was once again uncertain. It was particularly awkward for Prince Leopold who became seemingly rudderless and purposeless without his wife. He lingered quietly in London. However, one day his luck would turn full circle.

Clarence and the FitzClarences

The prince regent became King George IV in 1820. He was (now) childless, but he had many younger brothers. However, most of them had no legitimate heirs of their own. Several of them had conducted marriages (with actresses) outside of the Royal Marriages Act, which were not legal, and therefore their offspring were illegitimate and could not inherit the throne. The eldest of these brothers, Frederick, Duke of York, died childless, predeceasing his elder brother, George IV, in 1827. From then on, it became clear that the heir to the throne was the next Hanover brother, William, Duke of Clarence. With the king beginning to show signs of aging and ailment, probably owing to his gluttony and resulting obesity, it was time to prepare the heir presumptive for the throne.

Prince William, Duke of Clarence, being the third son of George III, had not been expected to inherit the crown. Therefore, he had been packed off into the Royal Navy at a young age. As there was less pressure on him to marry into another princely house, on his return to Britain, he took up with an Irish actress, Dorothea Jordan. The two of them were together for twenty years. They lived at Bushy House and had ten children together all with the surname FitzClarence. Even though she was given a generous annual allowance, Dorothea continued to perform at Drury Lane. She and the duke were arguably quite a modern couple, and it is thought that they had a happy family existence. However, by 1811, William found himself facing debt and money difficulties. He left Dorothea to hunt for an heiress, but none would have him.

He granted Dorothea a generous income and custody of their daughters, whilst he had custody of their sons. The condition for this arrangement was that she never return to the stage; however, when her family got into money troubles, she did return to the stage to help. William was furious; he stopped her allowance and took back their daughters. Dorothea Jordan died penniless and alone in Saint-Cloud, France, in 1816.

Following Princess Charlotte's death in 1817, there was a race amongst William and his brothers to produce a legitimate heir to the throne. He had the advantage, however, being himself likely to succeed his two childless elder brothers. He scoured the courts of Europe looking for a Protestant princess who would be amenable to him, his debts, and ten illegitimate children.

He eventually found what he was looking for. At Kew in 1818, William married Princess Adelaide of Saxe-Meiningen. Their wedding was a double wedding alongside William's younger brother, Edward, Duke of Kent and Princess Victoria of Saxe-Coburg-Saalfeld (the future parents of Queen Victoria). Adelaide took care of William and his debts. Initially, they lived relatively frugally in Germany, and it is believed that theirs was a happy marriage.

The Struggle for an Heir

That said, Adelaide suffered two failed pregnancies in Germany, after which William decided that they should move home so that his heir could be born on British soil. They moved to Bushy House where he had lived with his mistress Dorothea. Adelaide gave birth to a daughter, Princess Elizabeth, at St James's Palace in 1820; however, the baby died just months later. Around the same time, the family experienced a variety of other significant changes. The previous year, William's younger brother, Edward, the Duke of Kent, had produced a legitimate daughter – Princess Alexandrina Victoria of Kent. Edward died just a few months later in January 1820, the same year that William's father, George III, died and William's older brother, the prince regent, became king.

After Elizabeth, two more stillborn boys were born to William and Adelaide in 1822, and there may have been another pregnancy after that, but it was becoming clear that William and Adelaide were not going to be able to sire an heir. However, when his elder brother Frederick, the Duke of York, died childless in 1827, William became heir presumptive to his brother, George IV. Three years later, George IV died on the 26 June 1830 at Windsor Castle; he was sixty-seven. Weighing in at some twenty stone, he remained a passionate lover of food and indulgence to the end. William, Duke of Clarence, succeeded as King William IV.

KING WILLIAM IV

Early in his reign, the sixty-five-year-old King William recognised as his heir Princess Alexandrina of Kent, the daughter of his late younger brother. The future Queen Victoria was only about eleven at that time. William acknowledged his illegitimate children by granting the eldest, George, the title of Earl of Munster, giving all the others the courtesy title and dignity of being the younger siblings of a marquess, which entitled them all to put Lord or Lady before their name. The sons were also made knights of the Royal Guelphic Order. The FitzClarences became attractive prospects by association on the marriage market and married into the British aristocracy and gentry. Former Prime Minister David Cameron (Baron Cameron of Chipping Norton) is a descendant of William IV via his illegitimate daughter Lady Elizabeth FitzClarence.

King William IV reigned long enough to ensure that his successor would be of age – something of a personal crusade for him. This was to avoid any potential regency, which likely would have been influenced by his sister-in-law the Duchess of Kent whom he detested. William died in 1837 respected and liked by his subjects. During his reign, reforms had been made to the Poor Laws, and child labour and slavery had been further suppressed or abolished in most of the British Empire.

Queen Victoria

When William IV died, the crown passed to a girl of just eighteen. Princess Alexandrina Victoria made the decision to be styled Queen Victoria.

It is important to note that Queen Victoria was the only child and eventual heir of any of the first four sons of King George III – which is why she succeeded as Queen of Great Britain. However, the laws of succession for the Kingdom of Hanover (over which her uncles and grandfather had ruled) were different. Hanover was subject to Salic law, which is much more common on the continent. Salic law allows only males to inherit and rule. As a consequence, the crown of Hanover passed from William IV to his next surviving younger brother, Prince Ernest Augustus, Duke of Cumberland and Teviotdale. This ended the personal union via the monarch between Britain and Hanover which had been in place since George I in 1714.

King Ernest Augustus of Hanover eventually left London to take up his new kingdom. Many in government were relieved as Hanover had often been a thorn in the side of Britain during the continental wars of the previous two hundred plus years. It had also been a distraction of responsibility to several monarchs during that time. However, through familiar ties, Hanover would be a friend of Britain roughly until the First World War.

Queen Victoria, a Hanover on her father's side, ruled from 1837 to 1901. Though her reign is the second longest in Britain's history and is worthy of much investigation, it is perhaps too eventful to be fully included in this book. We will merely concern ourselves with the fact that she was the last British monarch of the House of Hanover, but as we shall see, she was just as much, if not more, a member of the House of Saxe-Coburg. Her marriage to her first-cousin, Prince Albert of Saxe-Coburg und Gotha produced nine children, which set the stage for the next dynasty to rule Britain. A new title was brought into the family in 1876, that of Empress of India.

Arguably, the House of Hanover ruled Britain from 1714 to 1901. Under their premiership, Britain went from a small seagoing country made of small, recently unified kingdoms into the largest and most powerful empire the world has ever seen. For the House of Hanover, it is certainly no small feat to go from a small German town to ruling a quarter of the world.

The House of Hanover continues to this day and remains on good terms with their British cousins. They were stripped of their British titles and privileges in 1917 following their fighting on the German side in the First World War, but these can be returned to them if the British sovereign ever wishes. The present head of the House of Hanover and senior male-line descendant of King George I is Prince Ernst August von Hanover (born 1954).

THE HOUSE OF SAXE-COBURG UND GOTHA

Edward VII, 1901-1910
George V, 1910-1936

THE HOUSE OF SAXE-COBURG und Gotha commenced its rule over England as Bertie (Edward VII) stood at the bedside of his dying mother Queen Victoria. Also at Victoria's side was her grandson, and Bertie's nephew, the German Kaiser Wilhelm II. Britain's relationship with the German states and kingdoms had for centuries been cordial and positive owing to the strong family ties of the royal family – who were effectively related to everyone! During the Saxe-Coburgs, however, Britain faced a united German Empire. The relationship became one of competition not of friendship and common values. This led to a war which pitched the Saxe-Coburgs against many of their cousins and relatives and changed the face of the monarchy in Britain forever.

At first glance, the House of Saxe-Coburg und Gotha looks like a relatively recent invention. Once again, the house takes its name from the territorial designation of a family title. The collection of these three names together first appeared for Prince Albert's father, Ernest I, Duke of Saxe-Coburg und Gotha, when he became the first sovereign duke of these territories in 1826 (and he remained so until his death in 1844).

Prior to this, he had been Duke of Saxe-Coburg-Saalfeld from 1806. These duchies were some of the Ernestine duchies (or Saxon duchies) in Thuringia in modern-day Germany. The word Ernestine refers to several cadet branches of the ruling House of Wettin that are named after Ernest/Ernst, Elector of Saxony from 1464 to 1486. The Ernestine branches were all dukedoms which (unhelpfully) all begin with the word *Saxe-*. Put quite simply, the House of Saxe-Coburg und Gotha was a very minor branch of the House of Wettin.

ORIGINS OF THE HOUSE OF WETTIN

The House of Wettin traces its lineage ostensibly as far back as Theodoric I of Wettin in Saxony who lived during the tenth century. His sons, Dedo and Frederick, are the first known Counts of Wettin, and they acquired or inherited Wettin Castle. Through the centuries, the family politicked and survived, garnering lands and titles. By 1423, they were invested with the Duchy of Saxony – making them Prince-Electors of the Holy Roman Empire, giving them a vote in the choosing of future emperors. However, from 1485, two Wettin brothers divided some of the territories and titles, forming two branches of the family: the Albertine line (after Albert, Duke of Saxony) and the Ernestine line (after Ernest, Elector of Saxony). Prince Albert (the prince consort) and his father were direct male-line descendants of John Frederick I, Elector of Saxony, the grandson of the aforesaid Ernest, Elector of Saxony.

In 1527, John Frederick I took as his wife Sibylle of Cleves – the sister of Anne of Cleves (who is more familiar to us as the fourth wife of Henry VIII of England). Sibylle and John Frederick had four sons. The second of these, John William/Johann Wilhelm (1530-1573), was made Duke of Saxe-Weimar. The title eventually passed to his second son, Johann II (1570-1605). Johann II had eleven sons and a daughter! His ninth (but sixth surviving) son became known as Ernest I, Duke of Saxe-Coburg.

Ernest I seemed to keep the family tradition of mass procreation alive. He and his wife/first cousin, Elizabeth Sophie, managed to have

EDWARD HILARY DAVIS

eighteen children. With this in mind, it is easy to understand why there were/are so many cadet branches of the House of Wettin. Their tenth (but seventh surviving) son, Johann-Ernest (1658-1729), became not only Duke of Saxe-Coburg but also Duke of Saalfeld. These titles were naturally merged making him the Duke of Saxe-Coburg-Saalfeld. His twelfth child, Francis Josias (1697-1764), eventually inherited the dukedom from his older brother.

Francis Josias passed the dukedom on to his eldest son, Ernest Frederick (1724-1800). He was married to Sophie Antoinette of Brunswick-Wolfenbüttel. Among her sisters were the Queen of Denmark and the Queen of Prussia. Their eldest son and heir, Francis (1750-1806), inherited the title of Duke of Saxe-Coburg-Saalfeld in 1800. His reign as duke was cut short by an early demise however. From his second marriage in 1777, he had ten children, seven of which survived to adulthood. Three of these children are of particular note to us: firstly, Ernest, the eldest son; secondly, Leopold, the youngest son; and thirdly, Victoria, the fourth daughter.

Ernest: The Scandalous Duke

The eldest son, Ernest (1784-1844), succeeded his father in the Dukedom of Saxe-Coburg-Saalfeld in 1806. He fought valiantly on the side of the allies against the French in the Napoleonic Wars (as a Prussian general at the Battle of Leipzig), for which he was much rewarded. After Napoleon's final downfall at Waterloo in June 1815, the Congress of Vienna awarded Ernest with a large estate around St Wendel. The following year the estate was recognised as the Principality of Lichtenberg.

However, Ernest actually sold the principality in 1834 to the Prussians. Following events and the deaths of various Wettin family members in 1825, the Ernestine duchies were reorganised. Ernest became Ernest I, Duke of Saxe-Coburg und Gotha, the following year. In 1817, he married his cousin, Princess Louise of Saxe-Gotha-Altenburg, and had two sons, Prince Ernest and Prince Albert (who went on to marry Queen Victoria).

Ernest and Louise's marriage was on shaky ground partly because both of them had extramarital affairs and were quite promiscuous. Ernest had a string of mistresses; Louise had affairs with a chamberlain and a stable master. He excused his own infidelities but was outraged by hers. The couple separated in 1824 and actually divorced in 1826. They were a scandal to the courts of Europe, and their reputation cast a dark cloud over their sons.

Uncle Leopold

Leopold, the youngest son of Duke Francis, was born in 1790. He is of particular note as he married the daughter and heir apparent of the Prince Regent of Great Britain, Princess Charlotte of Wales, in 1816. Though this was an ambitious dynastic match for him, the couple were happy. Both were enamoured of each other,, and thus when Charlotte succeeded as monarch, Leopold expected to be her consort and help her to rule the country.

It was widely anticipated that the House of Hanover would end and the House of Saxe-Coburg und Gotha would begin with their progeny. It did not happen. Tragically, Princess Charlotte died a year after their marriage whilst delivering a stillborn son. The country mourned. Many were devastated, but no one as much as Prince Leopold – whose prospects looked dashed.

Perhaps out of guilt or a desire to ease Leopold's disappointment, the London Protocol offered him the throne of Greece a few years later in 1830 following its war of independence. However, given its instability and volatility, Prince Leopold wisely turned it down. A year later, he accepted an offer to be King of the Belgians, who had successfully gained their independence too. They had seceded from the United Kingdom of the Netherlands in 1830. King Leopold I was sworn in as King of the Belgians on 21 July 1831 in Brussels. The following year he prudently took as his wife Princess Louise of Orleans, daughter of his powerful neighbour, King Louis-Philippe I of France.

However, as a new and freshly minted king on the European stage, Leopold needed powerful allies to shore up his reign. Who better than his old friends and the world's first superpower, Britain? He did not lose his ambition for a Saxe-Coburg on the throne of Britain, even if it could not be himself. Eventually, he would get what he desired.

Princess Victoria of Saxe-Coburg

Ernest's and Leopold's sister, Victoria (1786-1861), was first married in 1803 to Emich Carl, Prince of Leiningen, by whom she had a son and a daughter. After Emich Carl died in 1814, Victoria briefly served as Regent of Leiningen until their son came of age. Following the tragic death of her sister-in-law, Princess Charlotte of Wales, in 1817, Victoria received an offer of marriage from the Prince Regent's younger brother Prince Edward, Duke of Kent. The two were married in 1818 in a double wedding with Prince Edward's brother, the Duke of Clarence (William IV), and Adelaide of Saxe-Meiningen.

Effectively, the race was on to provide the country with an heir presumptive, seeing as George IV and his next three brothers had yet to produce any surviving legitimate children (though there were many illegitimate). On 24 May 1819 at Kensington Palace, Edward and Victoria got there first, as it were. Victoria gave birth to a daughter, whom they named Princess Alexandrina Victoria of Kent (the future Queen Victoria). Edward was fifty-one at the time and was especially proud of his daughter. He believed that it was highly likely she would one day be queen.

Edward, Duke of Kent, died of pneumonia in January 1820, less than a year after his daughter's birth. Six days later, his father, King George III, died.

Edward's daughter grew up at Kensington Palace during the reigns of her uncles, George IV and William IV. She was half a Hanover, half a Saxe-Coburg, and heir apparent to the throne. Princess Alexandrina Victoria's mother, the Duchess of Kent (also Victoria), got firm control over her schooling and upbringing. She kept her largely away from society and relatives where possible. This may have been mere motherly care but was possibly also a way to protect her own interests as her daughter was her chief means of advancement in the coming years.

As the aging King William IV appeared to be declining by the mid-1830s, there was much speculation as to who the young princess would marry and whether she would be old enough or need a regent to reign for her. Having been regent to her son in Leiningen, certainly the duchess hoped she might be regent of the United Kingdom for her daughter.

Ambitious Uncle Leopold, King of the Belgians, remained hopeful of a matrimonial alliance with Britain and sensed another great opportunity. He pushed his nephew forward as a candidate to marry Alexandrina Victoria. Albert was the younger son of Leopold's brother, Ernest, Duke of Saxe-Coburg und Gotha. Their courtship began from around May 1836, when a meeting was arranged. However, the plan for the match was hatched by the family from as early as 1821 – when the princess was just two years old!

Young Victoria

Princess Alexandrina Victoria of Kent succeeded to the throne on the death of her uncle William IV on 20 June 1837, having reached the age of 18 just weeks before – extinguishing the need for a regency. She chose as her regnal name Victoria. Queen Victoria was young, powerful and single. Naturally, she had many suitors on the royal marriage market, including Prince Alexander of Orange and other Hanoverian cousins. Despite it being a choreographed relationship and an arranged marriage, Victoria was smitten with her cousin Albert. It was a love match.

The pair were married at St George's Chapel, Windsor, on 10 February 1840, some three years into her reign – to the rejoicing of Leopold I of the Belgians. It seemed likely through the couple's issue that the House of Saxe-Coburg und Gotha would reign not just Belgium but also the

British Empire. Some may wish to note that it is this wedding which popularised the fashion for brides to wear white at marriage ceremonies.

Of course, Prince Albert, although highly influential in British life, history and development, did not reign as a monarch. He was prince consort to his wife. They had nine children together, many of whom married into other royal families as did their offspring – which gave Queen Victoria the sobriquet 'the grandmother of Europe'. Some of her grandchildren sat on the thrones of the United Kingdom, Germany/Prussia, Greece, Norway, Russia, Romania, Spain and almost Sweden. Meanwhile, other direct Saxe-Coburgs sat on the thrones of Belgium, Portugal, and Bulgaria. The House of Saxe-Coburg und Gotha, in the space of less than a century, went from being a humble provincial German princely family to being one of the most widespread and influential families among the crowned heads of Europe and indeed the empires of the world.

BERTIE: EDWARD VII

The first monarch of the House of Saxe-Coburg und Gotha was Albert and Victoria's eldest son, King Edward VII. Until our present king (Charles III), he was the longest serving Prince of Wales; that is to say, he spent the longest time as heir apparent to the throne – literally waiting to succeed his mother as sovereign for nearly sixty years.

Born Albert Edward in 1841, he was known by his family and friends as Bertie. In early adulthood, he began to gain a reputation for being a playboy. While a young army officer on practise manoeuvres at Curragh Camp in Ireland, fellow officers smuggled in actress Nellie Clifden – who was already known to him. It is thought that prior to the camp, he was a sexual novice. Bertie's father, Prince Albert, who always disapproved of extramarital carnal pleasures, was furious at such behaviour and soon travelled to Cambridge to meet with his son, who was studying there, to give him a dressing down.

Doubtless Prince Albert hoped to instill some Victorian morals into his son, but many agree that he lost all faith in his son following these incidents. It is said that they walked in the cold and wet for a long time during this corrective discussion. Then, just a few weeks later, Prince Albert died of typhoid fever in December 1861.

Queen Victoria's grief was all consuming. She attributed her husband's decline to the shock and constant worry Albert had about their son, as well as their chilly walk and talk. She directly blamed Bertie for his death. As a consequence, she never fully trusted her son after Albert's death. Throughout her reign, she sidelined him and did not make an effort to include him in the governing of the kingdom or empire, taking special effort that he should not see official state papers (which were and are carried in the famous red boxes).

Being mistrusted by his mother and sidelined from state business left Bertie relatively free to enjoy himself. He became quite the party prince and womaniser. He is famed for his appetite, shooting parties, mistresses, actresses, dancers and prostitutes. His appetite was immense, and he soon gained size and weight. It should be noted that it was he who started the tradition of having roast beef, horseradish and Yorkshire pudding on Sundays – the English Sunday roast.

Bertie travelled widely throughout the empire but became a regular and beloved figure in Paris. He was a frequenter of *La Chabanais*, a famous luxury brothel near the Louvre, which operated from 1878 until as late as 1946, and visited the now famous *Moulin Rouge* cabaret – which still runs today. At *La Chabanais*, he had a special chair made which enabled him (and his great gut) to enjoy 'activities' with two ladies at the same time. The siège d'amour (love chair) is now in the Musée d'Orsay. Historians and contortionists are still not in agreement on how it worked!

Scandals, Love and Marriage

At home, Bertie was involved with not only many mistresses but also a number of scandals. The Royal Baccarat Scandal, involving some cheating at baccarat at a house party in Yorkshire, resulted in a court case in

1891, causing Bertie to be the first British heir to the throne to be called to the witness stand in a court since 1411.

Through his dalliances, Bertie also broke other people's marriages. In one such scandal, a former lover, Harriet, Lady Mordaunt, went through a divorce trial with her husband – a rare event in those days. She was eventually committed to an insane asylum, and there are many who suspect that this was done only to silence her, lest she reveal untoward things about the Prince of Wales. It did not always pay to love a prince.

Unlike princes and kings of previous times, Prince Albert Edward did not officially or unofficially recognise any illegitimate offspring he may have had – as far as we know.

Despite being a playboy, Bertie did marry. Poignantly for this book, he married a Danish princess. He wed Princess Alexandra, daughter of Christian IX of Denmark, in 1863 at St George's Chapel, Windsor. Her father was King Christian IX of Denmark and of the relatively new House of Schleswig-Holstein-Sonderburg-Glücksburg – a cadet branch of the House of Oldenburg. More on them later. There had not been a royal match with a Danish prince or princess since Queen Anne's husband.

The poet, Alfred Lord Tennyson, summed up the feelings of a rather more historically aware British audience of the day in his ode *A Welcome to Alexandra*:

> *"Sea-kings' daughter from over the sea,*
> > *Alexandra!*
> *Saxon and Norman and Dane are we,*
> *But all of us Danes in our welcome of thee,*
> > *Alexandra!"*

This marital union between Britain and Denmark would arguably influence European history in the century ahead. The royal couple had three daughters and three sons – although the third son died after only a day. Their eldest son and heir, born in 1864, was named Albert Victor, in honour of the boy's paternal grandparents. He was quickly followed by his younger brother, George, born just seventeen months later.

Prince Eddy

Prince Albert Victor was later given the title Duke of Clarence and Avondale – Clarence being the medieval ducal title last used by Victoria's uncle, William IV, before becoming king. Being the third generation in a line of Alberts, he was known as Eddy. He was a sharp young man but not considered altogether bright. The Duke of Clarence and his younger brother, George, Duke of York, were educated and trained together in the navy on HMS *Britannia*. Soon after, in 1879, the two of them set out on a three-year tour of the world, visiting many places in the empire and beyond. Like true seamen, they reportedly both acquired many tattoos!

Eddy may have inherited some of his father's qualities – including a penchant for scandal and affairs – though little is provable. He was implicated with an actress who committed suicide (possibly after he had asked her to quit acting). He was connected to the Cleveland Street scandal – a male brothel in London – via his own equerry. Furthermore, he has long been associated with the Jack the Ripper murders in popular culture and conspiracy theories. He is often listed as a potential 'Jack', but the evidence shows that he was in London at the time of those atrocities. Regardless, these tales or connections do not paint a favourable picture of Eddy, particularly when you add that he was taking medicine for gleet – a loose term for gonorrhoea in those days. Perhaps the apple had truly fallen not so far from the tree.

Princess Mary of Teck

Prince Albert Victor found a suitable wife who would keep him respectable and prepare him for eventual kingship. His second cousin once removed, Princess Victoria Mary of Teck, was selected. She was the daughter of a German aristocrat (Franz, Duke of Teck) and Princess Mary Adelaide of Cambridge – grand-daughter of King George III. However, six weeks after the announcement of the couple's engagement, in January 1892, during the Russian flu pandemic, Eddy died of pneumonia at Sandringham.

There followed what can be described as some happily convenient family re-arranging. Princess Mary of Teck (as she was known)
and Prince George, Duke of York, naturally mourned Eddy together.
During this shared time of sorrow, they became very close. George's
grandmother, Queen Victoria, was always impressed by Mary's dignity and composure and was therefore a strong supporter of her being
a future queen consort. Put simply, Prince George was swapped in,
replacing his late brother in the previously arranged marriage.

Happily, theirs was a love match. George and Mary wed in July 1893
at St James's Palace – a little over a year after Eddy's death. The newly-
weds were quiet, slightly shy and relatively frugal. Interestingly, George
would later become the first British monarch for centuries who did not
grow up speaking German but learnt later as an adult.

Queen Victoria, the last British monarch of the Hanoverian line,
died surrounded by her family at her late husband's island retreat,
Osborne House, on the Isle of Wight in 1901. Her eldest grandson,
Kaiser Wilhelm II of Germany, held her hand to the last. At that time,
her reign was the longest of any British monarch in history – over sixty
years – which until recently seemed an unbeatable record. Also at her
bedside was her son, Bertie, who succeeded her as Edward VII, King of
the United Kingdom and also the first Emperor of India.

The Uncle of Europe

The aging King-Emperor, Edward VII, reigned only from 1901 to 1910.
However, in that short time he was particularly involved in international diplomacy, owing to his kin relationship with nearly all the royal
families of Europe. Like his mother, Bertie earned the affectionate title
of the 'uncle of Europe'.

Seeing the potential threat of German militarism and expansionism
under his nephew, Kaiser Wilhelm II, Bertie did much to strengthen
the bonds of friendship with his old friends the French and with Russia
as well. The Russian, Danish, Greek and British royal families were

often all on holiday together, and their family ties were strong. Kaiser Wilhelm was never invited to such gatherings.

Edward VII died at Buckingham Palace in May 1910 at the age of sixty-eight. With Albert Victor having predeceased his father, the crown was passed to Edward VII's second son, George, Duke of York – King George V.

THE HOUSE OF WINDSOR (1917-2022)

George V, 1910-1936
Edward VIII, 1936
George VI, 1936-1952
Elizabeth II, 1952-2022

TODAY, MANY PEOPLE have names that have been slightly anglicised. That is to say, a foreign surname that has been modified to sound more English/British/American so as to blend in more with society – or because the name is too hard to pronounce in English. (The latter is often true of people who have moved from East Asia.)

Many famous individuals and families have anglicised their names or adopted wholly different names in an effort to sound more British. This has often been the case for immigrant or refugee families. For example, many French Huguenot refugees settled in the south-east of England in the late seventeenth and early eighteenth centuries and adapted their surnames to their surroundings. Cartier became Carter; Carpentier became Carpenter; and Le Roy became Leeroy in some cases. Jewish immigrants/refugees to the UK and USA have often amended their surnames: Brook is used instead of Bruck/Bruch; Cohen, instead of Kohén; or Shaw, instead of Schultz. Individuals and families may have a variety of reasons for making these changes: to avoid prejudice or prejudgment, for political reasons, or to gain preference.

While it seems unlikely that the royal family of Great Britain, a centre of the establishment and British culture, would have to change their name for similar reasons, in 1917 that is exactly what happened.

WORLD WAR I

The First World War (1914-1918) pitted Britain, France, and Russia against the Central Powers: Germany, Austria-Hungary and the Ottoman Empire. In the decades leading up to war, many assumed that the stability of Europe was assured because many of its crowned heads were closely related to one another. Kaiser Wilhelm II of Germany, Tsar Nicholas II of Russia, and King-Emperor George V of Britain were famously all first cousins. Furthermore, the royal families of Europe were positively littered with the descendants or relatives of Queen Victoria and her husband Albert.

Their familiar links did not, however, prevent the Great War from starting following the events in Sarajevo in August 1914. Mere royal connections could not withstand the forces of nationalism, revolution, and political and strategic promises made by ministers between countries. In fact, the lifelong social ostracism that the Kaiser had experienced at the hands of the other royal families of Europe – for he was a difficult person to like or even tolerate – may have actually fanned the flames.

Many books, films and television dramas and documentaries (of a range of quality) have been made about the difficult moments the British royal family faced during the First World War. It is tempting to explore this more deeply. However, for the purposes of this book it is necessary to summarise.

Public Opinion

It almost goes without saying that the Great War was a long and terrible ordeal for the nations of Europe. As thousands of men were daily being fed into the giant killing factory that was trench warfare, there seemed to be no end in sight. Fighting on some fronts ended only in stalemate, and the war dragged on far longer than anyone had predicted. Naturally, in many countries, this led people to grow dissatisfied with the status quo and also with their rulers. In Russia popular discontent famously led to riots and then revolution. Other European monarchies experienced revolutionary rumblings too. Britain was no exception. There was anger that the war wasn't being won, that it was going on too long, that there were shortages, and that too many young men's lives were being lost.

With anti-German sentiment on the rise on the streets of Britain, there was concern about civil unrest. Some had pointed out that the king himself was a German; after all, his name was Saxe-Coburg und Gotha. The implication was that perhaps King George of the House of Saxe-Coburg und Gotha, with his many German relatives fighting for the enemy (the Kaiser being chief among them), was the reason Britain wasn't winning the war. While we may say that this idea was foolish and ignorant, it was nonetheless a growing sentiment during the second half of the Great War.

The peak of unrest came in March 1917 when the revolution started in Russia and George V's cousin and ally, Tsar Nicholas II, was forced to abdicate. A centuries-old monarchy was dismantled with just a few sheets of paper. The idea occurred to some that something similar might be possible in other European kingdoms. That same month, a newly developed German plane entered the war. The Gotha G.IV bomber was able to make Channel crossings and bomb parts of London directly. Incidentally, the plane was named after the company that built it, which in turn was named after the town in which it was founded: Gotha. The connection was not lost on the British people; Gotha was an ancestral land of King George's forebears and he shared part of his name with it.

The Royal Name

It became apparent that anti-German sentiment was reaching boiling point, and inspired by world events, anti-monarchist voices in

Britain were growing in strength. To address both these growing concerns, George V conceded that it would be sensible to change the name (or supposed surname) of the royal family to something more British. For this he turned to the advice of his private secretary, Lord Stamfordham.

Stamfordham was well versed in royal matters of a delicate nature. In previous years, he had been the one to explain the death (by Zulu ambush) of the Prince Imperial of France whilst serving in the British army in South Africa. He subsequently had to accompany the prince's mother, Empress Eugenie, to the site of the death in Zululand.

In order to solve King George V's surname problem, Stamfordham first asked the College of Arms, London, to help in coming up with alternative names. However, all of the names offered up by the college were considered by the king to be too German: Guelph, Wettin, and even Wipper. It seems the college rather missed the point, but they were immovable. Next, Stamfordham tried looking to past dynasties for ideas. He offered up 'Tudor-Stuart'. The king and queen were partial to Stuart on its own, but Herbert Asquith (who was consulting) pointed out that the last Stuart king was ousted by revolution. Royal family members gave their own suggestions in the form of the traditional royal titles: York, Lancaster, or even England. Nothing fit the bill.

THE CHOICE OF WINDSOR

There seems to be a consensus that it was Lord Stamfordham that suggested the name Windsor. It hadn't really been used as the name of a royal or nonroyal dukedom before, and the site of Windsor Castle had been occupied by most monarchs since William the Conqueror. Windsor had also been the burial place of many monarchs and lesser royals since at least the fourteenth century in a chapel dedicated to St George (where the Order of the Garter has its home). As a territorial style, Windsor had been used only by King Edward III (as Edward of Windsor), and he won famous battles in France!

The name seemed to fit perfectly. The king and his advisors felt the change needed to go deeper though. Whatever name they chose, the royal family were still in procession of various princely titles and ranks from the family's German possessions or homelands. These would have to go along with the surname. The king issued a statement to address these points on 17 June 1917:

> "...We, out of Our Royal Will and Authority, do hereby declare and announce that as from the date of this Our Royal Proclamation Our House and Family shall be styled and known as the House and Family of Windsor, and that all the descendants in the male line of Our said Grandmother Queen Victoria who are subjects of these Realms, other than female descendants who may marry or may have married, shall bear the said Name of Windsor. And do hereby further declare and announce that We for Ourselves and for and on behalf of Our descendants and all other the descendants of Our said Grandmother Queen Victoria who are subjects of these Realms, relinquish and enjoin the discontinuance of the use of the Degrees, Styles, Dignities, Titles and Honours of Dukes and Duchesses of Saxony and Princes and Princesses of Saxe-Coburg und Gotha, and all other German Degrees, Styles, Dignities. Titles, Honours and Appellations to Us or to them heretofore belonging or appertaining..."
>
> (London Gazette 30186. P7119. 17 June 1917)

The king and the government then went even further with the Titles Deprivation Act, which specifically stripped members of the extended royal family of their British peerages if they had been fighting for the enemy. The Duke of Coburg lost his British title of Duke of Albany. The Prince of Hanover lost the title of Duke of Cumberland.

British nobility who fought for the Central Powers were also deprived of their titles, such as Viscount Taaffe (an Irish peerage). German nobles who had previously had their titles 'recognised' in England as a courtesy, such as the Barons von Schroder, were also ear-marked for deprivation if they were found to be in league with the enemy. These deprivations were not in effect until 1919 however.

Other Royal Relations

On the Blighty side of the lines, many members of the extended royal family found themselves in the odd predicament of being resident in Britain, or even fighting for Britain, but being in possession of a German title. These were invited (effectively commanded) to follow the King's example. These families were allowed to exchange their German princely titles for a British peerage.

Famously, and important for this book, months after the king's proclamation, His Serene Highness Prince Louis of Battenberg, an admiral and former First Sea Lord, dropped his German name and titles to become The Most Honourable Louis Mountbatten, 1st Marquess of Milford Haven. Louis was married to the king's first cousin. At the time, no one could have known just how important this particular name change would be decades later.

Other titles and surnames which got changed in 1917 include the Duke of Teck (Queen Mary's family), who became the Earl of Athlone and the Marquess of Cambridge. Another Battenberg, Prince Alexander, was made Marquess of Carisbrooke. In the midst of these changes, King George V also restricted the use of the title of Prince or Princess to the close family members of the sovereign – the children and grandchildren of the monarch. This is a rule which still remains to this day, though exceptions have been made, and some have chosen to opt out of having the title altogether.

The royal change from Saxe-Coburg und Gotha to Windsor frustrated Kaiser Wilhelm, although it also amused him. With uncharacteristic wit, he reportedly remarked that he looked forward to returning to England to watch the '*Merry Wives of Saxe-Coburg und Gotha*' (instead of *Windsor* – the well-known comedy by William Shakespeare). The Kaiser was technically, by dint of being a grandson of Queen Victoria, a Prince of the United Kingdom. Needless to say, he certainly didn't use that title in his exile in the Netherlands following Germany's defeat at the end of the War.

Lord Stamfordham also is credited with advising the king not to grant asylum to the deposed Romanov cousins following the Tsar's abdication and incarceration. Attempts to rescue Nicholas II and his family were called off, and they were later executed by the Bolsheviks. Had they been given asylum somewhere in Britain (Balmoral possibly), they too might have abandoned their royal styles in favour of British peerages.

Edward VIII: Abdication

King George V died 20 January 1936 widely loved and respected by his people. He is credited as the forger of the modern monarchy we know and are used to today – opening Schools, engaging in charitable activities, being a patron of the arts and music and being the visible symbolic head of the nation and real head of the armed forces. On his death, the crown passed immediately to his son, Edward VIII.

Edward's very short reign is famously marred by the scandal of his choice of lover and wife (Mrs Wallis Simpson) as well as his politics and later connections to Nazi Germany. Though popular with the people, Edward found himself in opposition to the church and the government who insisted he give up Mrs Simpson. Unable to come to a compromise, King Edward abdicated as king and emperor on 11 December 1936 in favour of his younger brother the Duke of York, King George VI. Edward left the country and married the twice-divorced Wallis Simpson shortly afterwards.

Perhaps conveniently for all, Edward and Wallis did not have any descendants. Edward had long been regarded as unsuitable for the role of king by many in government and within his own family. In his younger brother George, they found a more reliable traditional man who would serve honourably.

George VI

The fact that George VI's real first name was Albert (aka Bertie) is fitting as he was the last king from the House of Saxe-Coburg und Gotha to rule as a consequence of Queen Victoria marrying Prince Albert. Thus two Alberts would bookend the dynasty.

There was reassurance in that George VI already had a stable marriage to a Scottish aristocrat, Lady Elizabeth Bowes-Lyon, and already had two legitimate heirs: Princesses Elizabeth and Margaret of York (born in 1926 and 1930, respectively).

A Lady from Scotland

Lady Elizabeth Bowes-Lyon (1900-2002) was the daughter of the 14th Earl of Strathmore and Kinghorne and hailed from one of the oldest noble Scottish families. Clan Lyon is thought to have some French origins but likely dates back to the Celtic times.

The first known progenitor of the family was John Lyon, Lord/ Thane of Glamis (c.1340-1382), a courtier of Scottish Kings David II and Robert II and Lord Chamberlain. Glamis Castle, which may be familiar from Shakespeare's *Macbeth*, became the home and fortress of the Lyon family. The Lyons became earls in 1606, and the name Bowes entered the family by dint of a large inheritance in 1767 when the 9th Earl of Strathmore and Kinghorne married Mary Bowes.

Centuries later, Lady Elizabeth Bowes-Lyon was courted by the king's son Bertie (the future George VI). After a few times of asking, she consented to be his wife. The king gave his permission, and the two were wed in 1923 at Westminster Abbey. Following Edward's abdication in 1936, Elizabeth became queen alongside her husband, George VI.

In the wake of WWI and with another war with Germany looming, Elizabeth was a welcome change from tradition. She was the first consort since 1707 not to be German or Danish and arguably the first person of non-German descent to possess the title of Queen since Queen Anne. She was also the first nonroyal consort (i.e. not a prince or princess) since Henry VIII's sixth wife, Catherine Parr.

World War II

King George VI ruled bravely through Britain's darkest hours in the Second World War. He had to overcome his shyness and a stammer to get through his royal duties. He looked on with trepidation as nearly all the other royal families of Europe were either deposed, exiled or occupied during the War. Despite the many threats, he and the family held firm; they remained in London even during the worst parts of the Blitz, showing their own sense of loyalty and duty to their people.

The Girl Who Would Be Queen

Following victory in the War, George VI's eldest daughter and heir, Elizabeth, married. She chose as her husband, a man who was tidied up and presented to the public as Lieutenant Philip Mountbatten RN, a nephew of a familiar national hero – Lord Mountbatten. The more honest telling of Philip's background was somewhat different. More on that later.

Though there was certainly some enthusiastic pushing by Lord Mountbatten, the match was evidently one of love. Their mutual affection is readily apparent in film reels taken of the couple during the early period of their relationship, and their lifelong dedication to each other stands as additional evidence of that fact. Philip was tall, handsome and a war veteran. Princess Elizabeth was young. He would not have been her family's first choice, what with him having about as much German ancestry as they and also having close family who had been involved in the Nazi Party. In the end, his charm, Lord Mountbatten's backing, and Elizabeth's love for him must have won over the king and queen. And so Princess Elizabeth returned to the tradition of so many

English monarchs before her – marrying a princely German or Dane.

The couple were married at Westminster Abbey on 20 November 1947 with jubilant crowds celebrating their union. They quickly produced an heir, Prince Charles, a year later on 14 November 1948.

George VI did not outlive his elder brother Edward VIII (by then Duke of Windsor). So, technically George never did become the senior head of the House of Saxe-Coburg und Gotha. The Duke of Windsor remained in that unofficial role. George VI was beset with ill health in the late 1940s owing to a life of excessive smoking and the stress of ruling through the War. He died on 6 February 1952 at Sandringham.

ELIZABETH II

The succession automatically passed to Princess Elizabeth, who was on a tour of Kenya at the time, and she became Elizabeth II. Her uncle, the Duke of Windsor, continued to live mostly in Paris. He died on 28 May 1972 at Villa Windsor in the Bois du Boulogne, ten days after a visit from Elizabeth.

Queen Elizabeth II was the longest-reigning sovereign the United Kingdom has ever had, reigning over seventy years from 1952 to 2022. In known world records, she is surpassed only by Louis XIV of France who reigned for over 72 years. (He succeeded at the age of four however, and lived to seventy-six.) Queen Elizabeth's reign was long and full of great change, inventions, wars, treaties, British successes and disappointments. However, we must concern ourselves with other matters.

Her Majesty died on 8 September 2022 at Balmoral Castle at the age of ninety-six. She was the last British monarch of the House of Saxe-Coburg und Gotha (known as Windsor since 1917). The dynasty had reigned for a century, from 1901 to 2022. Today the senior male-line Saxe-Coburg is now arguably Prince Richard, the Duke of Gloucester, the late queen's cousin and a grandson of George V.

At Elizabeth II's death, she was succeeded by her firstborn son, Charles III. Although he and his heirs will continue to be known formally as the House of Windsor, or sometimes Mountbatten-Windsor, his 'real' ancestral name (by ancient custom) is rather different – either Oldenburg or Schleswig-Holstein-Sonderburg-Glücksburg.

2 – Origins

THE HOUSE OF OLDENBURG

Iᴛ ᴡᴇ ᴡᴇʀᴇ to be strictly traditional and only take houses/surnames from the patrilineal line, the ruling house of the United Kingdom would not be Windsor nor Mountbatten-Windsor but Glücksburg. This is actually a shortening of the full name Schleswig-Holstein-Sonderburg-Glücksburg. This in turn is a branch of the House of Oldenburg. To put this into context, the House of Saxe-Coburg und Gotha was originally a branch of the House of Wettin. The House of Hanover was a branch of the older House of Welf/Guelph. The famous French House of Bourbon was a cadet branch of the House of Capet – which stemmed from one of France's early rulers, Hugh Capet. Put very simply, King Charles III's 'real surname' (whatever that means) is really Oldenburg.

Over the centuries from the 1100s onwards, the House of Oldenburg rose to great prominence having many different successful branches. Many of these branches had similar names that stemmed from titles or areas of land. Some cadet branches acquired royal status – usually by marriage – and some occupied a throne for decades or centuries. Prince Philip, the Duke of Edinburgh, was a member of such a cadet branch, which by the time of his birth had become the ruling family of Greece – the House of Glücksburg. On the death of his wife, Queen Elizabeth II, in 2022, their son, Charles III, also a member of that same house, became the King of the United Kingdom. The basic history of the recent monarchy of Britain is well known, but what is less well known is how the House of Glücksburg came to eventually sit on the throne. To understand this, we must look at the patrilineal ancestry of King Charles III – his father's father's father etc. We must start of course at the beginning with the House of Oldenburg.

As we have seen, houses and surnames are usually derived from a title, and that title is derived from a territorial designation. The House of Oldenburg is no different. Today the City of Oldenburg is in Lower Saxony in Germany. The settlement dates back to around the eighth century owing to some archaeological finds. However, the first documentary evidence can be found in 1108 which gives the name *Aldenburg*. The town was strategically important as it sits between the Rivers Hunte and Haaren and on the road from Bremen in the east to Groningen in the west. It was positioned by a ford on the Hunte, which is probably how the settlement started. Aldenburg Castle, located on the banks of the Hunte, is also mentioned in 1108. This served as the home of the family who became the Counts of Oldenburg.

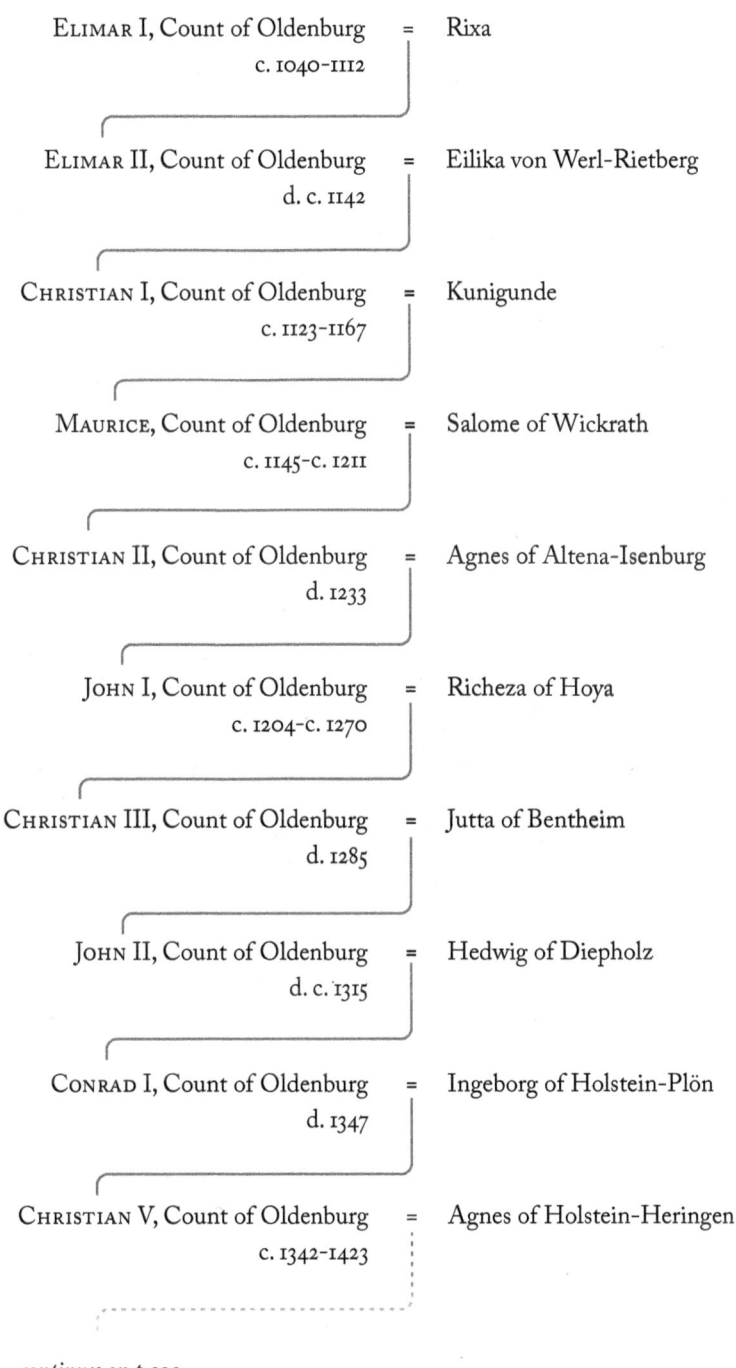

ELIMAR I, Count of Oldenburg
c. 1040-1112
= Rixa

ELIMAR II, Count of Oldenburg
d. c. 1142
= Eilika von Werl-Rietberg

CHRISTIAN I, Count of Oldenburg
c. 1123-1167
= Kunigunde

MAURICE, Count of Oldenburg
c. 1145-c. 1211
= Salome of Wickrath

CHRISTIAN II, Count of Oldenburg
d. 1233
= Agnes of Altena-Isenburg

JOHN I, Count of Oldenburg
c. 1204-c. 1270
= Richeza of Hoya

CHRISTIAN III, Count of Oldenburg
d. 1285
= Jutta of Bentheim

JOHN II, Count of Oldenburg
d. c. 1315
= Hedwig of Diepholz

CONRAD I, Count of Oldenburg
d. 1347
= Ingeborg of Holstein-Plön

CHRISTIAN V, Count of Oldenburg
c. 1342-1423
= Agnes of Holstein-Heringen

continues on p.202

Figure 2: The Emperor Charlemagne receiving the submission of Widukind at Paderborn in 785AD, by Ary Scheffer (1795–1858). Galerie des Batailles, Palais de Versailles.

Elimar I, Count of Oldenburg

(24xgreat-grandfather)

Born: *possibly as early as 1040*

Died: *before 1112*

Spouse: *Richenza*

Approximate concurrent English Monarchs: *Harold Harefoot, Harthacnut,*
Edward the Confessor, William I, William II and Henry I

THE FOUNDER OF THIS HOUSE and the furthest back patrilineal ancestor according to records of our present monarch (King Charles III)
was Count Elimar I (c. 1040-before 1112). Elimar is first mentioned in
writing as witness to a document of the local Archbishop of Bremen,
Liemar, in 1091. He is described as still growing up at that time. Elimar is
recorded later in 1108 as being accepted into a prayer society at the Iburg
Monastery in exchange for a membership fee which seems to have been
a bucket of ninety eels to be collected from Aldenburg/Oldenburg! It
would be hard to imagine royals today purchasing membership in societies with eels as currency. Elimar is also described as a powerful count
living on the border between Saxony and Friesland – roughly the border
between modern-day Germany and the Netherlands.

Elimar's origins and how he came into his presumed inheritance of
Oldenburg is unknown; there are few surviving sources. It is possible
he may have originated from the Osnabrück area, and he may have had
family connections in senior parts of the local clergy. There is nothing
that can conclusively confirm who his immediate relatives or ancestors were. According to Elimar's wife, however, he was descended from
the great Saxon warrior Widukind/Wittekind – which would suggest
Elimar may have Saxon origins. Precisely how he may have descended

from Widukind is unknown. Many other medieval Germanic dynasties also claimed descent from him, so perhaps he was in the line of Widukind or maybe it was just fashionable to claim as much. It may have been similar to the way in which Alfred the Great claimed descent from certain biblical figures for political advancement or legitimacy.

A historical but also legendary figure, Widukind (meaning child of the forest) was the leader of the pagan Saxons in the eighth century and is sometimes known as *Dux Saxonum* – Duke of the Saxons. He was the chief opponent of Charlemagne and Christianity in the area. He was the only Saxon noble who refused to be present in Charlemagne's court. Widukind regularly aligned himself with the Danes, the Frisians and the Westphalians in opposition to Charlemagne's Frankish Christian Carolingian Empire. The conflict between these opposing groups became the Saxon Wars of 777 to 785. Desecration of Saxon holy sites such as the Irminsul sanctuary (a sacred pillar or tree) were met with similar destruction of new Christian churches. Charlemagne massacred around 4,500 Saxon pagans at Verden in 782. As Charlemagne's forces pushed into Saxon lands, Widukind surrendered in the Bardengau in 785 in return for the promise that his life would be spared and no harm would come to him. Charlemagne's conditions were not surprising: Widukind had to be baptised and made Christian, which he was, with Charlemagne as godfather! Widukind's life produced many stories and legends, which unfortunately were wrapped in German nationalism during the twentieth century – mostly because he was seen as a hero for standing for Germanic pre-Christian traditions and against the Franks (which some might incorrectly read as the French)!

Elimar's connection to Widukind, though possible, has no conclusive evidence to support it besides the claims of his wife, Richenza (sometimes Rixa or Rikissa). Richenza was the daughter of Dedi of Adalgar and Ida of Elthorpe. Contemporary sources describe her mother, Ida, as the niece of both a pope and an emperor – but do not name them. For hundreds of years, genealogists have tried to solve this riddle without any clear success. One possibility is that her paternal uncle could have been Holy Roman Emperor Henry III and her maternal uncle, Pope Leo IX (Bruno von Egisheim-Dagsburg), but this is also unproven. (Pope Leo IX was instrumental in the Great Schism between the Catholic and Eastern Orthodox Churches.)

Very little else is known about Elimar. It is interesting that the founder of one of Europe's longest-lasting and successful dynasties (in terms of acquiring crowns and keeping them) has such vague and quiet origins. There is no great warrior founder or biblical hero, just the local ruler of a town in north-west Germany. Elimar could not have known that from his small county, his male-line descendants would one day occupy the thrones of Denmark, Sweden, Norway, Russia, Greece and the United Kingdom.

ELIMAR II, COUNT OF OLDENBURG

(23xgreat-grandfather)

Died: *c. 1142*

Spouse: *Eilika of Werl-Rietberg*

ELIMAR AND RICHENZA had three children. Elimar's successor was his son, Elimar II, Count of Oldenburg. Elimar II seems to have taken possession of the county. However, it is unclear if he actually occupied Oldenburg Castle. He married Eilika, daughter of Count Heinrich von Rietberg – who was a one-time associate of the Holy Roman Emperor. The couple had three sons and two daughters.

A theme throughout the story of the House of Oldenburg is propitious marriages and important inheritances. The significance of the latter was evidently apparent to Elimar II. He was forced to demand the inheritance of his grandmother, Ida von Elthorpe, from the local administrator of the county of Stade, which he probably acquired through successful politicking. Around 1141, Elimar II had a dispute with Counts Otto von Ravensberg and Ekbert von Tecklenburg over his claimed inheritance of lands to the north of Osnabrück. Elimar II's claim was based on his alleged descent from the warrior Widukind. Presumably, the dispute was resolved, as Elimar II's daughter married one of the von Tecklenburg clan. According to the German historian Bernd Hucker, Elimar II may have been killed by his brother, Count Christian, between 1142 and 1153; it is, however, difficult to prove this.

CHRISTIAN I, COUNT OF OLDENBURG

(22xgreat–grandfather)

Born: *c. 1123*

Died: *1167*

Spouse: *Kunigunde*

Approximate concurrent English monarchs: *Henry I, Stephen and Henry II*

ELIMAR II WAS eventually succeeded by his second son, Christian I, known as the Quarrelsome (c. 1123-1167). Elimar's lands were divided between Christian and his older brother, Henry, who ruled the lands of Wildeshausen. Henry's descendants are known as the Oldenburg-Wildeshausen line, a branch of the main house. Despite being the second son, Christian was the ruler of Oldenburg.

Christian married a woman called Kunigunde – a name more widely associated with Voltaire's *Candide* in modern times. Not much is known about this Kunigunde other than she probably hailed from the village of Versfleth, which has long been a submerged village beneath the River Weser. Christian and Kunigunde had at least two sons, Moritz/Maurice and Christian.

By 1166 Christian was in open opposition to his overlord, Henry the Lion, who was both Duke of Bavaria and Duke of Saxony. Christian also took part in the Italian campaigns of Emperor Frederick Barbarossa (1154-1155) and the campaign against Mecklenburg (1164). He attempted to gain independence from Henry the Lion by winning the support of the people of Bremen. However the Welfs attacked, and Christian was forced to fully retreat to Oldenburg where he died during the siege in c. 1167.

MAURICE I, COUNT OF OLDENBURG

(21xgreat-grandfather)

Born: *c. 1145*

Died: *c. 1211*

Spouse: *Salome of Hochstaden-Wickrath*

Approximate concurrent English monarchs: *Stephen, Henry II, Richard I and John*

MAURICE (C. 1145-1209) and his younger brother, Christian, were still juniors when their father Christian I died. Eventually Maurice inherited his father's lands and became the Count of Oldenburg. Christian, as the younger, sought his fortune on the Third Crusade with Frederick Barbarossa, but on his return from the Crusades he was murdered. Historians and chroniclers have pointed the figure at Maurice I The murder may have been the result of several inheritance disputes that were ongoing within the Oldenburg family.

Because primogeniture was not yet the custom in North Germanic states and counties, property, land and titles were divided amongst sons – not granted en masse to the eldest. Maurice probably wished to consolidate the Oldenburg lands lest they be divided further. He also clashed with the Wildeshausen branch of the family over yet more property disputes.

Maurice was a builder of castles on the outer extremities of his domains, which at the time provoked rebellions. It is also thought that he supported the Lords of Holstein, who were at that time hostile to the King of Denmark in the north. He married Salome, daughter of Count Otto von Wickrath and Adelheid von Hochstaden, and had five children.

CHRISTIAN II, COUNT OF OLDENBURG

(20xgreat-grandfather)

Died: *1233*

Spouse: *Agnes of Altena-Isenberg*

MAURICE I HAD two sons who succeeded him as Count of Oldenburg. One such son was Otto I (c. before 1209-1251). Like his father, Otto fought to claim and secure his inheritance. Otto was involved in the Stedinger War (1233-34) – a papally-sanctioned war launched by the Arch Diocese of Bremen (technically his feudal overlords) against the people of the Stedingen region to the north of Bremen. The Prince-Archbishop of Bremen, Gebhard, sought approval from Pope Gregory IX for a crusade against the people of Stedingen on the basis of heresy. The real reason was probably because they were in open revolt against Gebhard, his taxes and local property laws. The Stedinger people were free farmers but also subjects of the prince-archbishop.

The first initial crusading army was actually defeated, but a follow-up attempt the following year was victorious. During this war, Otto I was able to win parts of Stedingen, Moorriem, Holle and Elsfleth as well as other lands. This effectively secured his inheritance of the Versfleth, which came from his grandmother, Kunigunde von Versfleth. Cementing the family position further, Otto built castles at Berne, Lechtenberg, Lehe, and Delmenhorst – an area in the Stedinger lands formerly ruled by the Counts of Delmenhorst.

The House of Oldenburg was certainly on the rise and accumulating lands and counties. That said, Otto I seems to have constantly wrestled with the Wildeshausen cousins over ownership rights of various swathes of Oldenburg lands. Otto even had major disputes with the

Bishops of Munster over fiefdom claims. He founded a monastery in Menslage in 1244 but six years later had it moved to Borstel. This can be interpreted as an indication that he was unable to hold on to the northern possessions in Osnabrück. They were likely ceded to the Counts of Tecklenburg.

Otto's brother, Christian (died 1233), is confusingly known as Christian II of Oldenburg though he died before Otto. However, as we have learned, primogeniture was not yet commonplace; effectively, the two brothers jointly ruled their father's county. Christian married Agnes, daughter of Count Arnold von Altena, and had two sons. The eldest took Holy Orders and became an abbot. The younger son, John/Johann I would ultimately succeed as count.

Christian II of Oldenburg died in 1233. This may have been during the Stedinger War, but that is difficult to prove. He did, however, assist the Prince-Archbishop of Bremen in obtaining the support of the citizens of Bremen for the war. After Christian's death, Otto seems to have co-ruled with his nephew, John/Johann. Otto's own son, Henry, seems to have died in 1255 and did not rule Oldenburg.

JOHN I, COUNT OF OLDENBURG

(19xgreat-grandfather)

Born: c. 1204

Died: c. 1270

Spouse: *Richeza of Hoya*

Approximate concurrent English monarchs: *John and Henry III*

HAVING RULED OLDENBURG and its lands jointly with his uncle, Otto, from 1255, John/Johann I (c. 1204-1270) governed the county alone. He was now the Count of both Oldenburg and Delmenhorst.

As was tradition, he continued to dispute ownership of Oldenburg lands with his Wildeshausen cousins. The problem stemmed from the fact that the Oldenburg lands were divided between the dioceses of Munster and Bremen, which led to conflicts of interest and divided loyalties where feudalism and the two prince-archbishops were concerned. However, the choice was made easy for Johann when his cousin, Hildebold von Wunstorf, became Prince-Archbishop of Bremen in 1258.

John I married Richeza, daughter of Henry, Count of Hoya, and had at least four children. Sadly, John was not inventive with names; his three sons were called Christian, Maurice and Otto. After John's death, his lands were run by the boys' uncle (an abbot – who was infuriatingly also called Otto). When they came of age, the lands were divided between Christian and Otto (Maurice having predeceased his father). Christian received Oldenburg, and Otto received Delmenhorst, founding his own branch of the family (known as the Elder Line of Delmenhorst) which lasted five generations until 1436 when the lands reverted to the Oldenburg family. The famous Middle High German poet, Heinrich Frauenlob (Henry of Meissen), is said to have visited the court of Otto of Delmenhorst.

Christian III, Count of Oldenburg

(18xgreat-grandfather)

Died: *1285*

Spouse: *Jutta of Bentheim*

NOT A GREAT deal is known about the life of Christian III (d. 1285). By all accounts he was peace-loving and kind to the church. That said, during the early days of his stewardship of the Oldenburg lands, the ministeriales (a sort of free middling class) led by one Robert von Westerholt staged a rebellion. The rebels penetrated deep into Christian's ancestral lands, even invading the town of Oldenburg itself. Encircled and effectively trapped within Oldenburg Castle, Christian sent out men to carry out a scorched earth campaign. Like the Muscovites of 1812, his men burned the town and all its stores and supplies. Left with no proper shelter or hope of sustenance, the rebel forces eventually withdrew.

Of course, the razing of the town ultimately left Christian as the master of a burnt capital. He took his revenge, however. He pursued the rebels with his own force and caught up with them at the Tungeler marshlands where a battle ensued. Christian was not only victorious but captured von Westerholt and several other rebel leaders. Peace followed – albeit enforced. Chroniclers record Christian as pious but also a man who lived well and was fond of wine! Between his love of life and wine, he was unsurprisingly able to produce three sons with his wife, Jutta of Bentheim: Christian, Johan/John and Otto. Johan eventually would succeed him as Count John II. His youngest son, Otto, became the Archbishop of Bremen (in 1344) – which technically put the Oldenburg lands under the overlordship of another Oldenburg. It is good to keep these things in the family!

EDWARD HILARY DAVIS

JOHN II, COUNT OF OLDENBURG

(17xgreat-grandfather)

Died: *c. 1315*

Spouses: *1ˢᵗ Elizabeth of Braunschweig-Lüneburg*

2ⁿᵈ Hedwig von Diepholz

AFTER HIS FATHER's death, John II (d. c. 1315) was still very young. He was placed in the care of his uncle, Otto of Delmenhorst, from 1285 until about 1289. Local tradition paints a fairly negative view of John II as ruler of the Oldenburg lands. He reportedly attacked a monastery (Rastede) for reasons unknown and brought the county into a period of serious poverty. There were also some territorial losses caused by further feuds with neighbours during his time as count. At one point, John is thought to have been living in squalor not unlike a common peasant with a concubine or mistress.

John may have tried to make up for his failings by helping in the founding a Dominican monastery in Blankenburg near Oldenburg. The name effectively can be translated as white castle/hill – derived from the white habits of the Dominicans and the building/topography itself. It remained a monastery until the time of the Reformation. It was still in the Oldenburg family when it was secularised in 1623 and turned into a brewery (without a doubt the most cheery chapter of its history). Shortly afterwards, it was converted into a sort of hospital or care home for sufferers of the plague and then into a poorhouse and orphanage. From the late eighteenth century until the 1930s, it was an insane asylum. During the rule of the Nazi Party, many patients at Blankenburg fell victim to the national policy of euthanasia, particularly the children there. In 1941, as part of Aktion T4 – Hitler's order for involuntary euthanasia – 253 residents were 'removed' from the asylum. Eventually, after the war, Blankenburg became a tuberculosis hospital and nursing home. In more recent years, it has served as an initial reception facility for up to six hundred refugees in Lower Saxony and is part of the German Federal Office for Migration and Refugees.

John II married firstly Elizabeth von Braunschweig-Lüneburg and had three sons, inventively called Christian, John and Maurice. After Elizabeth's death, he married secondly Hedwig von Diepholz and begat another son, Conrad.

Conrad I, Count of Oldenburg

(16xgreat-grandfather)

Died: *1347*

Spouse: *Ingeborg of Holstein*

PROBABLY FOLLOWING THE wishes of their father (and learning from the mistakes of previous generations), Conrad I (d. 1347) initially shared power with his two older half-brothers, Christian IV and John III. This became the family policy, sharing power over all the Oldenburg lands, rather than dividing it amongst different sons and therefore splitting and diminishing the powerbase. Even after his elder brother's death in 1342, Conrad I ruled alone for just three years and then ruled jointly with his nephew, John IV (son of John III).

Together, Counts Conrad I and John IV acquired city rights for Oldenburg (under the city law of the Hanseatic city of Bremen). This made Oldenburg a more attractive market centre for foreign merchants and strengthened the economic base of the county through customs revenues.

Conrad I married Ingeborg, daughter of Count Gerhard von Holstein, and had two sons, Conrad and Christian. After Conrad I's death in 1347, the county continued to be co-ruled by his son Conrad II and nephew John IV. The latter died in 1356, and Conrad II ruled alone until 1368 when he was joined by his younger brother, Christian V.

Conrad II (d. 1401) was heavily engaged in political manoeuvres in an attempt to get his cousin, Maurice of Oldenburg (son of John II), made Archbishop of Bremen in 1348. Pope Clement VI instead favoured Gottfried von Arnsberg, who eventually was the successful candidate. Despite this failure to win the pope's blessing, Maurice was able to remain the coadjutor of the archbishopric and therefore exercised the actual power of government – allowing him to be a favourable ally of Oldenburg.

Perhaps due to his now having a relative set in a high place, Conrad II was able to expand the Oldenburg lands into Frisian areas. He formed alliances with many of the Frisian chiefs as well as the city of Bremen. However, the Bremen-Oldenburg campaign against Frisian Butjadingen (a northern part of a peninsula in north-west Lower Saxony) in 1368 was a catastrophic defeat in which many of the Oldenburg family lost their lives. There followed many so-called revenge campaigns. Eventually, Conrad was successful, and his victory led to the strengthening of Oldenburg's position as well as that of Bremen on the River Weser.

CHRISTIAN V, COUNT OF OLDENBURG

(15xgreat-grandfather)

Born: *c. 1342*

Died: *1423*

Spouse: *Agnes of Hohnstein*

Approximate concurrent English monarchs: *Edward III and Richard II*

IT IS POSSIBLE that Christian V (c. 1342-d. after 1399) was originally destined for life in the church, having been a canon at Cologne. However, in his twenties, he returned to Oldenburg to take up governance with his brother, Conrad II.

He may have even been ambitious enough to challenge his brother. He certainly consolidated his political position as chief of the Oldenburg clan and effectively obtained a blessing from Albert Brunswick-Wolfenbuttel, Archbishop of Bremen, in doing so. Christian actually married the Archbishop's niece, Agnes, daughter of Count Dietrich von Hohnstein-Heringen, in 1377. This union produced two sons, Christian VI and Dietrich, both of whom would rule Oldenburg eventually.

Christian's continued pursuit of sovereignty rights in individual lands within the Oldenburg estate (usually granted by Archbishop Albert) perhaps betrays his self-importance or wish to outshine his older brother. This evidently did not work out as Christian V died before his brother Conrad II, who returned to reigning alone for a time and died in 1401. From then, Conrad's son, Maurice II, succeeded alone but eventually shared authority with his cousins, Christian VI and Dietrich. It must have been an uneasy establishment since a lot of property, including Oldenburg Castle, was divided between them, – half being granted to Maurice II and the other half further divided between the two brothers, Christian VI and Deitrich. Maurice had no sons and died on 3 September 1420, and Christian VI died the following year with only an illegitimate son – which solved the problem of who was actually in charge and who owned the Oldenburg inheritance.

From 1421, Count Dietrich, son of Christian V, ruled Oldenburg alone. It is his descendants that would bring the House of Oldenburg to new heights of grandeur and form one of Europe's most successful dynasties.

Figure 3: Christian V. Section of a large illustrated Oldenburg family tree depicting Christian V, Gavno Castle Collection, copied and 'restored' from a damaged painted panel at Nyborg Castle, Funen, Denmark made in the reign of King Christian III of Denmark (1534–1559). (See Figure: 8.)

starts on p.183

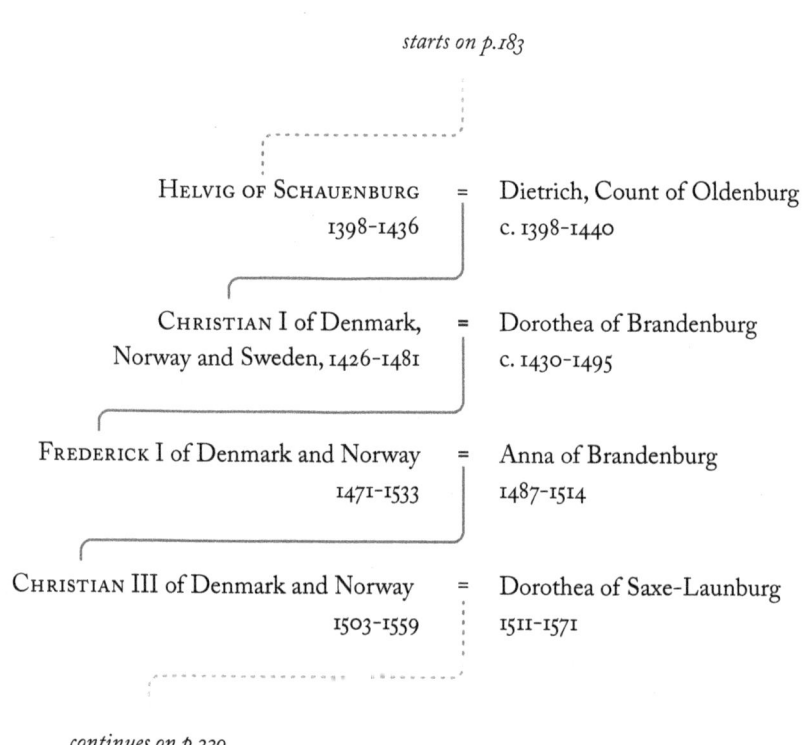

HELVIG OF SCHAUENBURG   =   Dietrich, Count of Oldenburg
1398-1436   c. 1398-1440

CHRISTIAN I of Denmark,   =   Dorothea of Brandenburg
Norway and Sweden, 1426-1481   c. 1430-1495

FREDERICK I of Denmark and Norway   =   Anna of Brandenburg
1471-1533   1487-1514

CHRISTIAN III of Denmark and Norway   =   Dorothea of Saxe-Launburg
1503-1559   1511-1571

continues on p.229

EDWARD HILARY DAVIS

3 – *A House on the Make*

THE ROYAL HOUSE OF OLDENBURG AND THE DUKEDOM OF SCHLESWIG-HOLSTEIN

Like the House of Tudor, it is possible for an obscure family with minor lands and titles, through chance and certainly advantageous marriages, to emerge as a powerful house and even take up the position of monarch and sovereign of a nation. Such was the House of Oldenburg. The family made the leap from mere counts in north-west Germany to Kings of Denmark, Norway and Sweden in just one generation. This obviously gave the House of Oldenburg potential that it could only have dreamed of in earlier generations – although doubtless there was great ambition. Luck, marriage and politics propelled the Oldenburgs to become the premier family in Scandinavia, one of the most important houses in Northern Europe and possibly the most successful dynasty to date.

Figure 4: Drawing of a Count of Oldenburg in fifteenth-century armour by Gustav Adolf Closs (1864-1938) in his "Deutschen Wappenkalenders" (c. 1938).

Figure 5: Dietrich, Count of Oldenburg. From a family tree painting at Rosenborg Castle, Copenhagen

DIETRICH FORTUNATUS ('THE FORTUNATE'), COUNT OF OLDENBURG

(14xgreat-grandfather)

Born: *c. 1398*

Died: *14 February 1440 at Delmenhorst*

Spouse: *1ˢᵗ Countess Adelheid of Oldenburg-Delmenhorst*

2ⁿᵈ Countess Helvig of Holstein

Concurrent English monarchs: *Richard II, Henry IV, Henry V and Henry VI*

DIETRICH, ALSO KNOWN as Theodoric, has been given the epithet 'fortunatus' or 'the fortunate' for a quite simple reason; he was rather lucky. Indeed, Dietrich was quite fortunate in three notable ways.

The first of these was the way in which he inherited – namely, in toto, without having to share with a brother, uncle or cousin. The (legitimate) lines of his older brother and cousins had died out, which meant that Deitrich was granted the entirety of the Oldenburg inheritance: Oldenburg Castle, the title of count and all of the lands to go with it. He did not, like so many generations of counts before him, have to share with other male relatives as had been the North Germanic/Saxon custom.

Secondly, in addition to his Oldenburg inheritance, Deitrich had the good fortune of acquiring the lands of the Oldenburg-Delmenhorst branch of the family in Delmenhorst. During the mid-fifteenth century, the then-last Count of Delmenhorst, Nicholas von Oldenburg-Delmenhorst, was Archbishop of Bremen. He repeatedly allowed himself to get into feuds with local landowning magnates, which sometimes spilled over into small military campaigns. His plan was to expand the archbishopric, acquiring more lucrative lands from neighbouring territories in the west (in Delmenhorst) in order to help pay some pre-existing debts. These speculative campaigns were financially costly, and at one point, Nicholas was captured by the Frisians. Remarkably, the council of Bremen were able to secure the archbishop's release without paying the ransom, but Nicholas was now saddled with additional debts from his unsuccessful land grab. His tenuous position in the diocese eventually led to his resignation.

At this point, Nicholas, reportedly being the senior-most and last legitimate descendant of the so-called 'elder line' or Delmenhorst branch of the House of Oldenburg, called on the help of his cousin, Count Dietrich. Nicholas signed over the lands of Delmenhorst to Dietrich in order to stop them from being used to pay his debts or indeed from becoming a permanent part of the diocese. Under the watchful eye of the Bremen council, Dietrich paid Nicholas two thousand guilders for Delmenhorst. Nicholas was a (Catholic) priest and so had no heirs to claim Delmenhorst – though he did have illegitimate issue. The title, Count of Delmenhorst, was transferred and joined to the Count of Oldenburg. The two lands and titles had been in the same family (but in separate branches) since 1278. Dietrich, however, was the first to re-combine them – fortunate indeed.

The third fortunate aspect of Dietrich's life was the way in which fate established for him and his family some very surprising royal connections. Princess Ingeborg of Itzehoe, Dietrich's Holstein grandmother, was eventual heir of her own grandmother, Princess Ingeborg of Sweden (d. 1290), daughter of King Valdemar of Sweden (1239-1302). King Valdemar's queen, Sophia, was the eldest daughter of King Eric IV of Denmark (1216-1250) – and she had no brothers. Owing to the lack of other living male-line descendants, Dietrich suddenly found himself in the line of succession to both King Valdemar and King Eric IV – he was heir to Sweden and heir to Denmark! Though Dietrich did not succeed to these kingdoms, his son did. He, along with his aforementioned forebears, is a male-line ancestor of the monarchs of Norway, Britain and Greece to this day – and Denmark as well up until 14 January 2024.

Dietrich's second marriage – from which his legitimate line descend – was to Helvig of Holstein (sometimes of Schauenburg) in 1423. She was the daughter of Gerhard VI, Count of Holstein – Holstein, being a province on the modern-day borders of Germany and Denmark, on the Baltic side. This pairing with the House of Schauenburg was later to prove a useful match for the House of Oldenburg. Her brother, Adolphus (1401-1459), became not only the Count of Holstein but also the Duke of Schleswig (c. 1439-1440) – a large fiefdom also in the southern borderlands of Denmark. The dukedom was granted to Adolphus (or he was recognised as the duke) by King Christopher III of Denmark following extensive petitioning. Dietrich's new ducal brother-in-law changed the fortunes of the Oldenburgs forever. Dietrich, however fortunate, would not live to see it though. He died in 1440 shortly after Adolphus's status was confirmed, leaving the County of Oldenburg to be ruled by his eldest son by Helvig, Count Christian.

Figure 6: Christian I, King of Denmark, Norway and Sweden.
Fifteenth-century portrait held at Frederiksborg Castle.

CHRISTIAN I, KING OF DENMARK, NORWAY AND SWEDEN

(13xgreat-grandfather)

Born: *February 1426 at Oldenburg*

Died: *21 May 1481 at Copenhagen Castle*

Spouse: *Princess Dorothea of Brandenburg*

Concurrent English monarchs: *Henry VI and Edward IV*

EIGHT YEARS AFTER Count Dietrich's death, King Christopher III, who ruled Denmark, Norway and Sweden, died without any clear heir in 1448. He was the last king of the House of Palatine-Neumarkt, a cadet branch of the House of Wittelsbach – then, as it is to this day, the ruling house of Bavaria. Possible successors were sought. Adolphus (Deitrich's brother-in-law) Duke of Schleswig and Count of Holstein was not only one of the most powerful politicians and greatest landholders in the Danish kingdom but also had a notable family connection to the throne. Through his mother, he was descended from King Eric V of Denmark and King Christopher I. He seemed the perfect candidate and was nominated as such by the Riksrådet – Danish Council of the Realm. Fate, it seems, had other ideas however. Duke Adolphus was old (for the time) and childless. At the grand age of 47, he did not feel up to the challenge. He nominated his nephew, the daughter of his sister Helvig, Count Christian of Oldenburg. The Riksrådet accepted Christian on the condition that he agree to the Constitution Valdemariana, an old agreement, made by King Valdemar III in 1326, that the Kingdom of Denmark and the Duchy of Schleswig should not be ruled by or be held as the sole possession of one person. The Riksrådet also required that Christian marry the Dowager Queen Dorothea of Brandenburg (Christopher III's widow), presumably to keep things tidy and maintain Danish influence and an ally in the Germanic lands to the south.

Conditions duly agreed to, on the first day of September 1448 in Viborg, Count Christian of Oldenburg was elected to the Danish throne as King Christian I. In October the following year, he was crowned in Copenhagen alongside his new wife Dorothea. In the space of a generation or two, the Oldenburgs had gone from North Germanic lords to Kings of Denmark. Since that day in 1448, the same House of Oldenburg (aka Schleswig-Holstein-Sonderburg-Glücksburg) ruled Denmark, right up until the abdication of Queen Margrethe II in 2024.

The union between the crowns of Denmark, Norway and Sweden had always been fragile and never assured. This union, personalised in the figure of the monarch of all three, was called the Kalmar Union. Earlier in 1448, before Christian I was made King of Denmark, the Swedes instead elected as their king Charles VIII – from the noble Swedish family Bonde. This put the Norwegians in a difficult position – having to decide between union with Denmark (Christian I) or Sweden (Charles VIII). Either would risk war. On 20 November 1449, Charles was crowned King of Norway in Trondheim. However, in a quick change of mind and keen to avoid a war with Denmark, the Norwegian nobility managed to persuade Charles to renounce his claim on Norway less than a year later. On 2 August 1450, accompanied by a large naval fleet for good measure, Christian came to Trondheim to be crowned King of Norway.

Denmark had for a long time been an elective monarchy. The monarchs were elected by a special council – rather like the Witan in England before the Norman Conquest. That said, the throne was usually passed through various family ties. Norway, by contrast, was technically an inherited monarchy, but for political reasons that had not been the recent reality when Christian took the throne. Weeks

EDWARD HILARY DAVIS

after his coronation, Christian I created a treaty of union between the Kingdoms of Denmark and Norway (the Treaty of Bergen), stating that they would have the same king in perpetuity and that the next king would be elected from the legitimate sons of such a king. Consequently, Norway was added to the territories ruled by the House of Oldenburg.

Another fortunate twist of fate led to the eventual addition of Sweden, reuniting the Kalmar Union under the House of Oldenburg, if only for a period. Charles VIII became an unpopular king in Sweden. He eventually went into exile, and Christian was invited to be the new king. However, Sweden was a country divided, with many opposing factions. Control of the country for Christian was illusive. The new regents of Sweden recalled King Charles VII twice, though he eventually died during his third reign in 1470. The following year, Christian took the opportunity to reassert his title and dominance over Sweden. This resulted in failure at the Battle of Brunkeburg near Stockholm, where he was defeated by the then regent, Sten Sture the Elder. Yet, rather like the English kings, who at that time still claimed kingship over France, Christian I continued to assert his title of King of Sweden until the end of his days.

Christian's uncle Adolphus died in 1459. Having already pre-inherited the crown through Adolphus, Christian now inherited his other lands and titles – most important of these was the Duchy of Schleswig and the County of Holstein. As we have seen, the Danish lands of Schleswig had some complicated statutes around its governance, but it effectively became a direct part of Christian's kingdom. Holstein was south of Denmark and was legally a Germanic county under the feudal overlordship of the Holy Roman Emperor. This oddly made the ruler of Holstein, in this case the King of Denmark, a vassal of the emperor. The then emperor, Frederick III, elevated Holstein to a duchy.

Christian I was a surprisingly well-travelled king for the Middle Ages, visiting Pope Sixtus IV in Rome as well as travelling to Milan, Burgundy and the Netherlands. In England at this time, the Wars of the Roses were raging, and English kings really only travelled abroad for short bursts of exile or fighting with the French. While with the pope, Christian gained permission to start a university in Copenhagen – which he founded in 1479.

One point that is particularly significant to us here in the UK is that Christian I's daughter, Margaret, married King James III of Scotland at Holyrood in 1469. The marriage was arranged as a way to offset the vast financial debt Scotland owed Denmark. The match was brokered by Charles VII of France, and once arranged, the vast debt was written off. Margaret was a popular queen in Scotland. She brought some much-needed colour, class and the latest European fashions to the Scottish court, and whilst she did not greatly care for her husband, she did provide him with three sons. It is believed she may have even taught them to speak Danish. This would not be the first or last time the Danes or the House of Oldenburg would form marriage alliances with British royalty – the most recent royal British-Oldenburg matches being Elizabeth II and Prince Philip of Greece in 1947 and Edward VII and Princess Alexandra of Denmark in 1863.

Christian I died at Copenhagen Castle on 21 May 1481. He was succeeded by his eldest son, John, who, like his father, managed to gain or be elected to the triple crown of Denmark, Norway and later Sweden. (He was known as John II in Sweden.) Owing to the ancient rules about the King of Denmark not also being allowed to also be the sole Duke of Schleswig, he shared the Duchy of Schleswig-Holstein with his younger brother, Prince Frederick. John ruled in Denmark from 1481 to 1513. Via his German wife, Christina of Saxony, he was succeeded by his son, Christian II.

King Christian II also shared the Schleswig-Holstein duchy with his uncle, Prince Frederick. Christian II attempted to keep the Kalmar Union intact, which eventually led to war in Sweden when Sweden tried to secede and Christian to fight to retake and hold it. Having won control of the country by 1520, Christian began systematically persecuting the rebellious Swedish nobility and churchmen. Shortly after

EDWARD HILARY DAVIS

his coronation in Stockholm, he effectively rounded up unsympathetic members of the Swedish court and hastily organised for them to be put on trial for heresy. Around a hundred people were executed in November 1520 in what has become known as the Stockholm Bloodbath or Stockholm Massacre. Needless to say, this made Christian II unpopular in Sweden, and the population branded him a tyrant. The following year, the Swedes rose up again and ousted him. By 1523 there was a new king in Sweden, Gustav I Vasa, whose family ruled the kingdom for more than a century. This marked the end of the Kalmar Union. The House of Oldenburg had lost one of its kingdoms.

On a lighter note, Christian II is also remembered in a piece of incidental music by Jean Sibelius: *Kung Kristian II* (Op.27). Sibelius wrote the music for a popular Swedish play of the same name written by his friend, Adolf Paul, in 1898. The play focuses on Christian's love affair with Dyveke. The music is in seven movements. The last movement, *Ballad*, is inspired by the Stockholm Bloodbath of 1520. Sibelius conducted the premier performance in 1898 at the Swedish Theatre in Helsinki, Finland. That same year, Jean Sibelius started work on his more famous first symphony (Op.39). Some say it exhibits some of the same traits as the final movement of his *Kung Kristian II*. A revised version of the first symphony was performed in Berlin in 1900, which launched Sibelius to international renown.

At home, Christian II sought to bring about quite radical reforms to law in Denmark, some of which would have given more rights to the common folk and peasantry. Naturally, this displeased the nobility and senior clergy, who were understandably anxious to protect their privileges. They rose up against their king in 1523 and exiled him to the Netherlands – specifically Lier, which is now in Belgium. He was replaced by his uncle, Prince Frederick, who became Frederick I. While on his 'down time' in Lier, Christian communicated with the great church reformer Martin Luther. For a time, Christian actually became a Lutheran and had the Bible translated into Danish.

Christian II's personal life was similarly a mess. Although he was married to Isabella of Austria (daughter of Holy Roman Emperor Maximillian I) in 1514 and 1515 (by proxy and in person), he brought with him to the marriage his Norwegian mistress, Dyveke Sigbritsdatter, who was of mostly Dutch extraction. It seems he loved Dyveke and so refused to give her up. Their love affair has inspired poetry in Denmark, despite the fact that not much is known about the romance. Dyveke (which means 'little dove' in Dutch) was at Christian's side from around 1507 until the end of her life. Her mother, Sigbrit Villoms, was made one of the king's chief councillors. This naturally antagonised the Danish nobles, Christian's wife and his powerful in-laws. Sigbrit was from the middling class of people, and her financial advice always favoured the plight of the working middling class in the kingdom. Eventually, the emperor intervened and demanded that Christian give up Dyveke. Christian refused and lost himself a powerful ally in the struggles to come. Dyveke died in 1517, probably from eating fruit that had been poisoned. In a rage, suspecting murder, Christian accused the popular nobleman Torben Oxe of the poisoning and had him quickly tried and executed despite the fact that there was little or no evidence of his guilt. This only alienated Christian further from the people of Copenhagen and Denmark at large. Not much is known about what happened to Sigbrit. Some say she was imprisoned for witchcraft – which seems believable given the times.

Christian did manage to do his duty with his wife and produced four sons, though none survived past childhood. His two daughters grew up to make fine marriages, but they would not inherit the throne.

Despite agreeing to his exile and to the rule of his uncle, Frederick I, in 1531 Christian attempted a coup to regain the throne. He reconciled himself with the emperor, returned to the Catholic faith and went with a fleet to Oslo but failed to take Norway. He agreed to an offer of safe conduct from Frederick I, which in truth eventually resulted in Christian being imprisoned in Sønderborg Castle and later Kalundborg

Castle for many years – though he was not overly confined and was, in fact, treated with great dignity.

After King Frederick I died in 1533, there followed a struggle known as the Count's Feud ('Grevens Fejde' in Danish). This conflict, lasting from 1534 to 1536, can be summarised as a war of Danish succession between two rival claimants: Christian II and Christian III (who was son of the late Frederick I). They were Catholic and Protestant, respectively, and the war between them can be seen as part of the European wars of religion that took place across the continent during the sixteenth and seventeenth centuries. The Count's Feud gets its name from Christian II's chief ally and commander, his cousin, Christopher, Count of Oldenburg – whose grandfather had been a younger brother of Christian I. The end result of the conflict was that Christian II remained in prison, Christian III stayed King of Denmark, and Lutheranism was established as the state religion.

Christian II died on 25 January 1559 whilst still a prisoner at Kalundborg, just days after his great rival Christian III. He must have been an interesting, erratic character – a schemer, theologian, murderous politician and loyal lover even to the detriment of his kingdoms. There is certainly a touch of Henry VIII about the man!

Figure 7: Frederick I, King of Denmark and Norway. 1539 portrait attributed to Jacob Binck. Frederiksborg Castle.

Frederick I, King of Denmark and Norway

(12xgreat-grandfather)

Born: *7 October 1471 at Haderslevhus Castle, Denmark*

Died: *10 April 1533 at Gottorf Castle, Schleswig*

Spouses: *1ˢᵗ Princess Anna of Brandenburg*

2ⁿᵈ Princess Sophie of Pomerania

Concurrent English monarchs: *Edward IV, Edward V, Richard III,*

Henry VII and Henry VIII

A S WE HAVE learned, Frederick was a younger son of King Christian I. He took over as king from his deposed nephew, Christian II. Frederick was of the older generation and a steadier pair of hands, having been co-Duke of Schleswig-Holstein with his brother John since childhood. He was in fact the last Catholic monarch in Denmark and Norway.

His early days as co-duke were punctuated by his brother King John's repeated attempts to gain control of Dithmarschen. This conflict culminated in the disastrous Battle of Hemmingstedt in 1500, in which the native peasant army inflicted massive casualties on the ducal Danish force, killing a great number of nobles and knights. The peasants, led by a farmer called Wulf Isebrand, broke local dykes, flooding the surrounding field lands and pushing the ducal army, which was less familiar with the terrain, onto narrow roads before launching an attack. The peasants were able to traverse the flooded areas on poles;

they knew where the ground would support weight and where it was boggy. Without that knowledge, as many as 7,000 ducal mercenaries and Danish soldiers perished or drowned. Allegedly, the peasant force of only about 1,000-1,500 captured the Dannebrog – the Danish banner and mascot carried on royal campaigns for centuries – until Frederick made them return it decades later.

When his brother, King John, died in 1513, a group of nobles from Jutland suggested that Frederick take the throne for himself. However, Frederick believed that his nephew, Christian, would have more support from the wider nobility of Denmark, and so the path was clear for Christian to become Christian II of Denmark. There is a possibility that Frederick did not speak Danish, only German, which may have been a reason for his hesitation. He spent much of his time at his estate around Gottorf Castle (Gottorp in Low German) in the north-east of Schleswig-Holstein, which is now in modern day Germany. A branch of the Oldenburg family, named after this castle and estate, would one day go on to rule Russia from Tsar Peter III to Tsar Nicholas II (1762 to 1918): the House of Schleswig-Holstein-Gottorp, though they preferred to be known as Romanov (sometimes known as the House of Holstein-Gottorp-Romanov). More on them later.

After Christian II was forced to abdicate, Frederick was elected King of Denmark and Norway in 1523 and 1524 respectively. Much of his early reign was spent quelling rebellions of those loyal to Christian II in Scania, Jutland and elsewhere. Frederick took a more liberal approach to the rise of Lutheranism in the kingdom than his predecessor. In fact, he encouraged that Catholics and Lutherans share the same churches, and he allowed and even supported the first official publication of the Bible in Danish. Hans Tausen, a Danish Lutheran theologian and reformer, was almost arrested by Catholic authorities for heresy. He was saved by Frederick, who quickly appointed him his chaplain – which gave Tausen immunity. At very nearly the same time that such things were transpiring in England, beginning around 1527, Frederick, despite being a Catholic, ordered the closure of many Franciscan priories in a (fairly successful) attempt to decrease the power of the bishops and the Roman Catholic Church in Denmark. That said, Frederick II managed to walk a difficult road avoiding a war between his Protestant and Catholic subjects. His death in 1533, however, caused tensions to rise and led to the Count's Feud – a war between Catholics and Protestants and a struggle for the succession to the throne. Ultimately, Protestantism and Frederick's son, King Christian III, emerged victorious.

With Frederick I and his successors began the centuries-long tradition of Kings of Denmark being officially named alternately Christian and Frederick (even if their first name at birth was different). This tradition continued through sixteen Kings of Denmark from 1533 until 1972. At that time, King Frederick IX died leaving the crown to his daughter, the present queen, Margrethe II. Fortunately, she decided not to change her name to Fred or Chris!

Figure 8: Christian III, King of Denmark and Norway. 1550 portrait by Jacob Binck, Frederiksborg Castle.

Christian III, King of Denmark and Norway

(11xgreat-grandfather)

Born: *12 August 1503 at Gottorf Castle, Schleswig*

Died: *1 January 1559 at Koldinghus Castle, Kolding, Denmark*

Spouse: *Princess Dorothea of Saxe-Lauenburg*

Concurrent English monarchs: *Henry VII, Henry VIII, Edward VI,*

Mary I and Elizabeth I

CHRISTIAN III WAS born the eldest son of Frederick I and his wife Anna of Brandenburg at Gottorf Castle in Schleswig. From an early age, he displayed great promise as a politician, leader and ruler. Following his father's accession to the throne, he subdued the population of Copenhagen – which had previously supported the deposed Christian II – and he expertly administered the provinces of Schleswig and Holstein as well as the Kingdom of Norway, of which he was viceroy from 1529. Although his father was a Catholic, Christian III was brought up with Lutheran tutors. As a young man, he was present at the famous Diet of Worms in 1521, where he heard Martin Luther himself speak – and where Luther was officially condemned as a heretic by the Holy Roman Emperor, Charles V, banning all imperial subjects from supporting or propagating Luther's views. These experiences left a mark on Christian III. As a consequence, he introduced Protestantism into his lands in Schleswig-Holstein, making Lutheranism the state church there from 1528.

When his father died in 1533, Christian III was proclaimed king; however, the council was predominantly made up of nobles and bishops who were ardently Catholic. Their disapproval led them to seek help from Count Christopher of Oldenburg to restore the still captive Christian II – a Catholic. A civil war followed from 1534 to 1536 which, as we have noted, is known as the Count's Feud. Using German Protestant mercenaries and enlisting help from the (new) King of Sweden, Gustav Vasa, Christian III was slowly able to win repeated victories and gain control of his various territories and kingdoms. Copenhagen finally surrendered to him in July 1536, and he was firmly back on the throne.

After the war, Christian was initially unpopular, which is not surprising bearing in mind he had conquered his own people using mostly German soldiers and Swedish allies. The government was divided between the Danish nobility and the many German advisers (from Holstein) that Christian kept around him. In the years that followed the Count's Feud, he enacted a policy to bring an end to Roman Catholicism in Denmark. He had racked up quite a lot of debt during the war and, like our Henry VIII, found it very convenient to confiscate church lands and use the profit from them to pay his creditors as well as increase his own wealth. Various bishops were arrested and excluded from the council, and Lutheranism was established as the Danish national church (or the Church of Denmark) in October 1536. Only two years earlier in 1534, Henry VIII of England had renounced papal authority in his own kingdom.

Before the reformation of the church in Denmark, the king's lands were a mere sixth of the kingdom. Afterwards, this number soared to roughly sixty percent, with many estates and parcels of lands being given as gifts to Christian's supporters. For us in England, this does sound awfully familiar! A year after solidifying his hold on both church and state in Denmark, Christian successfully did the same in Norway.

Through a coup d'état in 1537, the northern Kingdom of Norway was turned into an hereditary monarchy. No more would the King of Norway be elected by a council. The Norwegian succession was now (and in perpetuity) bound in blood to the House of Oldenburg.

That same year, Christian appointed Norway's first Lutheran bishop in the Church of Norway, thus ensuring that from here on Denmark and Norway would be Protestant kingdoms – as they are today. Christian did get involved with the English Reformation of the same period – if only for a moment. In 1553, following the accession of Mary I in England, many prominent Protestants there were at risk of arrest. It was clear that she would set out to purge England of heretics and burn them at the stake. One such fearful Protestant was Myles Coverdale, one-time Bishop of Exeter and a famous translator of the Bible into English. Coverdale was placed under house arrest. He feared the worst. However, his brother-in-law was able to alert King Christian III to the situation. Sympathetic to the Protestant cause, Christian intervened. He interceded with the English courts on Coverdale's behalf, obtaining him safe conduct passage to Denmark – and to have his baggage left unsearched. The nearly seventy-year-old cleric escaped the retribution of Mary's Catholic reprisals. However, despite Christian's kindness, Coverdale chose not to go to Denmark, instead journeying to Wesel in Germany, where many other English Protestants had fled.

Christian III had a powerful adversary in the Holy Roman Emperor, Charles V. Not only was Charles a Catholic, but his nieces (Dorothea and Christina) were the daughters of the deposed Christian II and could be seen as potential alternative heirs to the Scandinavian kingdoms. Christian aligned himself with various Protestant German princes and declared a pre-emptive war on Charles in 1542. He stopped all shipping through the Danish straits, which strangled commerce in Northern Europe and led to neighbouring states urging Charles to abandon the war, which he did the following year, abandoning also the claims of his nieces.

Up until 1544, Christian III had continued to rule over the Duchies of Schleswig (in Denmark) and Holstein (part of the Holy Roman Empire) – being Danish and iImperial fiefs, respectively. He ruled on behalf of his younger half-brothers during their minority, as the three of them technically shared the joint duchies. Christian's half-brothers were John the Elder (known as Duke of Schleswig-Holstein-Haderslev) and Adolf (known as Duke of Holstein-Gottorp, who founded the house of the same name which later ruled Russia). Despite being technically in two different countries and with their revenue divided amongst three brothers, the duchies were by no means unimportant to Christian. Their divided nature effectively meant that the duchies could not be rallied into a strong unified force to challenge the monarch. Furthermore, they served as a buffer between Denmark and the lands of the Holy Roman Emperor to the south.

EDWARD HILARY DAVIS

Figure 9: A fan pedigree of King Christian III of Denmark and Norway (1503–1599), showing all sixteen of his great-great-grandparents painted onto a panel at Nyborg Castle, Funen, Denmark.

Christian III died on New Year's Day 1559 at Gottorp Castle. He and his queen, Dorothea of Saxe-Lauenburg, reportedly enjoyed quite a happy marriage and had five children together. However, after Christian's death (or possibly just before), Dorothea fell in love with Christian's younger half-brother, John the Elder. Following her mourning, she made it clear that she intended to marry John. This met with opposition from courtiers and clerics alike. Across the water in England, they had seen a country descend into religious chaos (nominally) following the marriage of a prince to his dead brother's widow. Henry VIII's case for divorce centred on a passage from Leviticus saying that such a marriage was unorthodox and would not bear children (or sons, as he understood it). In Denmark, however, there was also politics and dynasty to be considered should she have a son with John. That said, Dorothea was about 48, so that was unlikely. For a few years, she campaigned for the marriage to no avail. Dorothea's eldest son, the new King Frederick II also opposed the match, causing a deep rift between mother and son. But Frederick got a taste of his own medicine soon enough.

Frederick wanted to marry a nonroyal woman with whom he was very much in love. This proposed match was also unpopular at court and with his mother. It also flew in the face of the convention of royals marrying other royals for state and strategic reasons. After a drawn-out period of arguing, Frederick married a cousin, Sophie of Mecklenburg, which evidently turned out to be a very happy marriage – producing seven children in the ten years following their wedding. Dorothea, alas, did not get to marry John, and she died at Sonderburg Castle in 1571. Of interest to us is her second son, who – by what seems poetic justice – was named John.

4 – Go Forth and Multiply

THE HOUSE OF SCHLESWIG-HOLSTEIN-SONDERBURG

Figure 10: A recent photo of Sønderborg Castle, South Jutland by Kim Toft Jørgensen, Museum of Sønderjylland.

FOLLOWING THE DEATH of Christian III, the Oldenburg line from Elimar I to our King Charles III went through a nonroyal phase, passing as it did through a younger son of the king. From then on, it formed its own house – what we call a cadet branch of the parent house. These are often formed when a strong house produces several younger sons whose subsequent dynasties are equally, if not more successful, over time.

A more famous example can be shown in the royal house of France. The dynasty started with the early medieval Hugh Capet who was followed by the Capetian line of kings. However, most of us are more familiar with the House of Bourbon. This was itself a junior branch of the House of Capet and started around the late thirteenth and early fourteenth centuries with Robert of Clermont (sixth son of King Louis IX of France) and his son, Louis, 1st Duke of Bourbon, after whom the cadet branch was named. Centuries later, several cadet branches of Capet (such as Valois) had died out, and the cadet branch of Bourbon found itself the senior line. Subsequently, France had its first Bourbon monarch in Henry IV in 1589. This was the beginning of the Bourbons, including the most famous French kings, Louis XIV, XV, and XVI, who were all in the direct male line from Henry IV of Bourbon. All subsequent French monarchs from 1589 to 1830 have been of this line (with the great exception of the Bonapartes and the Orleans, another branch of Capet, which usurped the Bourbons in the nineteenth century). Incidentally, thanks to cadet branches of the cadet branch, Bourbons currently sit on the thrones of Spain and Luxembourg. Philip VI of Spain (born 1968) and Henri, Grand Duke of Luxembourg (born 1955), both descend in the male line from Louis XIV of France.

So it is quite possible, after some generations, that a branch of a royal family that began as very minor royalty can, quite suddenly, be propelled forward as a ruling family – such as with the Bourbons. Similarly, there were many cadet branches of the House of Oldenburg, and the House of Schleswig-Holstein-Sonderburg was one of them – having different minor branches itself. We will follow the branch to which the king and his late father, the Duke of Edinburgh, belong. It is not a monarchical family, but, as with the Bourbons, fate determined that this cadet branch would return to a throne and a crown one day. For the time being, this branch of the Oldenburg family became not so much minor royalty as perhaps junior royalty on the European stage.

continues from p.202

JOHN (OF DENMARK),   =   Dorothea of Saxe-Lauenburg
Duke of Schleswig-Holstein-Sonderburg   1511-1571
1545-1622

ALEXANDER,   =   Dorothea of Schwarzburg-Sondershausen
Duke of Schleswig-Holstein-Sonderburg   1579-1639
1573-1627

AUGUST PHILIPP,   =   Marie Sibylle of Nassau-Saarbrucken
Duke of Schleswig-Holstein-   1628-1699
Sonderburg-Beck
1612-1675

FREDERICK LOUIS,   =   Louise Charlotte of
Duke of Schleswig-Holstein-   Schleswig-Holstein-Sonderburg
Sonderburg-Beck   -Augustenburg
1653-1728   1658-1740

PETER AUGUST,   =   Princess Sophie of
Duke of Schleswig-Holstein-   Hesse-Philippsthal
Sonderburg-Beck   1695-1728
1697-1775

PRINCE KARL ANTON AUGUST   =   Countess Charlotte of
of Schleswig-Holstein-   Dohna-Leistenau
Sonderburg-Beck   1738-1785
1727-1759

FRIEDRICH KARL LUDWIG,   =   Countess Friederike Amalie
Duke of Schleswig-Holstein-   of Schlieben
Sonderburg-Beck   1757-1827
1757-1816

FRIEDRICH WILHELM,   =   Princess Louise Caroline
Duke of Schleswig-Holstein-   of Hesse-Kassel
Sonderburg-Glücksburg   1789-1867
1785-1831

continues on p.275

ALL THE KINGS' FATHERS

Figure 11: Hans/John (II), Duke of Schleswig-Holstein-Sonderburg, by an unknown painter. Frederiksborg Hillerod Museum, Denmark.

John, Duke of Schleswig-Holstein-Sonderburg

(10xgreat-grandfather)

Born: *25 March 1545 at Haderslev, Denmark*
Died: *9 October 1622 at Glücksburg, Schleswig-Holstein*
Spouses: *1ˢᵗ Duchess Elisabeth of Brunswick-Grubenhagen*
2ⁿᵈ Princess Agnes Hedwig of Anhalt
Concurrent English monarchs: *Henry VIII, Edward VI, Mary I, Elizabeth I and James I*

JOHN (KNOWN AS HANS IN DANISH) was born in 1545, the third son of King Christian III and Queen Dorothea. His eldest brother, Frederick II, succeeded in 1559 as the new king in Denmark and Norway (simultaneously, as his father had combined the two as hereditary monarchies). John's other elder brother was Magnus. Technically and owing to custom, all three of the other brothers inherited an equal share of the Duchies of Schleswig and Holstein. That said, Magnus eventually gave up his rights to the duchies, having become a prince-bishop. Later, while in Moscow, he was named and crowned King of Livonia by the then ruler of Russia, Ivan the Terrible – although Magnus later had to relinquish his kingly claim.

A senior clerical position was considered for John also. Back towards the Oldenburg heartlands, there was an opportunity to try and push John forward as the next Prince-Archbishop of Bremen. However, thanks to a new war with Sweden (the Northern Seven Years War 1563-1570), King Frederick II was in vital need of German allies in the south.

Securing all the best bishoprics and offices for his brothers would not be prudent in light of the war and might even lose him friends. So John did not go to Bremen. Instead, he was made duke, and Frederick tried to divide the family's duchies and give John one half of the territory to rule. However, the Danish Estates of the Realm refused to accept this division of Danish lands into effectively separate countries. In the end, John was given Sonderburg Castle, the title of Duke of Schleswig-Holstein-Sonderburg, and an income from the lands. He was not, however, the de facto ruler of the territories. Real power over the territories lay with his brother the king. In truth, this put John in a less promising position than he might have originally anticipated. Most dukes in North Germanic territories were effectively sovereigns of their own states (however small or large) – not so for John. He was not permitted to mint any coinage or have a standing army. He can be called the first 'partitioned-off' duke – a term used in Schleswig-Holstein for a duke whose territory is not really under their control and is not formally recognised by the Estates of the Realm. This was the status of the joint duchies (and their dukes) from John onwards.

When his brother Frederick II died in 1588, his nephew Christian IV was too young to rule, and a regency council was formed. Rule of the joint duchies lay with his widowed sister-in-law, Queen Sophie, who was regent for her son. It is possible that John had ambitions of marrying Sophie, which would have been seen as a political play to get closer to the throne and have more control of Schleswig-Holstein; however, it did not happen.

John could be described as a prolific procreator. With two wives, he produced twenty-three children, although not all survived to adulthood. Lovers of cheap chocolate will be delighted to know that John's eldest surviving son, Christian, was the Duke of Aero (or Ærø)!

Curiously, even though he was the eldest, John had hopes of getting his son Christian a senior position in the Catholic Church – despite not being a Catholic! The hope was that he would land the prominent role

EDWARD HILARY DAVIS

of Bishop of Strasbourg. He was enrolled by the cathedral chapter as canon, and he was successfully elected to be bishop. The chapter continued to give him the stipend of an unmarried priest. Christian knew that, if he married, he would likely lose both his position and his stipend as well as any other opportunities within the church. When it became clear that Christian intended not to marry, his father passed him over as main heir and instead gave him Ærø. Thus, Christian became yet another partitioned-off duke with the territorial designation of Duke of Schleswig-Holstein-Sonderburg-Ærø. Far from being chocolate, Ærø is a Danish island in the Baltic Sea. He did not have sovereignty over the island, but owing to the merging of farms into various manors, it was still quite a prosperous place for Christian.

He was content to live amongst the farms and manors there. Instead of making a great dynastic marriage, as might have been expected of him, he formed a relationship with his housekeeper, Katharina. The two of them produced a daughter in 1600, Sophie Griebel. She was gifted land and given various tax exemptions. However, upon Christian's eventual death in 1633, the majority of his estates were divided up amongst his brothers and nephew, Augustus Philip, the senior. More on him shortly.

The chief and eventual heir of Duke John was his younger son, Alexander. However, from John's other sons, more cadet branches of Schleswig-Holstein-Sonderburg formed (Plön, Norburg and Glücksburg). If we were to follow all of these it would only serve to confuse any reader. That said, it should be mentioned that one of the younger sons, Philip (1584-1663), was given a castle and land in Glücksburg and was subsequently dubbed the Duke of Schleswig-Holstein-Sonderburg-Glücksburg – what a mouthful! He formed a cadet branch of the same name which lasted for four further generations until the last Duke of Schleswig-Holstein-Sonderburg-Glücksburg died in 1779. This is known as the Glücksburg elder line because, shortly afterwards, in 1825, the title was revived for a distant cousin (another descendant of Duke John), Prince Frederick William – whom we shall meet later. The present House of Schleswig-Holstein-Sonderburg-Glücksburg should therefore technically be called the 'junior' or 'newer' line. However, as this line boasts crowned heads of at least four kingdoms, it is doubtful that would catch on.

Duke John died in 1622, leaving Sonderburg castle and its estate to his younger son, Alexander. As the senior heir, Alexander continued the House of Schleswig-Holstein-Sonderburg.

Alexander, Duke of Schleswig-Holstein-Sonderburg

(9xgreat-grandfather)

Born: *20 January 1573 at Sonderburg*

Died: *13 May 1627 at Sonderburg*

Spouse: *Countess Dorothea of Schwarzburg-Sondershausen*

Concurrent English monarchs: *Elizabeth, James I and Charles I*

ALEXANDER WAS BORN at Sonderburg Castle in 1573. He married Dorothea, daughter of Count John Gunter von Schwarzburg-Sonderhausen, on 26 November 1604. Dorothea's mother was also an Oldenburg, so the nuptials took place in the old family domain of Oldenburg. Though Alexander and Dorothea spent much of their time at his father's castle at Sonderburg, they were able to acquire from Dorothea's Oldenburg relatives their own 'home' – the knightly estate of Beck (or Haus Beck), a manor in the Eulenburg district of the town of Löhne in Westphalia (modern day North-Rhine Westphalia). They

Figure 12: Woodcut of Alexander, Duke of Schleswig-Holstein-Sonderburg. Sonderburg Castle, Denmark.

became the owners around 1605, and established their own family there. It is certainly where their eleven children spent much of their childhoods.

On Whitsun morning, 13 May 1627, Alexander died at Sonderburg Castle. He left many serious debts. Knowing that this would likely be the case, he had stipulated in his will that his wife should inherit the entire estate – as opposed to it being broken up amongst his various heirs, as was the old Danish/Germanic custom. This was to enable her to have the best chance of paying off the debts he had accrued in his lifetime – although she was not able to pay all the debts, some of which were eventually passed to their eldest son and heir, John/Hans Christian.

While John Christian inherited debts from his father, he received a more favourable inheritance from another source. John Christian's uncle, Christian, Duke of Ærø, died six years after Duke John. As Christian had no sons, a portion of the Ærø inheritance therefore went to John Christian. Today the island of Ærø is still part of Denmark and is endeavouring to become entirely self-sufficient with regards to energy. It has launched many new initiatives in renewable energy, including a solar plant, wind turbines and a green energy electric car ferry. Ærø even has the world's largest solar collection system for heating. There is perhaps a strange link here between King Charles and his ancestral homelands.

Once again, with more sons came more cadet branches of the Schleswig-Holstein, now Schleswig-Holstein-Sonderburg line. Alexander and Dorothea's second son founded a short-lived Catholic line of the family by morganatic marriage. This died out in the following generation. Their third son, Ernst Gunter, founded the Augustenborg line of the family, which was so named after the palace and home he built for himself at Stavnsbøl Birk. He bought the land from his cousin King Frederick III of Denmark in 1651 and converted a manor farm into a great house. He then named the palatial house after his wife, another distant cousin, Princess Augusta of Schleswig-Holstein-Sonderburg-Glücksburg (of the elder line). Thus, Ernst was known as Duke of Schleswig-Holstein-Sonderburg-Augustenburg.

Eight years after Alexander's death, his youngest daughter, Sofie

Katrine, was engaged to be married to a distant cousin Count Anton Gunter – the last Count of Oldenburg. At the wedding in 1635, Sofie Katrine's mother and eldest brother presented the Beck estate as a dowry. Anton and Sofie's marriage was childless, and Anton died in 1667. The Oldenburg-Delmenhorst estates and titles passed to his closest male relative – King Frederick III.

Duke Alexander and Dorothea's fifth son, August, was particularly keen to acquire his old childhood home of Haus Beck for himself. He purchased it off his sister around 1645 and founded the new cadet branch of Schleswig-Holstein-Sonderburg-Beck.

Figure 13: A 1791 family portrait of Princess Katharina (of Holstein-Beck) seated next to a bust of her father, Peter August, Duke of Schleswig-Holstein-Sonderburg-Beck (carved by Alexander Trippel). To her right: her son Prince Ivan Baryatinsky, her daughter Anna with the latter's husband Count Nikolai Alexandrovich Tolstoy. Charlotte holds a miniature of her late husband, Prince Ivan Sergeevich Baryatinsky. By Angelica Kauffman RA (1741-1807). Pushkin Museum of Fine Arts.

The House of Schleswig-Holstein-Sonderburg-Beck

I N England, we are familiar with the traditional plight of younger sons in aristocratic, gentry or wealthy families. Typically, they have to get a job. This is because, unlike in the continental tradition, most if not all of the wealth and estates in a family are passed solely to the eldest son. Until the mid-nineteenth century, however, there were very few jobs that were appropriate for a gentleman. Effectively the options were limited to the army, the church or sometimes politics – with enough financial backing. Lesser or more eccentric families might send a third or fourth son into the navy. Even lesser families might send a younger son into law or academia – God forbid! Younger sons faced a cold reality back then, and many still do to this day. They must carve out their own place in the world.

Some younger sons have had such successful careers that they end up outshining their relatives and earlier ancestors. For example, Arthur Wellesley, the Duke of Wellington, was the fourth son of the 1st Earl of Mornington. Naturally, as a field marshal and a duke with a line of important military victories behind him, he rose far above his kin – even becoming prime minister and a prince (of Waterloo) in the Netherlands and Belgium.

Another Prime Minister, Sir Winston Spencer-Churchill, though he did not accept a grand title, surpassed his paternal family and arguably his great ancestor John Churchill, 1st Duke of Marlborough, in his achievements and grandeur. Sir Winston was himself the eldest son of the third son of the 7th Duke of Marlborough. On different occasions, he was actually offered the titles of Duke of Dover and Duke of London – neither of which he accepted.

What, however, are the options for minor royalty, the far offshoots of a royal dynasty? Well, if younger sons of nobility have to get a job, younger sons of royalty (and their sons after them) have to do the same, though naturally the jobs fit for (even minor) royalty are at a higher level than those for (mere) gentlemen. A younger royal son might fast track to Bishop or Cardinal. In a military career, he could buy a commission and be a general within a matter of years. Such was the case for many of Duke Alexander's offspring and descendants. Sons of his formed their own new cadet branches of Schleswig-Holstein-Sonderburg – branches of branches of what had become the Danish royal family.

Connected by the blood royal to the Danish kings and in possession of sizable estates and castles, the family were not without influence, though their influence dwindled as the generations drifted further apart. Some of the family found careers and homes in other duchies, provinces and kingdoms – sometimes working for other distant cousins. Naturally, some also entered a life of religion. For most of the men we shall concern ourselves with, the army was the career of choice.

Of course, as minor royalty, there was always the possibility that enough uncles and cousins would die without heirs and that one's chances of a great inheritance or even succession would increase dramatically. Such a happenstance had occurred before in the Oldenburg family. Such a happenstance could recur.

Figure 14: August Philipp, Duke of Schleswig-Holstein-Sonderburg-Beck.
Unknown artist. English school.

August Philipp, Duke of Schleswig-Holstein-Sonderburg-Beck

(8xgreat-grandfather)

Born: *11 November 1612 at Sonderburg, Duchy of Schleswig*

Died: *6 May 1675 at Haus Beck, Westphalia*

Spouses: *1ˢᵗ Countess Clara of Oldenburg*

2ⁿᵈ (Abbess) Countess Sidonie of Oldenburg

3ʳᵈ Marie Sibylle of Nassau-Saarbrücken

Concurrent English monarchs: *James I, Charles I, Lord Protectorate and Charles II*

August Philipp was born on 11 November 1612 at Sonderburg. Although a great-grandson of a king (Christian III), he was a fifth son of a third son of a second son. He barely counted as minor Danish royalty. It was clear that he would need to make his own way in the world. When he was about twenty-one, he left the Danish provinces for Germany. He began to make his way by firstly acquiring his own estate to base himself. He chose his childhood home of Haus Beck, which he purchased from his sister. Following this, he was known as the Duke of Schleswig-Holstein-Sonderburg-Beck (or Sonderburg-Beck or just Beck for short). The new Duke of Beck both redesigned and restructured the house on the same site and made it into more or less the building we see today. In recent times, it has been a training and exhibition centre with outbuildings leased to furniture companies. Much of the medieval remains of the former residence are no longer visible.

August Philipp made a life for himself in the army, becoming an officer in his early twenties, around the time he purchased Beck. Having set himself up with a title, a big house, and a military career, he naturally began to look for a wife to start his own new dynasty, which would of course derive its name from his new residence, Beck. August Philipp married three times. His first marriage may well have been a play at dynastic politics. As seemed to be tradition in the family, in 1645, he married a distant cousin, Clara of Oldenburg, who was daughter of the reigning Count of Delmenhorst – Count Anton II of Oldenburg-Delmenhorst. However, this marriage was childless, and Clara died two years after the wedding.

The Duke of Beck searched for another wife. He did not look far though. He took his shot at Sidonie/Sidonia of Oldenburg (1611-1650) – his deceased wife's sister. Bizarrely, she was actually brought out of a convent to marry August. Formerly, she had been the Abbess of Herford Abbey in Westphalia. The couple were married in June 1649. They had a daughter together the following year, but Sidonie died shortly after the birth.

On his third attempt, in April 1651, August Philipp took as his bride Marie Sibylle, daughter of Count Wilhelm Ludwig of Nassau-Saarbrücken. The third time seems to have been a charm, for it produced eleven children between 1652 and 1672, most of whom lived into adulthood and produced children of their own. The House of Beck was on the rise.

German military life (or military life of some kind) became a theme in following male generations of the Beck branch. August Philipp's eldest son and heir, Augustus (1652-1689), became a major general in the Brandenburg army. The family seat of Beck was within the Principality of Minden, which itself had been under the Electorate of Brandenburg since 1648, so this was effectively the local native army. Being of high aristocratic birth was one of the principal qualifications for becoming a senior officer in most German armies of the day. Although he became a major general, Augustus succumbed to a common soldier's disease, dysentery, and died in Bonn in 1689.

Augustus's own son and heir, Frederick Wilhelm (1682-1719), also took up a military career but with a different army. He converted to Roman Catholicism and joined the army of the Holy Roman Empire. He served in the War of the Quadruple Alliance (1718-1720). The war involved the Spanish attempting to recapture lost territories in Italy. These attempts were held off by a (quadruple) alliance of the British, French, Austrians and the Dutch. Meanwhile in Scotland, the Spanish were backing the Jacobite Rising of 1719, trying (and failing) to restore the Catholic Old Pretender James Francis Edward Stuart to the throne.

For his part, Frederick Wilhelm, Duke of Beck, fought in the Holy Roman Empire's Army at the Battle of Francavilla in Sicily (20 June 1719) against the Spanish – who were victorious. Frederick Wilhelm, along with over three thousand of his comrades, died of his wounds within days of the battle. He was thirty-seven. As he had no legitimate male heirs, his estate and title eventually passed to his paternal uncle, Frederick Louis (1653-1728) – the second son of Duke August of Beck and another army officer. More on him shortly.

August Philipp, the Duke of Beck, spent the remaining decades of his life back at his childhood home of Beck of which he was so fond. He died there in 1675 at the age of sixty-two. He must have hoped that his new 'humble' dynasty, an offshoot of an offshoot of a royal dynasty would grow in stature. He could not have known how high that stature would come to be in the coming centuries.

August Philipp was the seventh great-grandfather of Prince Philip, Duke of Edinburgh – who bore part of his name. In 2021, a direct descendant and namesake of August Philipp was born; Princess Eugenie of York's first son was christened August Philip Hawke Brooksbank at the Royal Chapel of All Saints, Windsor Park. A ten-times great-grandson.

Figure 15: Miniature portrait of Frederick Louis, Duke of Schleswig-Holstein-Sonderburg-Beck (1653–1728). Painter unknown. Pushkin Museum of Fine Arts.

Frederick Louis, Duke of Schleswig-Holstein-Sonderburg-Beck

(7xgreat-grandfather)

Born: *6 April 1653 at Haus Beck, Westphalia*
Died: *7 March 1728 at Königsberg, Prussia*
Spouse: *Louise Charlotte of Schleswig-Holstein-Sonderburg-Augustenburg*
Concurrent British monarchs: *Lord Protectorate, Charles II, James II, Mary II,*
William III, Anne, George I and George II

FREDERICK LOUIS (OR Friedrich Ludwig) was the second son of his father, August, Duke of Beck, and Marie Sibylle of Nassau-Saarbrücken. Born at Beck in 1653, as it happened, he was actually only the titular duke, since he did not possess the Beck estate – although eventually the estate and title were actually purchased by his eldest son, another Frederick Wilhelm (1687-1749). Frederick Louis continued the family military tradition, gaining quite an impressive career. He was commissioned as a colonel in the Brandenburg-Prussian army in 1676. By 1697, he had been appointed a full general of both infantry and cavalry in the Duchy of Prussia. A year later, he was made Governor of Minden (a town in Westphalia). He seems to have enjoyed serving under the Prussians. In 1694, his kinsman Christian V of Denmark made him a knight of the Order of the Elephant and offered to make him a general in the Danish Army and even Governor of Norway. Frederick Louis refused the offers.

At Königsberg in 1701, Frederick Louis was a part of the ceremony in which the Elector of Brandenburg was crowned the first King of

Prussia. The new King Frederick I of Prussia was a grateful master, and more awards and governorships came Frederick Louis's way.

Among the many members of his family who built careers in the military, Frederick Louis has the distinction of serving in a British army, or at least serving in an army which was overall commanded by a British general – and not just any general, John Churchill, Duke of Marlborough. (Frederick Louis maintained that distinction until centuries later when his direct male-line descendent, Prince Philip of Greece, would also serve under British command in World War Two.)

Under the command of General John Churchill, Frederick took part in the War of the Spanish Succession between Louis XIV of France and the Habsburg Empire, a titanic struggle seemingly for control of Europe. Again, such a topic is better explained in a great many books and volumes, not least of which are Winston S Churchill's four volumes, *Marlborough: His Life and Times.* However, for the uninitiated or those short of time, we will summarise.

The War of the Spanish Succession is so named because there was indeed a succession crisis. The Habsburg King Charles II of Spain (1661-1700) was childless and without an obvious heir. He suffered from bouts of ill health, possibly owing to the severe levels of inbreeding in the Habsburg family at this time. Certainly, he had a very pronounced 'Habsburg jaw', which may have led to him not chewing food properly, swallowing it nearly whole and suffering from stomach issues as a result. Although Spain was weaker than it had been in the previous centuries, it was still a global power with an empire which included much of South and North America, the Philippines, large parts of Italy, and the Spanish Netherlands as well as its vast territory on the Iberian Peninsula.

The two most prominent heirs of Charles II were Philip of Anjou (1683-1746), the grandson of Louis XIV of France, and Archduke Charles of Austria. Shortly before his death, in 1700, Charles proclaimed his great-nephew, Philip of Anjou (a Bourbon), as his heir – as opposed to any Habsburg. This threatened to place the great Spanish

Empire under the influence of France and specifically Louis as well as swing the balance of power in Europe. Charles's proclamation quickly led to declarations of war. France and Spain would defend the succession against the Grand Alliance of nations who were uncomfortable with France's new potential to become a superpower. These included Britain, Austria, the Holy Roman Empire, the Dutch Republic, Prussia, Savoy and Portugal – though most of the allies were heavily subsidised by the British.

The wider war was fought in nearly all parts of the globe where the British, French, and Spanish were. It has sometimes been seen as the first truly world war. The war touched Europe, North America, South America, India, the East Indies and West Africa. In a way, it eventually became a struggle for international dominance. The French held a significant advantage economically and militarily in the initial stages of the war, but as time drew on, and thanks to John Churchill at the Battle of Blenheim (1704) and Ramillies (1706), France lost control of the Spanish Netherlands and was soon on the defensive.

As a senior leader in the Prussian forces around the start of the war, General Frederick Louis (of Beck) was by now a knight of the Order of the Black Eagle, a statthalter in the Kingdom of Prussia and subsequently Governor of Königsberg, the capital of East Prussia. He was sent to the Netherlands to help lead Grand Alliance troops against the French. He saw action at the Battle of Oudenaarde on 11 July 1708. He was part of the allied force of around eighty thousand men led by John Churchill, Duke of Marlborough, and Prince Eugene of Savoy, and they faced a French force of perhaps ninety thousand led by Louis Duke of Burgundy – another of Louis XIV's grandsons – and the Duke of Vendôme.

In the initial stages of the engagement, much of the French reserve forces were, for an unknown reason, not ordered up to battle. Both sides took positions on opposite sides of the river (Diepenbeck and the Scheldt). The infantry of both sides advanced and were locked in battle. Marlborough executed a flanking manoeuvre which relied on the expertise of the allied cavalry and advance guard under Lord Cadogan. This ensured a rout of the French infantry. Witnessing mounting numbers of casualties, Vendôme and Burgundy had to withdraw the French from the field; French losses may have been around double those of the allies. Frederick Louis may well have been in the thick of the allied cavalry action during the course of the day.

Huge tactical errors were made by the French during the battle. They did not engage around half their force – perhaps a cowardly error by Burgundy or more likely a miscalculation. Such a force could have easily destroyed the allies' right wing. Marlborough and Prince Eugene's reputations were greatly enhanced by this victory, and the Grand Alliance were able to march on to lay siege to Lille – which Frederick Louis was also present for. The French garrison capitulated on 10 December 1708. The siege had lasted just short of four months.

Oudenaarde was not the only Marlborough battle Duke Frederick Louis of Beck in which saw action. The following year, in 1709, he was present at the Battle of Malplaquet. The war was taking its toll, and there had been multiple mutinies and a harsh winter so that by mid-1709 France was effectively bankrupt. Louis began seeking terms with the allies and instructed his military commanders to avoid battle at all costs. Sensing that France was near collapse, Marlborough was keen to advance through her defences. In June, he and the allies laid siege to Tournai, which capitulated in September. Frederick Louis of Beck was again present for this siege. The Grand Alliance then advanced on Mons. At this point Louis XIV ordered his marshal, the Duke de Villars, to hold Mons at all costs, impressing on him that the safety of France was at stake. De Villars marched out and took position in the gap of Malplaquet to the south-west of Mons.

As with many battles of the time, it commenced with an artillery bombardment. When that had ceased, the Grand Alliance assaulted the French lines in the Sars woodland with a large Brandenburg-Prussian contingent of the army led by Counts Schulenberg, Lottum and

Finckenstein. Duke Frederick Louis of Beck was likely part of this valiant contingent. Heavy and close hand fighting ensued, and both sides took heavy losses. When the Dutch contingent engaged on the French right flank, they were forced back, rescued or covered by the Prussian cavalry. Once again, a flanking move was used against the French through the Sars wood with a British and Dutch contingent – forcing Villars to remove battalions from his centre to bolster the flank – a grave error. As the French left flank faltered and with the allies concentrating a strong drive forward in the centre, the French were forced to withdraw. The allied armies were too exhausted to follow. Whilst the allies were victorious on the field and eventually took Mons in October 1709, they sustained far greater losses than the French by most accounts. The figures are debatable, but at worst the allied losses may have been double. To this day it is debated whether Malplaquet was an allied success or a French strategic victory – as she kept her army largely intact and Louis XIV was able to negotiate a peace from a more positive position later.

Having fought in such famous and bloody battles in Europe, Frederick Louis certainly cemented his reputation within his wider house and family as a fighting Schleswig-Holstein. A man of formidable stature, he was made a field marshal by 1713. During his governorship in Prussia, he successfully guaranteed eventual Prussian neutrality from the Great Northern War between the Russian Empire and Sweden (1700-1721). Frederick Louis lived to the grand age of seventy-four. He died on 7 March 1728 at Königsberg and was buried with honours at the cathedral there.

On the home front, whilst a young man and still only a colonel, he took as his wife a (first) cousin in 1685, once again repeating a sort of family tradition of intermarriage between different parts of the House of Oldenburg. (It actually continues into the twentieth century.) His bride was Louise Charlotte, daughter of Ernst Gunter, Duke of Schleswig-Holstein-Sonderburg-Augustenburg, his uncle, who had founded his own separate cadet branch from the Becks at his palace at Augustenborg – his family name derived from the family home and thus both named after his wife, Augusta (another cousin)!

Frederick Louis and his bride, Louise, had eleven children together between 1685 and 1700 – five sons and six daughters. Owing to his growing influence amongst the Prussians and the new reigning House of Hohenzollern there, it is unsurprising that their eldest daughter married George, Margrave of Brandenburg-Bayreuth and a member of the extended Prussian royal family. Frederick's eldest son was Frederick Wilhelm II, Duke of Schleswig-Holstein-Sonderburg-Beck.

Born in Potsdam in 1687 and brought up in Königsberg, Frederick Wilhelm, like his father, followed a career in the Prussian army after his education. As a young man, he served in his father's own regiment as a captain and by 1704 had been promoted to lieutenant colonel. At the age of twenty-six, he was made full colonel and served in the Prussian Holstein regiment. During the Great Northern War, Frederick Wilhelm distinguished himself at the siege of Stralsund (1711-1715) in Swedish Pomerania – in present day Germany (Mecklenburg-Western-Pomerania). An alliance of Russians, Danes and Prussians laid a long siege to the town, eventually forcing it to surrender, although King Charles XII of Sweden escaped.

In recognition of Frederick Wilhelm's valiant service in the war and siege, his master and namesake, King Frederick Wilhelm I of Prussia, granted him a castle and estate called Friedrichshof near Ludwigswalde in East Prussia in 1717. A second estate with the same name was also gifted to him in Kasebalk near Königsberg. Sensibly, Frederick Wilhelm decided to rename the castle there Schloss Holstein. After becoming a major general in 1721, Frederick Wilhelm was given command of his father's old regiment (the Eleventh Infantry).

By 1728, Frederick Wilhelm's father was dead, and he became the titular Duke of Holstein-Beck, but the title and estate were once again joined in 1732 when he purchased the Beck estate from his cousin's (Frederick Wilhelm I's) widow, having raised the money for the purchase from the sale of one of his Prussian estates. The following year he was promoted to lieutenant general, and he took part in the Polish Wars of Succession from 1734 to 1735. However, it was here that his military career almost came a cropper.

His new master in the Prussian army was King Frederick II of Prussia, known today as Frederick the Great. In the First Silesian War, a militarised expansionist Prussia sought to wrestle the territory of Silesia away from the Habsburg Austrian Empire. The first battle of this war was the Battle of Mollwitz (1741). It was also Frederick the Great's first battle and first major test on the world stage. Many serious military blunders were made by both Frederick's Prussian forces and by the Austrian army. It was a Prussian victory; however, at one point, King Frederick had had to flee the field in retreat. It very nearly could have been a defeat for Prussia. One of the other great blunders of the day was that Frederick Wilhelm's regiment, which was held in reserve, arrived too late to the battle and were unable to make any meaningful contribution. Unaware of the perilous situation the Prussian Army was in, Frederick Wilhelm actually marched his men right past many Austrian units. Though this inflamed the frustrated and humbled King Frederick the Great, he was reportedly fond of the Duke of Holstein-Beck and referred to him as 'the good old Holsteiner'. Oddly, his mistakes at Mollwitz were rewarded with a promotion to field marshal that same year, and Frederick Wilhelm, like his father, was awarded the Order of the Black Eagle.

In 1721, Frederick Wilhelm II married for a second time (his first wife having died childless). He took as his wife Ursula Anna (1700-1761), daughter of Christopher, Burgrave and Count of Dohna-Schlodien, a fellow Prussian general who had also served at Stralsund. Frederick Wilhelm and Ursula had just two children, a daughter and a son, imaginatively named Frederick Wilhelm III.

Frederick Wilhelm II sold the Beck estate out of the immediate family in 1744-1745 to the Baroness von Ledebur-Königsbrück, but he retained the name Beck within his title. Two years later, he was appointed to the prestigious post of Governor of Berlin in the heart of Prussia, but owing to illness he never fully took up the post. He died in 1749 in Königsberg at age sixty-two.

The only son and heir, Frederick Wilhelm III, was born in 1723. Following his father and grandfather, he entered military service in the Prussian army. He commissioned and gained the rank of colonel, commanding the Prussian Forty-sixth Fusilier Regiment, known as 'the Old Württemberg'. Again, like his forefathers, he was highly decorated, although this time it was with the Order of the Red Eagle – not the black which is more senior. He took part in the European campaigns of the Seven Years War, in particular the Battle of Prague (6 May 1757). This conflict was really part of the Third Silesian War, in which Frederick the Great had again to assert his control over the territory. A force of sixty-four thousand Prussians pitted themselves against a slightly lesser force of Austrians outside Prague. It was a Prussian victory, but owing to his heavy losses, Fredrick the Great decided not to attack the city. Frederick Wilhelm III, however, lay among the dead. He was thirty-three and unmarried.

The chief title of Duke of Schleswig-Holstein-Sonderburg-Beck then passed to Frederick Wilhelm III's uncle, Charles Louis, who was a younger son of Frederick Louis. Charles Louis was yet another officer in the Prussian army. Unlike the former Dukes of Schleswig-Holstein-Sonderburg-Beck, however, he was a convert to Roman Catholicism. When his nephew died in 1757, he became the senior figure of the Beck cadet branch. By that time, he was a lieutenant general in the Prussian army, but he eventually left Prussian service to instead give his services to the Tsardom of Russia. This may initially sound odd, but it sounds less odd when we are reminded that his kinsman and distant cousin Peter, Duke of Schleswig-Holstein-Gottorp, was named as heir to the Russian throne in 1742 by his aunt Empress Elizabeth. In 1762, Peter succeeded her as Peter III of Russia. Like the Becks, he was a member of a cadet branch of the House of Oldenburg.

With his sixth cousin soon to inherit the throne of Russia, Duke Charles Louis of Beck was made a governor in Russian-held Reval (modern day Tallinn in Estonia). Peter III also appointed Charles a field marshal in the Russian army in 1763. Charles declined on account of his age (seventy-three) and having not really served in the Russian army. However, it is likely that this was more of an honorary appointment because they were kin. Charles Louis of Beck returned to Königsberg and died childless there in 1774 at the age of eighty-four.

The title of Beck and the headship of the cadet branch passed to the next surviving son of Frederick Louis. This was Charles's younger brother, Peter August, Duke of Schleswig-Holstein-Sonderburg-Beck.

Figure 16: Peter August, Duke of Schleswig–Holstein–Sonderburg–Beck. Painter unknown.

Peter August, Duke of Schleswig-Holstein-Sonderburg-Beck

(6xgreat-grandfather)

Born: *7 December 1697 at Königsberg, Prussia (now Kaliningrad, Russia)*

Died: *22 March 1775 at Reval/Tallinn, Estonia*

Spouses: 1st: *Princess Sophie of Hesse-Philippsthal*

2nd: *Countess Natalia Nikolaievna Golovina*

Concurrent British monarchs: *William III, Anne, George I, George II and George III*

P ETER AUGUST WAS the fifth son of Louis Frederick and Louise and was born in Königsberg in 1697, where so many of his family had been based for many years. Following family tradition and being a younger son, he too followed a military career. Rather than copy his father and brother, he did not immediately enter the Prussian ranks but instead gained a commission in the army of the Landgrave of Hesse-Kassel, where he served as a colonel. This move was almost certainly related to the fact that in 1723, he took as his first wife, Princess Sophie of Hesse-Philippsthal, the niece of the Landgrave of Hesse-Kassel, William VII. His commander in chief was therefore his uncle-in-law, but Peter August did not stay in Germany. He saw potential in another kingdom to the east.

Perhaps due to lobbying by Peter's mother, Louise, around 1734, he was able to enter the service of the Empress of Russia, Anna Ivanova; he was able to keep his rank of colonel and was given a regiment to command. He served under the prominent Russian statesman and general, Count Burkhard Christoph von Münnich, a man coincidently from Oldenburg who had served under the Duke of Marlborough. Having been promoted to major general, Peter August took part in the Russo-Turkish War (1735-1739). The war stemmed mostly from Russia's struggle for access to the Black Sea. The hot points of this conflict were the Balkans and the Crimea – both of which are familiar to us today. Russia's gain in the war was the town of Azak (now Azov), situated near to the Black Sea on the Sea of Azov. Russia did not, however, gain the Crimean Peninsula.

After the death of Empress Anna and her short-lived son, Tsar Ivan VI, the Empress Elizabeth succeeded as ruler of Russia from 1741. While serving in the Russo-Swedish War (1741-1743), Peter August was promoted to lieutenant general in 1742. This war, oddly known as the War of the Hats, was instigated by a Swedish political party, called the Hats, that had ambitions of regaining territories lost earlier in the Great Northern War (another war with Russia). The war was a disaster for Sweden, and she lost yet more territory to Russia.

Empress Elizabeth's older sister was married to one of Peter's distant cousins, Frederick Charles, Duke of Schleswig-Holstein-Gottorp. Perhaps not so coincidentally, Peter August was appointed Governor of Tallinn in Estonia from 1743 to 1753, a post also held at one time by his older brother, Charles Louis. Elizabeth also appointed Peter August general in chief, and he led the Russian College of War from 1755 to 1758.

Peter August's namesake and sixth cousin, Peter of Schleswig-Holstein-Gottorp, succeeded to the Russian throne as Tsar Peter III in January 1762. (He was overthrown and then died in July that same year.) During that short reign, Peter August was appointed to the Imperial Council of the Russian Empire and was made a field marshal. Unlike his elder brother, he seems to have had no problem accepting this dignity. Peter August also got to hold the impressive position of General Governor of St Petersburg. In his short time as governor, the use of livestock in the city streets was banned, fees were introduced for taxis, new wells were constructed for the local population, and St Nicholas Naval Cathedral was completed and consecrated. Many a Russian naval memorial can be found there, including one to the crew of the Kursk (K-141).

Tsar Peter III was ousted in a coup by his wife later that same summer; her name was Catherine the Great. That said, it is important to remember that their issue would continue to rule Russia for the next few centuries. This meant that branches of the House of Schleswig-Holstein sat on the thrones of both Denmark and Russia, which put the House of Beck once again in a favourable position with potential patrons to the east and to the west. Catherine the Great actually thought highly of Peter August and left him to continue as Governor of Reval/Tallinn.

The title of Duke of Beck was passed to Peter August on the death of his elder brother in 1774; however, this was only titular as the Beck estate had been sold about thirty years earlier. He did not, however, have time to enjoy this title as he died a year later at the age of seventy-eight in his governorship of Reval/Tallinn in Estonia. Having lived so long, he tragically outlived his son and heir, Charles Anton. By the time of Peter August's death, he had been showered with honours from Russia and elsewhere, including the Russian Orders of St Andrew, St Anna and Alexander Nevsky as well as the Prussian Order of the Black Eagle.

From his marriage with Princess Sophie, Peter August had a daughter and two sons the first of whom died an infant. The second-born son was named Charles Anton. Sophie died in 1728 when she was only thirty-three. Years later, in 1742, Peter took as his second wife Natalia, daughter and heiress of Count Nikolai Golovin and Sophia Pushkina. Natalia came with a substantial inheritance from her father. Together, she and Peter August had two sons and a daughter, Katharina. Peter August died in Tallinn in 1775 and is buried in the Church of St Nicholas there. The titular designation of Duke of Holstein-Beck (aka Schleswig-Holstein-Sonderburg-Beck) passed to his grandson, Frederick Charles.

By now, the family was well established as a feature of St Petersburg and Russian aristocratic high society. The Holstein-Becks, like characters in a Tolstoy novel, knew everyone. Peter's daughter, Katharina, was considered one of the finest beauties of the Russian court and a highly desirable bride. In 1767, she married Prince Ivan Sergeevich Bariatinsky (1738-1811), a diplomat and general in the service of Catherine the Great. The couple seems to have had several affairs, however. In fact, they attended the coronation of Louis XVI of France (as special envoys) while Katharina was pregnant with another man's child! Nonetheless, she is credited as improving the fashion at the Russian court on her return as she brought with her many new Parisian dresses. To add yet more glamour to this Russian offshoot of the family, Katharina's daughter, Princess Anna Ivanova Baryatinska, married Count Nikolai Alexandrovich Tolstoy – an important figure on the Russian side of the Napoleonic Wars and a relation of the famous author of *War and Peace*. There is a story that he was present at the meeting of Tsar Alexander I and Napoleon at the Congress of Erfurt. As is normal at diplomatic meetings of heads of state, gifts were exchanged, in particular medals. In this case, the French Legion of Honour and the Russian Order of St Andrew were exchanged. Presumably both of these were placed on the table before the delegation. Tolstoy is rumoured to have untactfully exclaimed that the Legion of Honour was not worthy to be next to the (far older) Order of St Andrew. Napoleon, overhearing this, replied that Tolstoy himself was not worthy to receive the Order of St Andrew. In truth, Tolstoy never did, despite receiving many other Russian orders and France's Legion of Honour while they were allies. Another Russian version of this story holds that Tolstoy was offered the Order of St Andrew but would not accept because its worthiness had been sullied by the fact that it had at one time been awarded to Napoleon!

A slight digression here: The Napoleon/Nikolai Tolstoy story brings to mind the BBC adaptation of Leo Tolstoy's *War and Peace* of 2016 – yes, the Lily James one. There was much commotion in the press after the first episode aired seemingly showing a Russian courtier oddly wearing the French Legion of Honour. Major General Alastair Bruce took to Twitter to point out this mistake. However, in truth, several members of the tsar's court had been awarded such an honour before Napoleon's invasion of Russia. Unfortunately, the dressers on the set put it on the character of Vicomte de Mortemart, a French exile who loathed Napoleon. It was a stifling blunder but an easy one to miss. The historical advisor, Professor Dominic Lieven, graciously expressed regret for the mistake. Alastair Bruce is the historical advisor of Downton Abbey which, whilst very lovely, is not without its share of blunders! (Remember the water bottle?) However, having been on the set myself, it is easy to see how things might slip through the net. Regardless, I am certain that Leo Tolstoy would be delighted that another gaff about the Legion of Honour was made more than two centuries after his kinsman Nikolai made an even worse one!

Katharina Baryatinskaya (née Holstein-Beck) and her family were painted by Angelica Kauffman, a noted artist and one of only two female founding members of the Royal Academy of Art in London in 1768 (the other being Mary Moser). It is likely the Baryatinsky-Tolstoy family were painted by Kauffman on one of her tours of Europe, which at one time included St Petersburg.

*Figure 17: Miniature portrait of Charles/Karl Anton
August, Prince of Schleswig-Holstein-Sonderburg-Beck
(1727-1759). Painter unknown. Pushkin Museum of
Fine Arts.*

Prince Charles Anton August of Schleswig-Holstein-Sonderburg-Beck

(5xgreat-grandfather)

Born: *10 August 1727 at Marburg, Hesse*
Died: *12 September 1759 at Stettin, Prussia (now Poland)*
Spouse: *Countess Friederike Charlotte Antoinette of Dohna-Schlobitten-Leistenau*
Concurrent British monarch: *George II*

C HARLES (KARL) ANTON was born at Marburg in 1727. As we have seen, he did not live long enough to succeed to the Holstein-Beck title of duke and was outlived by his father. As was becoming the family custom by now, Charles entered military service. By the time he was commissioned as a major, Russia was taking part in the Third Silesian War. As Charles Anton's uncle had fought in the First Silesian War for the Prussians, he did likewise in the third. By now of course, sections of the family were becoming both Russian and Prussian, so there may well have been some difficult decisions made. Russia allied with the chief enemy of Prussia in the conflict, Austria. Once again, the war turned out in Prussia's favour. However, while they may have won the war, they did not win all the battles.

One such battle was the Battle of Kunersdorf (12 August 1759) near Frankfurt an der Oder, at which Charles Anton was present. Around fifty thousand Prussians under Frederick the Great faced off against a combined force of about sixty thousand Russians and Austrians under Count Peter Saltykov. By the time of the battle, Frederick was already one of the great and skilled commanders of his day. However, the Russians and Austrians had arrived at the battlefield two weeks earlier and had already selected the most favourable positions in which to entrench themselves. The terrain was difficult and complex, but they had time to strengthen and construct causeways between ponds and through marshland to make manoeuvring easier. The Russians and Austrians also anticipated Frederick's usual tactic of oblique order (a tactic by which an army attempts to overwhelm their enemy's flank by deceptive strength in numbers in a certain part of the line). Thanks to the causeways, they were able to present Frederick with a united front.

The fighting was fierce at Kunersdorf, and losses on both sides were significant. However, the prior preparations and weight of numbers on the Russian/Austrian side was enough to hold off the Prussians, who for the first time retreated in mass disarray. Frederick was only able to keep control of three thousand men out of his initial fifty thousand. This was arguably his most significant and complete battle loss. On both sides, there were significant losses to the general staff; many colonels and generals were killed or seriously wounded. Charles Anton was on the Russian staff. He received many injuries during the battle and died as a consequence exactly one month later. He was thirty-two. By 1763, however, Silesia was confirmed as a Prussian territory.

Before his death in battle, Charles Anton had kept up another family tradition, a union with a cousin. In 1754, he married Countess Friederike Charlotte (1738-1786), daughter of Count Albrecht of Dohna-Schlobitten-Leistenau, when she was fifteen. The Don or Dohna family is one of the very oldest in Saxony. Friederike's mother, Princess Sophie, was the daughter of Frederick Louis, Duke of Holstein-Beck, making the new couple first cousins.

After three years of marriage, Charles Anton and Friederike produced a son, Frederick Charles, in 1757. However, three years later, Charles Anton died from wounds received at Kunersdorf, and baby Frederick Charles became heir to his grandfather (who still lived) and the Holstein-Beck legacy. Much later, Friederike married a man from a famous Prussian military family, Count Friedrich Detlev von Moltke, in 1777. He held the desirable title of oberjägermeister under King Wilhelm III of Prussia. (This means chief hunting master, not chief drinker of the Jägermeister!) This marriage was childless.

The Beck dynasty effectively skipped a generation. The title and headship of the cadet branch bypassed the unfortunate Prince Charles Anton, owing to his death from battle injuries. His son, young Frederick Charles, inherited the titular designation of Duke of Holstein-Beck upon the death of his grandfather, Peter August, in 1775.

Figure 18: Frederick Charles, Duke of Schleswig-Holstein-Sonderburg-
Beck, circa. 1800, by Johan Friederich August Tischbein (1750-1812).
State Tretyakov Gallery, Moscow.

Frederick Charles,
Duke of Schleswig-Holstein-Sonderburg-Beck

(4xgreat-grandfather)

Born: *20 August 1757 at Königsberg, Prussia*

Died: *24 April 1816 at Wellingsbüttel Manor, Hamburg*

Spouse: *Countess Friederike Amalie Antonie von Schlieben*

Concurrent British monarchs: *George II and George III*

FREDERICK CHARLES GREW up as the heir to his paternal grandfather, Peter August, Duke of Holstein-Beck. Born in Königsberg in 1757, he was brought up by his maternal grandmother (who was also his great-aunt and a fellow Holstein-Beck). During the short-lived reign of his distant cousin, Peter III of Russia, in 1762, some of the Holstein-Beck family were offered courtly positions or military rank in the Russian army, such as Charles Louis of Holstein-Beck, who turned down becoming a field marshal. The five-year-old Prince Frederick Charles was also invited to come to Russia with the hope that he would one day enter the service of his cousin the tsar, but his family delayed and indeed prevented him going. They must have known something was afoot in the Russian court. Later that same year, Tsar Peter III was ousted in a coup led by his wife, Catherine the Great. He died in captivity – possibly by assassination. The Holstein-Beck family had tactfully avoided getting involved and did not suffer reprisals from Catherine the Great and her allies. That said, their cousins the Holstein-Gottop family technically regained the rule of Russia as Peter III's and Catherine the Great's son, Paul, eventually succeeded this mother in 1796.

With a grandfather so prominent and successful in the Russian court, Frederick Charles was keen to get to know him and of course visit him in Estonia – where his grandfather was governor. In 1775, he prepared to do just that, hoping also to ultimately enter military service in the Russian imperial army. However, that same year, Frederick Charles's grandfather died, and his hopes and prospects seemed blighted. That said, he was now officially the Duke of Holstein-Beck. Around the same time, the Prussian war machine was still rumbling in Europe but needed feeding and fuel to continue on and make up for losses – money. It needed money from taxes from its subjects and estates to pay for its wars. As the family were still settled in Prussia, they were approached for war 'contributions'. Frederick Charles's mother was not able to make these contributions. Instead, King Frederick the Great of Prussia agreed to take young Frederick Charles into military service in lieu of payment.

For his initial military schooling and training, King Frederick sent Frederick Charles to the Metz Military Academy in France around June 1775. He was not there long. The following year, he seems to have done a leg of the Grand Tour of Europe and Italy, which was no doubt part of his education. When he fell ill, the tour was cut short, and he returned to Prussia. In 1777, he was commissioned a major in the Prussian Twenty-seventh Infantry Regiment based at Stendal. In that guise, Frederick Charles took part in the War of Bavarian Succession.

The junior line of the House of Wittelsbach had died out with the death of Maximillian III Joseph, the Elector of Bavaria, in 1777. Naturally, Prussia (the House of Hohenzollern) wished to acquire this fertile territory for itself. The trouble was that the Habsburg Austrians felt the same way. The war began in 1778 and lasted roughly a year. Prussia did not gain the territory, but in truth, neither did Austria fully. Another branch of the Wittelsbach family succeeded as Dukes and Electors of Bavaria. Both sides wielded huge, massed armies, but the only battles were small-scale skirmishes. Famously, the war is known as the Potato War (or even the Plum Fuss) owing to the serious famine that persisted during the conflict. Thousands died of disease rather than battle. Major Charles Frederick, Duke of Holstein-Beck, survived however.

Following the war and the Peace Treaty of Teschen of 1779, Charles Frederick was made a junior staff officer of the von Schlieben regiment. He considered this, at worst, a demotion or, at best, a sideways promotion, and he requested to be released from the assignment. In September 1781, he was promoted to lieutenant colonel. Perhaps dissatisfied at his slow promotion, he briefly left service to attend to his own affairs and estates. A year earlier, he had married Countess Friederike, daughter of the Prussian minister of war, Count Leopold von Schlieben, after whom the regiment was named. The Holstein-Beck family were not pleased with this marriage. Generations of their family had married princesses or nobility from some of the oldest European families. The von Schliebens were new by comparison, so Frederick Charles was considered to have married beneath himself.

Frederick the Great was succeeded by Frederick Wilhelm II as King of Prussia in 1786. He recalled Frederick Charles into service as a full colonel in December that year giving him command of a grenadier battalion. By 1789, Frederick Charles, like men of previous generations of his family, rose to the rank of major general. Shortly afterwards, he commanded the Eleventh Infantry Regiment and, in 1794, suppressed the Kościuszko Uprising. In this Polish revolt, led by General Tadeusz Kościuszko, Polish forces sought to overthrow the occupying force and prevent the partitioning of Poland by Prussia and Russia. How history does like to repeat itself!

Kościuszko himself had actually fought in the American War Revolutionary War – or American War of Independence – for the colonists. He now fancied taking the spirit of independence back to his countryman in Poland, a country often ruled or occupied by neighbouring Prussia and Russia. He raised an army of peasants and had some initial successes taking on a Russian garrison, but the uprising was eventually crushed by the might of the two greater powers in the region who had large professional armies. Though Warsaw was held by the Polish forces, it eventually had to surrender to the Russian Army.

Following his service in putting down the uprising, Frederick Charles was promoted lieutenant general in the Prussian army and was made the commander of Prussian-held Kraków in modern day Poland. Putting down such a rebellion may have left a nasty taste in his mouth however. In 1797, he resigned his Prussian commission – the same year he achieved what may have been his childhood ambition – becoming a lieutenant general in the Russian army. He later left the Russian army in 1798, so it is possible that the appointment may have been a gift from his distant cousin, Tsar Paul I (of Schleswig-Holstein-Gottorp), whose coronation had been the same year as the appointment (1797).

Frederick Charles seems to have then taken something of a sabbatical. He went to study sciences at the University of Leipzig. In 1800, he returned to his East Prussian estate at Lindenau, and he later became a regional official there.

With his wife Friederike, Frederick Charles had three children: two daughters and a son. The eldest daughter, also Friederike (1780-1862), married into the now-famous von Richtofen family – they of the Red Baron in WWI. The second daughter, Luise (1783-1803), married the Duke of Anhalt-Köthen. The Holstein-Beck's only son and heir, Prince Frederick Wilhelm, was born in 1785.

As a young man, he went into military training like so many relatives before him. However, in contrast to the Prussian and Russian leanings of recent generations of his family, he returned to the ancestral Kingdom of Denmark where the House of Oldenburg ruled.

By 1808, Prince Frederick Wilhelm was at Copenhagen, and his father Duke Frederick Charles went to visit him. During this trip, their distant cousin, the King of Denmark, made Frederick Charles a lieutenant general in the Danish army. Additionally, in 1810, he was granted a manor house and estate at Wellingsbüttelin near Hamburg by Frederick VI of Denmark. By this time, the manor was its own separate fiefdom, allowing Frederick Charles to ostensibly live like a true duke. He remained there for most of the rest of his life, dying there in 1816 at the age of fifty-eight. That said, life in Denmark was not without its dramas. At times, the Holstein-Becks had to vacate the manor. During the Napoleonic Wars as Napoleon was expanding the lands under his influence, Hamburg was more than once a city under pressure and, at times, siege. A volunteer force of Prussian soldiers was stationed there, and by 1813 (the year of the Siege of Hamburg), it was used by the Russian general Count Alexander Ivanovich Osterman-Tolstoy – another member of the Tolstoy clan. Later, in 1868, Wellingsbüttelin was annexed by Prussia and became part of its province of Schleswig-Holstein. In the late twentieth century, the house was co-owned by the German states of Bremen, Hamburg and Schleswig-Holstein as a student hall of residence. More recently, it has become a nursing home.

By the time of his death in 1816, Frederick Charles, Duke of Holstein-Beck, had the impressive position of being a lieutenant general in the Prussian, Russian and Danish armies. Like his predecessors, he had picked up an impressive collection of honours and awards over the course of his career: Palatinate Hubertus Order (Bavaria); the Order of the Red Eagle (Prussia); the Alexander Nevsky Order (Russia) and, returning to the patronage of his Danish kin, the Order of the Elephant (Denmark). Ties with his cousins, the Kings of Denmark, were indeed becoming closer again. He passed his estates and title to his son, Frederick Wilhelm, who was the last Duke of Holstein-Beck.

Figure 19: A Photograph of Glücksburg Castle taken in 2018 by Matthias Süßen.

THE HOUSE OF SCHLESWIG-HOLSTEIN-SONDERBURG-GLÜCKSBURG

THE OLDENBURGS HAD EMERGED from an obscure North German backwater fiefdom to sit on the thrones of Denmark, Norway and Sweden in the fourteenth century. Originally this was because of family links and ties which stretched back many generations before that succession. Such was the succession of Christian I of Denmark. In a way, history was to repeat itself in the nineteenth century. From a modest castle by a small town in what is now Germany, another branch of the House of Oldenburg, the House of Glücksburg, rose to prominence becoming the eventual successor to the throne of Denmark. Other members of this cadet branch eventually became the monarchs of Greece, Norway and, as of 2022, the United Kingdom. Its full and proper name is of course Schleswig-Holstein-Sonderburg-Glücksburg.

Like the dynastic branches of the Oldenburg family before it, the House of Glücksburg takes its name from a place or estate. In this case, it is the town of Glücksburg, specifically the castle there. The town is located in the Schleswig-Holstein area on the eastern side of the (Danish) Jutland Peninsula on what is now the border between Germany and Denmark.

Following the end of the Napoleonic Wars, the end of French dominance in Europe, and the humbling of the Austrian Habsburg Empire, a new power was rising in Europe during the nineteenth century. The Kingdom of Prussia, with its military strength, would soon influence most of the Germanic kingdoms and states. With the rise of revolutions, nationalism and a desire to see German-speaking peoples unite, Prussia became a formidable and looming adversary on the southern borders of Denmark. Once more, the House of Oldenburg faced a difficult and troubling time during what has become known as the Schleswig Wars. Despite this, the new ruling branch – that of Glücksburg – became one of the most influential and well-connected European royal families of its day.

It is not completely relevant but perhaps of note that Glücksburg Castle was the site of a scandalous WWII jewel heist or theft. This scandal involved members of the Glücksburg family as well as British Special Forces who were tasked with rounding up prominent Nazi leaders who had gone into hiding in northern parts of Germany and Europe in the days immediately following the end of the war. In particular, one such British unit was seeking to capture alive Albert Speer (Hitler's former armaments minister), who had holed himself up at Glücksburg Castle with his staff and a small detachment of SS guards. Also taking refuge in the royal castle were several members of different German (and Danish) royal families, who were not actually Nazis. This group included the head of the House of Schleswig-Holstein-Sonderburg-Glücksburg, Duke Friedrich Ferdinand.

In short, while taking Speer and his men prisoner, the British soldiers, led by celebrated SAS officer Major Geoffrey Gordon-Creed DSO MC, also robbed many of the resident royals of their valuable jewels at gunpoint, even though most of the royals were private citizens. Gordon-Creed is thought to be one of the inspirations for Ian Fleming's character James Bond. The British soldiers made off with their ill-gotten loot despite protest from Duke Friedrich Ferdinand of Glücksburg (the then owner of the castle). The soldiers did not however count on the fact that most of these royals were cousins of their commander in chief King George VI. Most of them wrote to him personally to complain. Some of the loot was returned, owing to the intercession of the king's mother, Queen Mary, who was herself a niece of the Duke of Glücksburg. It was a shameful episode for the British army and the careers of the men involved.

Today, Glücksburg Castle is a museum owned by its own foundation headed by the Schleswig-Holstein-Sonderburg-Glücksburg family. It houses many surviving family heirlooms and documents. Arguably, since the accession of King Charles III of the United Kingdom, who hails from the same family and bloodline, there is now a kinship between Glücksburg Castle and Windsor Castle.

continues from p.229

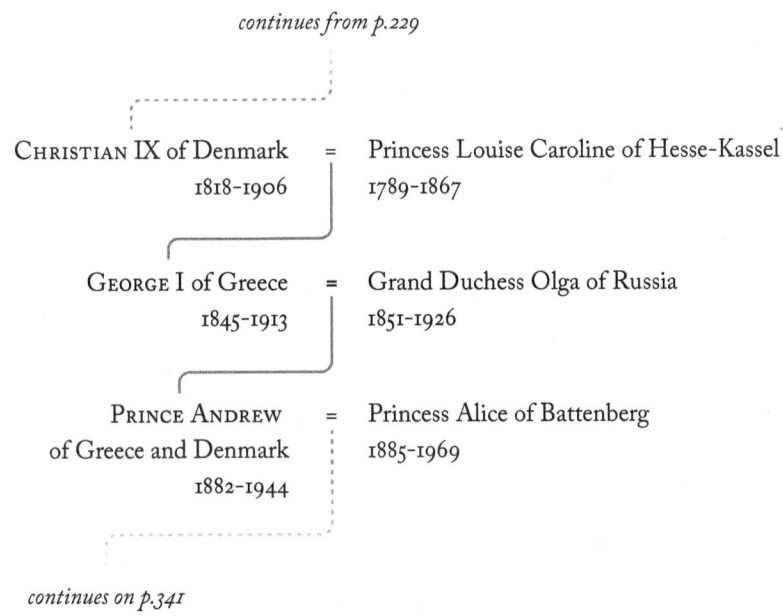

CHRISTIAN IX of Denmark = Princess Louise Caroline of Hesse-Kassel
1818-1906   1789-1867

GEORGE I of Greece = Grand Duchess Olga of Russia
1845-1913   1851-1926

PRINCE ANDREW = Princess Alice of Battenberg
of Greece and Denmark   1885-1969
1882-1944

continues on p.341

Figure 20: A print of Frederick William, Duke of Schleswig-Holstein-Sonderburg-Glücksburg. Possibly by Albert Emil Kirchner in 1830–1831. Royal Danish Library.

Frederick William,
Duke of Schleswig-Holstein-
Sonderburg-Glücksburg

(3xgreat-grandfather)

Born: *4 January 1785 at Lindenau, Prussia (now Poland)*
Died: *17 February 1831 at Gottorp Castle, Schleswig*
Spouse: *Princess Louise Caroline of Hesse-Kassel*
Concurrent British monarchs: *George III, George IV and William IV*

PRINCE FREDERICK WILLIAM was born the third child and only son of his parents at their residence in Lindenau, Prussia, in 1785. Naturally, by this point, the family had made their home in Prussia and truly established themselves as part of the nobility and upper-class of Prussian society despite their Danish origins. It had already become something of a family tradition that the men enter military service in the Prussian military. However, this was not necessarily the case for Frederick William. From 1799 to 1802, the young prince was educated at the Ritterakademie in Brandenburg and later at the University of Leipzig until 1803.

Following his education, his father sent him to Denmark to become an officer in the army. His godfather, King Frederick VI of Denmark, saw to it that he obtained a cavalry commission in 1804 and became a member of the Royal Horse Guards the following year. This may have been out of a nostalgic urge that the family should not lose its ties with its ancestral country. However, it seems more likely that this decision came about as a result of Frederick William's father having fallen out of favour with the Prussian king and his court since his retirement. Consequently, Frederick William entered military service as part of the Danish army during the mid-Napoleonic Wars.

It may be surprising, but Denmark, though technically neutral, was eventually forcibly dragged into the war on the side of the French following pressure from Napoleon and his Russian allies to join the Continental System – a policy of barring Britain from any trade with Europe. This culminated in the two Battles of Copenhagen (1801 and 1807). The second of these was a devastating surprise bombardment of the Danish capital by Britain, which resulted in the surrender of the entire Danish fleet. Britain had been concerned that Napoleon might garrison troops in Danish territory and commandeer its navy to block access to the Baltic or harass British shipping in the North Sea. Consequently, British troops were sent to Øresund together with the Royal Navy. This pre-emptive attack on a technically neutral country was widely criticised in the courts of Europe, and Britain found itself at war with Russia too (until 1812).

Frederick William served in Copenhagen for roughly a year. On his own request, in 1805, he was transferred to Holstein in the south, where the Danish army guarded the southern borders. There he remained as a second lieutenant in the Life Regiment Dragoons up until 1807, performing guard duty and reconnaissance missions. Frederick William arrived too late to be involved in the 1807 Battle of Copenhagen, but it is exciting to think of the King of the United Kingdom's great-great-great-grandfather fighting in the army opposing the British!

Frederick William may have been involved in a small military action against the Swedes in 1808, but little is known of this. Through his early military career, he seriously considered transferring to join the Prussian Army and thus continuing the family's tradition, but his father put a stop to this. As fate would have it however, he found himself fighting in a successful skirmish against Prussians troops at Straslund in 1809. He was subsequently honoured with knighthoods from France,

Holland and Denmark. That same year, he was promoted to the rank of major and placed on the general staff based at Gottorp Castle under the command of General Field Marshal Prince Charles of Hesse-Kassel – a grandson of King George II of Great Britain.

While garrisoned at Gottorp Castle, Frederick William was able to make the acquaintance of his commanding officer's daughter, Princess Louise Caroline. The couple were hastily wed there on 26 January 1810 amid the wars. Her father did not attend. Once again, the importance of fortuitous marriages in the House of Oldenburg cannot be understated. Louise Caroline had connections not only to British royalty but also Danish. Her older sister, Marie Sophie of Hesse-Kassel, was Queen of Denmark and married to the then king, Frederick VI. This made Frederick William the king's brother-in-law as well as a distant cousin and godson!

To further add to the mix, Louise Caroline's mother was a Danish princess (Louise, daughter of Frederick V) and was consequently of the senior Oldenburg line. This would become an important point in future years.

At the age of 31, Prince Frederick William became the head of the House of Beck upon the death of his father in 1816. He and his wife went on to have ten children together. However, as Prince Frederick William did not possess a great estate of his own, the family lived in an apartment or wing of Louise Caroline's father's castle at Gottorp. Fate would provide though.

One of the many other cadet branches of the House of Schleswig-Holstein-Sonderburg was the House of Glücksburg, which began with Philip the fourth son of John (Hans), Duke of Schleswig-Holstein-Sonderburg. The name and title of Glücksburg had been taken from a castle of the same name inherited by Philip in 1622. The last of Philip's line, Duke Frederick Henry of Schleswig-Holstein-Sonderburg-Glücksburg, died childless at the age of thirty-one in 1779. There were no more Dukes of Glücksburg.

Duke Frederick Henry's widow remained at Glücksburg Castle until her own death in 1824. With no obvious immediate heirs, it was not clear what would now happen to the castle and estate, and they passed into the hands of the Danish Crown. After deliberation, King Frederick VI decided to give the castle to his 'homeless' cousin/godson/ brother-in-law, Frederick William, who became Duke of Schleswig-Holstein-Sonderburg-Glücksburg – seeing as he did not own Beck.

Frederick William and Louise Caroline moved their large family to Glücksburg, but he did not have many years to enjoy it. Having caught a cold, he suffered from pneumonia and possibly scarlet fever and died on 17 February 1831. He was laid to rest in Schleswig Cathedral. Little did he or his family know that he had founded the house that would one day rule Britain.

Figure 21: Photograph of King Christian IX of Denmark. Royal Danish Library.

Christian IX, King of Denmark

(great-great-grandfather)

| 1818–1863 | 1863–1903 | 1903–1906 |

Born: *8 April 1818 at Gottorp Castle, Schleswig*

Died: *29 January 1906 at Amalienburg Castle, Copenhagen*

Spouse: *Princess Louise of Hesse-Kassel*

Concurrent British monarchs: *George III, George IV, William IV,*
Victoria and Edward VII

K ING CHRISTIAN IX was the fourth son of his parents Princess
Louise Caroline and Prince Wilhelm Frederick, Duke of
Schleswig-Holstein-Sonderburg-Glücksburg. He was born in 1818 at
Gottorp, his maternal grandparents' castle in the Duchy of Schleswig.
He was named after his godfather, his mother's cousin, King Christian
VIII of Denmark – who personally attended the christening at Gottorp.
This indicates how close the Glücksburgs had become with their rul-
ing cousins from the senior Oldenburg line. That said, little Prince
Christian was thought to be considerably far from the succession to the
Danish throne. He descended in the male line from Christian III, who
ruled centuries earlier, and he was only the fourth son of his father. At
most, he might establish yet another minor branch of the Oldenburgs.
Once again fortune, not just marriages, eventually changed this.

Youth and Marriage

The early years of his life were spent at Gottorp Castle and then later Glücksburg Castle when the family moved there in 1825 following Christian's father's elevation to Duke of Glücksburg (founding what is known as the younger Glücksburg line to differentiate it from the previous line of the same name). After his father's unexpected early death in 1831, the family was left with little money (despite a large house) and ten children to support. At the suggestion of his godfather, the king, Christian was enrolled in army training at Copenhagen in 1832. Much of his tuition at the Land Cadet Academy was private owing to his position. In 1835, he was confirmed into the Danish Lutheran Church in Copenhagen, and the following year he joined his father's old regiment, the Royal Horse Guards, as a junior officer. Christian was billeted at the regimental barracks by the Frederiksholms Kanal in simple army conditions.

Christian's eldest brother, Karl, naturally had inherited the title of Duke of Glücksburg upon their father's death. In 1838, Karl cemented the tight links between their family and the senior Danish royal family by marrying the king and queen's daughter, Princess Vilhelmine Marie. (They were second cousins.) The year after this marriage, Christian was invited by the king to move from the barracks and make his home at the Yellow Palace, a large townhouse close to the royal palace of Amalienborg.

As a young officer and prince with very creditable royal connections in Europe, Christian was in want of a wife. Owing to his status as a sort-of royal and a fourth son, he was justifiably ambitious in his selection. Having officially represented the Danish king at the coronation of the young Queen Victoria of Britain, he decided to try his luck. His offer of marriage was politely declined, as Queen Victoria was all too happy to go along with her family's arrangement of marrying her cousin, Prince Albert of Saxe-Coburg-Gotha. That said, she reportedly appreciated the offer and found Christian very agreeable indeed. It mattered not. Years later, her eldest son and heir, the Prince of Wales, would marry his eldest daughter – but more on that later.

EDWARD HILARY DAVIS

Between 1839 and 1841, Prince Christian continued his education and also travelled a little, as all young royal or aristocratic men of his day did. He studied law and history at the University in Bonn, visited many sites throughout the German states and even made the obligatory Grand Tour visit to Venice. Reportedly, on his journey back through Germany to Copenhagen, he was offered a commission in the Prussian Army by the King of Prussia himself – an opportunity to follow in the steps of his grandfather and great-grandfather. Fortunately for Christian, he declined.

On his return to the Danish capital, Christian finally found a wife. His bride, Princess Louise of Hesse-Kassel, was the daughter of General Prince William of Hesse-Kassel, the Governor of Copenhagen and Princess Charlotte of Denmark – the king's sister. This made Princess Louise the niece of Christian VIII, and thus the bonds between the Glücksburgs and the Danish royal family grew ever tighter. (The young couple were second cousins.) They were married in May 1842 and lived together at the Yellow Palace, where they began to have children – five in their first ten years of marriage. Though they were extended members of the Danish royal family, Christian and his family remained relatively understated, modest and fairly unknown.

The Danish Succession Problem

During the 1840s, it became clear that there was a complicated succession crisis brewing in the Danish court and royal family. It was clear that King Christian VIII wasn't going to have more children, nor was his son, the crown prince (later Frederick VII), nor his childless brother, Prince Ferdinand. None of them were going to sire any further male heirs. It seemed likely, therefore, that the senior line of Oldenburg was going to become extinct in a matter of years. The complication was only worsened by the fact that different parts of the Danish territories had different succession laws.

Since the reign of Frederick III (1648-1670), Salic law was in effect in the Kingdom of Denmark. Thus only eldest males were eligible to inherit. If all the male members of Frederick III's line died out (as was likely about to happen), the law stipulated that semi-Salic law should be adopted – that is to say, succession could pass to the most senior female line or relative. However, there was some vagueness as to whether that meant that a woman could actually inherit or that the heir should be the next male in the senior-most female line from the last king. Adding to this confusion Schleswig and Holstein were held separate from the Danish kingdom. Although separate duchies (with the king as their duke), their succession customs were slightly different. Their laws were indeed also Salic but also allowed for the succession of other male lines that predated Frederick III.

As we have seen, there were many junior branches of the House of Oldenburg, many of which went back to Christian I. Thus there were many potential heirs and possible ways to interpret succession to Schleswig and Holstein, but a great many of the potential heirs of Schleswig and Holstein had no rights to the Danish throne per se. The two duchies were indeed separate but were 'forever undivided' according to the 1460 Treaty of Ribe and had to be ruled by the same person – which for centuries had conveniently been the Kings of Denmark.

It is worth mentioning that the Kingdom of Norway was no longer an issue by this point. In 1814, Norway had declared itself separate and independent from the Kingdom of Denmark and had instead, as part of the peace treaties following the Napoleonic Wars, chosen as their monarchs the Kings of Sweden. The union between Sweden and Norway lasted from 1814 until it was peacefully dissolved in 1905.

This Danish succession crisis was made yet even more complex owing to the backdrop of the political situation at the time. Since the end of the Napoleonic Wars, nationalism had been on the rise in continental Europe, particularly in many German and Italian states, but also in Denmark. Part of the goal of popular nationalism in those days was to see peoples of the same culture and more importantly, the same language, join together as a nation or union. In the many German kingdoms and duchies this was not an uncommon hope, and it was becoming more popular. This sentiment was later harnessed by military expansionist Prussia (under Bismarck) to establish Prussia as the foremost nation in a German confederation of states and, later, an empire. The sticky points were areas on the fringes – at the outside edges of the territory inhabited by predominantly German-speaking peoples. In other words, where does Germany end and Denmark begin? This proved a dangerous question.

Following the Napoleonic Wars, many of the German states and kingdoms had been brought together in a German-speaking grouping of nations known as the German Confederation – with Prussia and Austria, the largest two states within it, vying for dominance. Denmark was not part of the Confederation. However, the King of Denmark *was* duke of two duchies to the south which were part of the Confederation: Holstein and Lauenburg. The Duchy of Schleswig was not part of the confederation but had a mixed German- and Danish-speaking population. These three duchies (Schleswig, Holstein and Lauenburg), though not technically part of Denmark, provided around half of the Danish Crown's income and were therefore prized processions. Neighbouring Prussia looked on covetously.

The problem of succession deepened when Christian VIII died and was succeeded by his childless son, Frederick VII, on 20 January 1848. The question of who would rule after him in either the kingdom or the duchies remained unresolved.

The Schleswig-Holstein War

In 1848, nationalist uprisings and revolutions exploded all across Europe. From Paris to Germany, Italy and Hungary, the downtrodden revolted in the name of national unity and the right to self-determination – in some cases. Denmark too had its share of nationalist uprising. Nationalist Danes wanted to disambiguate the status of the southern duchies and establish a more clearly defined Denmark. They asserted that Denmark stretched from the top of Jutland south to the Eider River – which happened to be the border between Schleswig and Holstein. They wanted to effectively subsume Schleswig into the Danish state, and they became known as 'Eider Danes'. This antagonised the many Germans who lived in Schleswig. (By contrast, the population of Holstein, to the south, was majority German.) Furthermore, it was the common belief in Schleswig (and Holstein) that Schleswig-Holstein ought to remain 'undivided forever', and that Schleswig should join the German Confederation along with Holstein. The British foreign secretary, Lord Palmerston, is reported to have exclaimed that the whole affair was so complex that only three men ever understood it: Prince Albert (who was by that time dead), a particular German professor (who then went mad), and Lord Palmerston himself (who claimed to have forgotten)!

Lists of demands were presented to the Danish king (and duke), Frederick VII, by the Eider Danes and the German nationalists. Unsurprisingly, the king decreed in favor of the Eider Danes. This quickly led to the German nationalists setting up a provisional government in opposition to the Danish government in the southern duchies. Nationalist movements in Denmark claimed Schleswig; nationalist movements in the German Confederacy did the same. War seemed inevitable. Men living inside the duchies had a difficult decision to make: to be Danish or German, to join one army or the other. Such a decision split families from all classes. For local farmers and the peasantry, it may have been a more simple choice, but for many aristocrats it was a choice between their nationality (or sentiment) and their king/ liege/lord. The forthcoming conflict is known as the Schleswig Wars – there are two.

At the outset of the First Schleswig War, both Denmark and the independent Schleswig-Holsteiners asked for support from neighbouring Prussia. As a German nation, Prussia had great sympathy for the Schleswig-Holsteiners and entered Schleswig with troops in April 1848 – commencing the First Schleswig War. The war is complex and owes much of its result to poor leadership as well as tactics which had not yet caught up with technological advantages in the field, but this is not a book on the Schleswig Wars regrettably. The overall outcome, despite Denmark being seemingly outnumbered and outgunned, was inconclusive. This was still rightly seen as a Danish victory since it still held the Duchy of Schleswig. Furthermore, the dragging on of the war forced Frederick VII to make many political concessions to his parliament, and Denmark consequently became a constitutional monarchy in 1849.

By 1850, both Denmark and Prussia were under immense pressure from other countries to end the war as it was a destabilising influence on Europe as a whole and upset trade in the Baltic. Russia was an advocate for peace at the time. The two sides signed a tentative peace deal in July. The agreement was simply to lay down arms and stop fighting. However, Denmark then launched a surprise offensive at the Battle of Idsted (25 July 1850). The Danes failed to break the German-Holstein army at Idsted, but the attack negated the peace agreement and so the war dragged on into 1851.

Resolving the Succession

Meanwhile, the issue of Danish succession was still not settled. Everyone had an opinion. One contender was the Duke of Augustenburg (another branch of the ancient Oldenburg line). However, some of their family had sided with the Prussians in the war. Christian was from a junior line (the Glücksburgs), but it was to his credit that he was close to the previous Danish monarchs, had grown up as a Dane not a Prussian and had served in the Danish army. The trouble was that he was a fourth son and therefore not the senior man of his family.

After much consideration, the Schleswig-Holstein matter was resolved in London in the presence of Britain, France, Austria, Prussia and Russia. The London Protocol of 1852 decided the Danish succession and marked the end of the (First) Schleswig War. In summary, Prince Christian was chosen as heir presumptive to the Danish throne (despite having older brothers) after Frederick VII's aging, childless uncle, Prince Ferdinand (who predeceased Frederick VII anyway). Denmark was internationally recognised as holding Schleswig as a direct fief and Holstein and Lauenburg as separate fiefs but still in the German Confederacy. This essentially brought the area back to its pre-war status. None of the issues over which the war was fought had really been resolved. The objective of Britain, France, Russia and Austria in the agreement was really to curb the dominance of Prussia. Needless to say, the Germans in Schleswig-Holstein and the Prussians felt hard done by.

Whilst living as second-in-line to the Danish throne (after Ferdinand), Christian had mixed popularity. He was largely ostracised from domestic politics, owing to his conservatism and his disapproval of the way King Frederick VII conducted himself – especially with regards to his third wife who was an actress. Christian continued to chiefly reside in the Yellow Palace and merely waited for his time to succeed. His stature in the courts of Europe, however, had increased tenfold. As the soon-to-be King of Denmark with a healthy brood of children (three sons and three daughters), the Glücksburgs were suddenly quite desirable on the royal marriage market. No longer very minor royals on the fringes of court life, the Glücksburgs were among the first rank of European royals.

The year of 1863 was a momentous one for Christian and his family. On 10 March, his eldest daughter, Princess Alexandra, married the Prince of Wales (the future Edward VII), cementing the family's place in the European club of royals. Just ten days later, Christian's second son, Prince William, was elected to become King of the Hellenes (Greece) following a referendum. In June that year, Prince Ferdinand died, making Christian first in line to the Danish throne. On 15 November, Frederick VII died, and Christian finally succeeded to the throne as King Christian IX of Denmark.

Yellow Palace (Bergum's Mansion) town mansion next to Amalienborg Palace in Frederiksstaden district building entrance in Copenhagen, Denmark.

The Second Schleswig-Holstein War

At almost the same time as Christian's accession to the throne, the country was plunged back into conflict. The German nationalists set up a rival claimant Duke of Schleswig-Holstein, Duke Frederick of Augustenborg – a distant cousin who was overlooked for the kingship of Denmark. (He was also father-in-law of the future Kaiser Wilhelm II.) Duke Frederick became a symbol for the Germanic independence movement in the southern duchies, though his claims were not recognised by the London Protocol. Under some pressure from the Eider Danes, Christian agreed to legislation which brought Schleswig more under the direct rule/authority of the Danish state and made the inhabitants thereof more Danish. This was a clear break with the London Protocol and could only lead to war again. The Second Schleswig War began in February 1864 when Prussian and Austrian troops of the German Confederation, together with the German nationalists of Schleswig-Holstein, crossed the Eider and entered Schleswig.

Once again, this war was complex and is worthy of many large volumes. In summary, however, the Danish military leadership were overconfident that they could defend the territory a second time. The Prussians were faster and more organised and had better artillery. The Danish military leadership were also hindered by the fact that they were directed by their politicians which led to several avoidable setbacks. At the Battle of Dybbøl (18 April 1864), the Danes lost ten percent of their entire army. Following this, there was a truce so that some negotiations could begin. Prussian Chancellor Otto von Bismarck was willing to divide Schleswig, but Danish politicians continued to insist that Denmark extend to the Eider River. It appeared that the war would continue with no foreseeable end.

It has been discovered quite recently that Christian IX actually secretly communicated with Bismarck and Prussia during this time. He suggested that Denmark, as a whole, join the German Confederation, thus removing the need to fight. Bismarck, however, rejected this proposal fearing that ethnic strife between Danes and Germans would probably continue. Also, war against the confederation's neighbours was Bismarck's way of creating a path towards German reunification. The revelation of these communications was only recently published in 2010 by Danish historian Tom Buk-Swienty, who had been given access to the royal archives by the late Queen Margrethe of Denmark.

Following another Danish defeat at the Battle of Als (30 June 1864) with the Austro-Prussian forces occupying most of Jutland and thousands of Danes dead or surrendered, Denmark was forced back to the negotiating table in October 1864. This time, the Prussian demands were far higher. They asked that the duchies of Schleswig, Holstein and Lauenburg be separated from the state of Denmark and be subsumed into the German Confederation.

Defeat

Throughout the Second Schleswig War, Christian and his government had sought aid from other great powers who might help them with military support against their stronger adversaries of Prussia and Austria. However, Britain was closely aligned with Prussia, due to the fact that Queen Victoria's eldest daughter was married to the Prussian crown prince. That said, there were British attempts at mediation, but these failed. In Russia, Christian's distant cousin, Tsar Alexander II, was still licking his wounds from his defeat in the Crimean War. Russia also owed Prussia for its help putting down a Polish rebellion in 1863. Finally, troops promised by King Charles XV from Sweden and Norway never came to Denmark's aid. There was no help to be found in Europe.

Denmark had suffered humiliation, defeat and the loss of a huge swath of land. It was a wakeup call. Denmark stood no chance in a military conflict against its German neighbours – especially if alone. (Denmark did not fight in a war again for over a century, being neutral in the world wars. Danes living in Schleswig-Holstein, however, were conscripted into the German army.) This has led to some lasting resentment. At the end of the First World War, however, a plebiscite (direct vote) was arranged by the victorious powers, and northern Schleswig was returned to Denmark in 1920.

The Father-in-Law of Europe

Following the war, Christian IX's reign was, perhaps understandably, not regarded enthusiastically by Danes. His support for the Danish nationalist cause seemed half-hearted at best – which turned out to be true. His popularity grew through his later reign due to a number of democratic, parliamentary and welfare reforms he enacted in Denmark. In fact, due to his long reign, Christian IX eventually became something of a national icon. It was during his reign that Iceland was permitted its first constitution – though still ruled by Denmark.

Owing to his links with multiple royal families, Christian IX earned the nickname 'the father-in-law of Europe'. By the end of his life, his three daughters had become the Queen of England, the Empress of Russia, and the Crown Princess of Hanover. Christian's eldest son and heir, Frederick VIII, married a Swedish princess. His second son, Prince William, as we will see, was elected the King of Greece. As for Christian's third and youngest son, Prince Valdemar, he was elected to be the new Sovereign Prince of Bulgaria following a coup which toppled the previous monarch, Alexander of Battenberg. However, both Valdemar and his wife turned down the offer, making him the only one of his siblings not to sit on a European throne.

Christian and the Danish royal family enjoyed hosting family holidays, which incorporated their royal relatives from both Britain and Russia. The Prussian royal family was often left out – for obvious reasons of bitterness. It has been conjectured that the feeling of being left out and the closeness of his British and Russian cousins may have contributed towards Kaiser Wilhelm II's bitterness towards the two countries and thus paved part of the way toward the First World War. These family gatherings often took place at the Fredensborg Palace and were known affectionately as 'Fredensborg Days', immortalised in a painting by Tuxen in 1886.

Christian IX died peacefully in 1906 at the age of 87 having reigned for over forty-two years. He was buried next to his wife at Roskilde Cathedral. where the Kings of Denmark had been buried since Christian I in 1481. Most of the European royal families today descend from Christian IX, this includes reigning monarchs such as Kings Charles III; Frederick X of Denmark; Philippe of Belgium; Harald V of Norway; Philip VI of Spain and Henri, Grand Duke of Luxembourg.

Figure 22: 'The Family of Christian IX of Denmark' – by Laurits Tuxen – depicting the family group in the Garden Hall of the Fredensborg Palace, 1886. Now on display at the Christiansborg Palace, Denmark.

The thirty-two individuals depicted are (from left to right): Prince Albert Victor, Duke of Clarence and Avondale (Charles III's great-great-uncle); Edward VII, then Prince of Wales (Charles III's great-great-grandfather); Queen Alexandra, then Princess of Wales (Charles III's great-great-grandmother); Princess Ingeborg of Denmark; Prince Harald of Denmark; Prince George of Cumberland; Princess Marie of Cumberland; Princess Thyra Duchess of Cumberland; Princess Alexandra of Cumberland; Queen Louise of Denmark; Prince Valdemar of Denmark; King Christian IX of Denmark; Prince Christian of Denmark (later Christian X); the Tsarevich of Russia (later Tsar Nicholas II); Grand Duke Michael Alexandrovich of Russia; Tsarina Maria Feodorovna of Russia; Grand Duchess Olga Alexandrovna of Russia; Tsar Alexander III of Russia; the Crown Prince of Denmark (later Frederick VIII); the Crown Princess of Denmark (later Queen Louise); King George I of Greece; Princess Thyra of Denmark; Princess Alexandra of Greece; Queen Olga of Greece; Princess Marie of Greece; Princess Louise of Wales (later Princess Royal); Prince Carl of Denmark (later King Haakon VII of Norway); Grand Duke George Alexandrovich of Russia; Princess Victoria of Wales; Princess Maud of Wales (later Queen Maud of Norway); Grand Duchess Xenia Alexandrovna of Russia and Princess Louise of Denmark.

Figure 23: Photograph of King George I of the Hellenes/Greece circa. 1912.
National Portrait Gallery.

George I, King of the Hellenes

(great-grandfather)

Born: *24 December 1845 at the Yellow Palace, Copenhagen*
Killed: *18 March 1913 near the White Tower, Thessaloniki*
Spouse: *Princess Olga Constantinovna of Russia*
Concurrent British monarchs: *Victoria, Edward VII and George V*

WHILE HIS FATHER Prince Christian was still living a relatively quiet life as a minor Danish royal in Copenhagen, Prince William (as he was originally known) was born in the Yellow Palace at the end of 1845, his parents' second son and third child. At the time, it seemed unlikely, though possible, that his father would become King of Denmark. At the same time, it must have seemed unthinkable that this baby prince would become king of a Mediterranean country hundreds of miles away and found a wholly new royal family, but that is what happened. Once again, fate, luck, fortune and convenient marriages seemed to follow the House of Oldenburg – now the House of Glücksburg.

Youth

Prince William was baptised Christian William Ferdinand Adolph George but was known by the name William – which was the name most used by both of his grandfathers. It should not escape the reader's attention that it is also the name of the present Prince of Wales, who is his great-great-grandson.

It is safe to assume that Prince William of Denmark's life changed a little once his father was officially announced as the heir to the throne in 1852. That said, by royal standards of the era, Prince William lived a relatively normal, low-key life. His education was fairly simple and was in fact conducted mostly by his parents and an English governess – making English his second language. Like many royal second sons of the day, he decided to embark on a career in the Danish navy. He entered as a cadet at the Søofficersuddannelsen in Copenhagen to train to become an officer. There he gained a reputation for having a sense of humour and being a jolly fellow. He reportedly liked to play practical jokes. The carefree practical joker had to get very serious very soon.

William's family had undoubtedly moved up in the world, and their rise was about to make a major jump. When he was seventeen, his older sister Alexandra (a year older than he) married the heir to the British throne, Bertie, Prince of Wales (future Edward VII), on 10 March 1863 at Windsor. William attended with his parents. However, that year was to significantly change the young prince's life in many other ways as well.

A Greek Kingdom?

Greece had struggled for independence for centuries. When the Ottomans captured Constantinople in 1453, it was only a matter of time before they pressed their advantage westwards into Europe, which they did. By 1458, the Ottomans had captured Athens and large parts of the Balkans. By the end of the fifteenth century, they occupied most of the plains and islands of Greece. However, large groups of the Greek people had retreated into the Greek hills and mountains. There they were out of the reach of the Turks and continued to resist the invaders by means of guerrilla warfare. Still, Greece was effectively under Ottoman–Turkish rule for the next four centuries.

In the early 1800s, many secret societies and groups organised revolts and uprisings of the Christian Greek peoples against the Muslim Turkish occupiers. Small revolts were put down by the Turks, but by 1821 the Greek War of Independence had begun. Readers will not be surprised if we brush over this bloody conflict, and no doubt many will be

EDWARD HILARY DAVIS

aware that Lord Byron volunteered to fight in this war (only to die of fever in 1824). The Greeks were assisted by the French, the Russians and the British (who possessed the Ionian Islands). The Ottoman Empire became overstretched as it entered into a war with Russia in 1828. As a consequence, it was forced to accept Greek autonomy, and Greece was recognised as an independent state in 1830. However, Europe was evidently not yet ready for a kingless state. The hunt began for someone to take up the role of the new country's monarch – the King of Greece.

The ideal candidate would be from the existing stocks of European royals and have a loose connection to Greece, perhaps ancestrally. Many princely candidates were considered. It was initially offered to Prince Leopold of Saxe-Coburg und Gotha (the uncle of Queen Victoria). He looked at the precarious and unstable situation of the new country of Greece and passed on the opportunity – instead becoming King of the Belgians a year later. Some hopefuls actually put themselves forward for consideration as potential king, including one Wexford Irishman, Nicholas Macdonald Sarsfield Cod'd, who claimed alleged descent from the ancient Palaiologos family of Byzantine emperors. Alas, his claim was overlooked.

By 1832, Greece was still unstable as a new country. It needed leadership and a clear sovereign head. Foreign secretary Lord Palmerston convened a meeting of the three great powers – Britain, Russia and France – in London to settle on a candidate once and for all. They settled on a neutral candidate (not from their territories) who was also young and malleable. They chose the teenage Prince Otto of Bavaria, second son of King Ludwig I of Bavaria, to be the first king of modern Greece. He arrived in Greece that year as the new king, sporting Greek national dress but also accompanied by 3,500 Bavarian soldiers and a British battleship just for good measure. Initially though, he was popular.

Though he reigned long and expanded the Greek territories, pushing out the Turks, Otto often interfered with internal Greek political matters. He tried to rule as an absolute monarch, sometimes relying on his German troops, and didn't put Greeks on his council. Otto's prestige was heavily reliant on the support of the great powers, but following an open revolt in 1843 and the Pacifico Incident in 1850, the British actually blockaded several Greek ports. To make matters worse, Otto and his wife Queen Amalia were still childless. There was an attempt on her life in 1861. Then, the straw that broke the camel's back was when Otto unwisely dismissed his prime minister, an old hero of the Greek War of Independence who was very popular with the people. This provoked a rebellion and a military coup.

The British told Otto not to resist the coup (which had successfully set up a provisional government calling for there to be a new and better king). The royal couple escaped on a British steam frigate, the Scylla, and headed home to Bavaria with their tails between their legs. Greece now needed a new king.

A Referendum to find a New King

Though the great powers were happy to select another European prince for the job, a 'novel' idea occurred to the Greeks, perhaps the people should decide –because referendums are always a good idea! Greek politicians decided to hold a plebiscite, or referendum, on who the new monarch of Greece should be. The referendum began in late 1862, and the results were announced in February 1863 at the national assembly. There were a large number of princely candidates considered, including the Emperor of France, the Tsar of Russia and a French marshal. Of the nearly quarter million votes, there was an overwhelming majority of 95% for Prince Alfred (later Duke of Edinburgh) – Queen Victoria's second son. This was problematic, as the three great powers had agreed years before that, in order to maintain their balance of power, no prince from one of their families should be the Greek monarch. Plus Queen Victoria didn't approve and forbade Alfred from accepting the crown. The Greek assembly proclaimed Alfred king, but he declined the crown.

The great powers of Europe needed a candidate who was not too

British, not too French and not too Russian. The runner up, the Duke of Leuchtenberg, was a grandson of Napoleon Bonaparte's stepson, Eugene de Beauharnais, but was also a nephew of the Tsar of Russia. Quite far down the list of candidates in the Greek referendum was Prince William of Denmark, a boy of 17. He was thought sufficiently neutral, despite some British and Russian connections. Although he only received six votes in the referendum, he was selected as the successful candidate. The Greek assembly unanimously elected William as their king on 30 March 1863 – which was better in appearance than having a king imposed on them. To differentiate between the new king and his disastrous predecessor, William was proclaimed King of 'the Hellenes', and he adopted the regnal name of George I (Γεώργιος Α΄ or Geórgios I). Oddly, he had a ceremonial enthronement that summer in Copenhagen rather than Athens. However, the ceremony was attended by Greek dignitaries. As a gift to the new monarch, the British gave him/Greece the Ionian Islands – perhaps an uncharacteristically generous gift from the British but more likely a ploy to gain favour with the new king (and the British already had a well-established Mediterranean naval base at Malta).

King of Greece

Before arriving in Greece as the monarch, the new seventeen-year-old king first made official visits to London, Paris and St Petersburg. This was perhaps to show deference to the great powers who had made his election possible. On 30 October 1863, he finally arrived at his new kingdom, landing at Piraeus to cheering crowds. King George I of the Hellenes was keen not to make the same mistakes as his predecessor. He learnt to speak Greek, sensibly appointed Greek advisors and was keen that his kingdom would not be overly influenced by Denmark or by other European powers.

The Greek assembly, however, was divided over the details of their constitution. In 1864, the young king showed the colour of his character and good nature. George bravely pointed out that he had only agreed to be king if there was a settled constitution in place; if there was not, then he was well within his rights to leave and go back home – or worse, impose laws at whim. The assembly quickly settled its differences of opinion and George was able to take an oath to defend the new constitution as a constitutional monarch not unlike those in Denmark or the UK.

As part of the new constitution, Greece was the first European country (in modern times) to have universal male suffrage. All men could vote. However, this new proud nation faced a variety of challenges. There was a long-held culture of corruption in Greece. Also, most men were illiterate, yet they truly believed that they were culturally and ethnically descended from, and the inheritors of, Alexander the Great, Plato, Socrates, Leonidas, Agamemnon, Odysseus and the Byzantine Emperors. Therefore, any European minister or outsider who (quite correctly) questioned the validity of this, found themselves open to a frosty reception. Ruling the population was like riding a wave of energetic cultural beliefs about identity and nationalism. Crete was a sticking point for this as the largely Greek population there was still ruled by the Turks. In an effort to help the nationalists unite all the Greek peoples (and territory), King George used his influence with his brother-in-law, the Prince of Wales, to try to gain British support in taking the island. Despite Bertie's efforts, British ministers did not want to get involved, and so the Greek revolt in Crete was brutally put down by the Turks.

The Right Wife

At the outset of his reign, it was apparent that King George was in need of a wife to support him in his new role. Having travelled to Russia in 1863 to thank Tsar Alexander II for his support in the Greek election, George met the Tsar's daughter, Grand Duchess Olga, for the first time. He was seventeen at that time; she was a mere twelve years old. The next time George returned to Russia in 1867, it was as the King of Greece.

On paper, he was visiting his sister Princess Dagmar, who had married the Tsarevich (the future Alexander III), but in truth, he had come to find an appropriate wife. He believed that an alliance with Russia was going to be useful to Greece, and a union with a specifically Orthodox princess was sellable to his largely Orthodox Greek subjects. By then, Olga was just fifteen, but she reportedly fell in love with the new young king – indeed, she was enthusiastically smitten. Her father took some persuading owing to her age, but it was agreed that she would be free to marry King George once she had attained the age of sixteen. She reached this milestone in September 1867 and was married in October in the St Petersburg Winter Palace. After a very short honeymoon in Russia, the new royal couple returned to Greece, and Olga learnt to speak Greek and English within a year.

George and Olga were of course of the same royal house – albeit distantly. He was of the House of Schleswig-Holstein-Sonderburg-Glücksburg, and she was of the House of Schleswig-Holstein-Gottorp, which since the mid-eighteenth century had also adopted the name of Romanov. The founder of the House of Schleswig-Holstein-Gottorp was Prince Adolf of Denmark (1526-1586) who was made Duke of Holstein-Gottorp by his father, Frederick I of Denmark. His descendant, Duke Peter of Holstein-Gottorp, succeeded as Tsar of Russia in 1762 but was deposed by his wife Catherine the Great. That said, the House of Holstein-Gottorp-Romanov (a cadet branch of the Danish House of Oldenburg) sat on the throne of Russia until 1917.

Put more simply, the new King and Queen of Greece were members of different cadet branches of the House of Oldenburg. They were both descended in the male line from King Frederick I of Denmark (1471-1533). These two great cadet branches were now (re-)united in the Greek royal family. Like many in their respective families, King George and Queen Olga were accomplished procreators. Between 1868 and 1888, they had five sons and three daughters, all of whom married other princes or princesses of Europe.

Constitution and Expansion

As King, George promoted and defended the constitution of Greece. This included elections by secret ballot and universal male suffrage (with no property prerequisites). George's familiar relationship to so many powerful European royal families such as Britain, Prussia and Russia (and, to a lesser extent, Denmark) meant that Greece had many friends in diplomacy. However it could also sometimes put her at the centre of international affairs. There was much lawlessness in Greek towns and cities. British tourists (there to look at ancient archaeology) were sometimes kidnapped and held hostage or murdered. Politically, there was much instability in the country. In the eleven years since George's nomination as king in 1863, Greece had more than twenty governments, none of which lasted more than about eighteen months. In order to keep stability and exert any influence he could, George had to support, or at times impose, a minority government. This led to him being accused of behaving like an autocrat in some Greek newspapers at the time.

The second half of the nineteenth century was a time of change in many parts of the eastern Mediterranean and also a time of Greek expansion. The newly found national identity of the Greeks, together with their common Christian faith, created a will to expand territory and reclaim islands and lands around the peninsula. Appetite for this may have started with the British gift of the Ionian Islands in 1864. However, particular attention was on lands originally taken by the Turkish Ottoman Empire centuries earlier, such as Thessaly (north of Greece), Epirus (Greek Albanian border lands) and the island of Crete. Thessaly was ceded to Greece in 1881, but Greece received only part of Epirus (with the help of the influence of Britain and France).

Greece's territorial expansion, however, was stewarded and limited by the great powers of the day, particularly Britain. For example, despite its alliances, Greece was stopped from entering into the Russo-Turkish War (1877-1878) by Britain and France, who likely feared Russian expansion and wanted to avoid upsetting the Ottomans unnecessarily. Having made certain territorial gains after that war, the Greek government and politicians were poised to take an opportunity in the north, where a revolt had taken place in Bulgaria. They mobilised the Greek army, but the British navy swiftly and effectively blockaded Greece to halt any military action. The officer in charge of the blockade was in fact the man that the Greeks had overwhelmingly voted for to be their king – Prince Alfred, Duke of Edinburgh. It is not surprising that the Greeks took notice. To add to the awkwardness of the escalation, the British First Lord of the Admiralty at that time was the Marquess of Ripon. His brother-in-law had been a hostage and murdered by Greek revolutionaries not sixteen years earlier. George had to ask his government to back down.

Olympic Reign

By 1888, King George had reached his silver jubilee year. This included many celebratory events, the highlight of which must have been a special lunch for over five hundred guests held on top of the Acropolis in a massive tent of blue and white. His sister and brother-in-law, the Princess and Prince of Wales, were among the special visitors which of course included the Danish and Russian royal families too. Even dignitaries from the Ottoman Sultan came with gifts of Arabian horses.

Greece was growing and becoming prosperous, and the country entered a period of peace. Greece now had an identity and sense of her place in the world. It became popular to celebrate and indeed recreate its ancient history. The most notable recreation being the first (new) Olympic Games, which were held from 6 to 15 April 1896. The games were famously the creation of the French noble Baron Pierre de Coubertin. In them, 241 athletes from fourteen invited nations took part. All were Europeans with the exception of those from the USA, and around two thirds of the contestants were in fact Greek. The athletes competed in just nine sports (viz: athletics, which we would call track and field; cycling, both road and track fencing; gymnastics; shooting; swimming; tennis; weightlifting; and wrestling). Confusingly, the winners won a silver medal and the runners up a copper medal. The highlight of the games for the Greeks was the marathon victory of Spyridon Louis – a poor mineral water seller and sometime policeman and farmer. He ran from Marathon to the refurbished ancient Panathenaic Stadium. Towards the end of the race, he was met with great cheers as he entered the stadium, and King George's sons, Crown Prince Constantine and Prince George, ran alongside Louis in his last lap. His victory set off great celebrations across all of Greece. (Of course, it should be noted that of the seventeen runners in this first Olympic marathon race, thirteen of them were Greek!) King George had naturally opened the games at the stadium. Crown Prince Constantine had been president of the organising committee, and Prince George had adjudicated the weightlifting – being something of a strong man himself. The success of the games kept them in the popular eye of the Greek people for a long time.

War

Tensions with the Ottomans grew in the face of Greek nationalism and the will to unite the Greeks as a people under one nation. Greek troops were also sent north into Macedonia, an ambitious land grab which sparked a formal declaration of war from the Ottoman Sultan Abdul Hamid II in 1897. Despite the nationwide patriotic support for this expansion into the 'lost' realm of Alexander the Great, the Greek army was woefully underprepared for such a conflict. In fact, it is fortunate that it only lasted thirty days, but its Greek moniker is fitting – the Unfortunate War. They were soundly beaten back by the Ottomans. The resulting border arrangements could have been worse but for the close relationship King George had to Britain and Russia, who brokered the peace. However, Greece had to give up official ambitions in Crete, give other small territorial concessions and pay four million pounds in reparations to the Turks. The Greek peoples of Crete then revolted against Turkish rule, and so King George sent his son Prince George to claim and hold the island for Greece, in spite of the previous peace agreement. The great powers of Europe were not pleased and tried to mediate between the Greeks and the Turks. In 1898, Turkish troops left Crete, and a national Cretan government and Muslim-Christian assembly was established. Prince George, who was still in his twenties, was made governor. He had already proven himself as a man several years earlier when he saved his cousin (the future Tsar Nicholas II) from an assassination attempt in Ōtsu in Japan in 1891. Crete was (and is) a complicated place to govern, and Prince George eventually resigned and returned to Athens in 1906.

The great popularity and esteem in which King George and his family were held by the Greeks now diminished in the wake of territorial loss and humiliating reparations to the enemy. George briefly contemplated abdication in the face of such failure. He regained some respect by bravely surviving an assassination attempt in February 1898 in Phaleron. Coming back from the beach in an open carriage, two gunmen shot at the king. George's first instinct was to shield his daughter Maria who was next to him. Though they and their staff survived, George had the gunmen hunted down and eventually beheaded.

The Goudi Coup

Despite a regaining of respect, the stain of the Unfortunate War remained. A group of disgruntled officers formed a military league which demanded that the Greek royals be stripped of all their military commissions and titles. Pre-empting possible embarrassment, King George's sons resigned their commissions. In August 1909, the Goudi Coup took place in Greece, beginning in a barracks in Goudi just east of Athens. A large group of military officers began demanding immediate reform of the country, its political systems and the armed forces. King George initially was not moved and continued to support the elected government that was in place, but after large public demonstrations and overbearing tension the king was forced to give in and replace his prime minister, although this only caused a stalemate between liberal-republican and conservative-monarchist factions. Eventually the Cretan politician Eleftherios Venizelos was promoted by the coup leaders as someone who would respect liberal values and allow new elections. Venizelos became prime minister in October 1910.

King George and Venizelos were aligned in their beliefs that Greece needed a strong military to redress the humiliation of 1897. Crown Prince Constantine was eventually made commander in chief, and the army and navy were enlarged and improved with the assistance of the British and French. It was obvious to many in Europe that the Ottoman Empire was coming close to collapse. Venizelos allied Greece with other Christian countries in the Balkans who were also hostile to the Ottomans. Montenegro, Serbia and Greece declared war on the Turks in 1912 – the First Balkan War. This campaign was a marked improvement on the previous war. The Greeks won many victories. The people gathered in thousands to cheer their king as he rode triumphant through the streets of Thessaloniki in November 1912. The following year was also to be George's golden jubilee – fifty years on the throne. It is known that, seeing that he was an old man, he intended to abdicate in favour of his eldest son, Crown Prince Constantine, after the celebrations.

Assasination

On the afternoon of 18 March 1913, George took his daily walk in the streets of Thessaloniki. As usual, he had minimal protection as, at that time, he was popular and highly regarded by the people – so there was no thought that extra care would be needed. He was walking near the White Tower (a medieval fortification) with his aide-de-camp discussing his upcoming visit to a German battlecruiser (*Goeben*). They were accompanied by just two policemen, who politely kept their distance.

Reaching the corner of Vasilissis Olgas Avenue and Agia Triada Street, the king was approached from behind by a man in his forties, Alexandros Schinas. Schinas shot George in the back at point-blank range. The king collapsed and was rushed to hospital by carriage, but he died on the way, the bullet having hit his heart. He was sixty-seven. Schinas did not flee and was apprehended by the aide-de-camp and officers. It is said that Schinas asked for their protection from the resulting angry crowd. He is thought to have been an anarchist. However, his profile, motives and background remain largely a mystery. During the subsequent interrogation in prison, he 'fell' out of a window to his death. This may have been suicide. Crown Prince Constantine was away with the army in Epirus, securing yet more successes for Greece. He was eventually informed of his father's assassination and that he was now king.

The king's body was embalmed and shipped back to Athens. He lay in state for three days at the Metropolitan Cathedral with both the Greek and Danish flags draped over the coffin. The Dowager Queen Alexandra of Britain, his sister, was particularly downcast – having also lost her husband three years earlier. The funeral took place at the Cathedral of the Annunciation on 2 April 1913. The next month, the First Balkan War came to an end, having seen much Greek success and territorial expansion. A few years later, a bust of George was erected near where he was assassinated on the street renamed King George Street. The Greek crown passed to Constantine I, whose reign was marked by war and turbulence. Married to the sister of Kaiser Wilhelm II of Germany, he struggled to navigate the deadly politics of the First World War. He abdicated once in 1917 and again in 1922.

With his wife Queen Olga, King George I of the Helenes had four sons after Constantine. The second son, George, married a Bonaparte princess and heiress, Marie. She was a friend and sponsor of Sigmund Freud and was also one of the first people to scientifically research the female orgasm – with varying results! Their third son, Nicholas, married another Russian princess, Archduchess Elena Vladimirovna (granddaughter of Tsar Alexander II). We however will concern our-selves with their fourth son, Andrew, who married Princess Alice of Battenberg. It is also worth mentioning that their fifth son, Christopher, initially married an American actress named Nonnie May Stewart who was older than he and twice married previously! King George I of Greece is buried at the Royal Cemetery at Tatoi Palace on the slopes of Mount Parnitha in Greece.

Figure 24: A photograph of Prince Andrew of Greece and Denmark taken between 1910 and 1920. From the George Grantham Bain Collection, Library of Congress..

Prince Andrew of Greece and Denmark

(grandfather)

Born: *2 February 1882 at Tatoi Palace, Athens*

Died: *3 December 1944 at Hotel Metropole, Monte Carlo*

Spouse: *Princess Alice of Battenberg*

Concurrent British monarchs: *Victoria, Edward VII, George V,*

Edward VIII and George VI

PRINCE ANDREW (ΑΝΔΡÉΑΣ or Andréas) of Greece and Denmark was the fourth son and seventh child of King George I and Queen Olga of Greece. The Tatoi Palace where he was born in 1882 was the summer palace for the Greek royal family. Andrew's father had purchased it and the surrounding estate about ten years earlier with his own money (that is to say, not with funds given to him by the Greek government). Like his other brothers and sisters, Andrew received a solid education and was fluent in several languages: Danish (from his father), Russian (from his mother), English, French and German However, as he grew, he made a special point of only speaking Greek to his family – asserting his identity a man of the Hellenes. It has been argued that, perhaps owing to his tutors (a Mr Dixon for example), his first or best language at an early age was in fact English though. Unlike his father, who held onto his Lutheran faith, Andrew was brought up in the Greek Orthodox Church.

As a young royal prince with so many family connections, he was able to visit the courts of several other countries. He visited his grandfather

King Christian IX of Denmark, his grandfather Grand Duke Constantine of Russia, and his uncle Prince Ernest Augustus of Hanover (then also 3rd Duke of Cumberland in the UK peerage). His teachers and tutors were very strict, and by the time he was a teenager, he was deemed to be quite a cultured and well-educated young man. In line with the tradition of European royals having a close attachment to their native armed forces, he was enrolled at the Evelpides College, the Greek military academy, in Piraeus for training. It was here that he became a college comrade of the future dictator of Greece, Theodoros Pangalos. Prince Andrew suffered from some degree of short sightedness and often wore glasses and then later a monocle. Having successfully passed many military tests and studied politics and military history, Andrew was commissioned as a cavalry officer in the spring of 1901.

Battenberg(s)

A year into his military service, Prince Andrew was invited to accompany his brother Crown Prince Constantine of Greece to the coronation of their aunt Alexandra as Queen of the United Kingdom alongside the new King Edward VII at Westminster Abbey. Because of Britain's place in the world at that time and the fact that the late Queen Victoria was related to nearly every royal house in Europe, the event was widely attended by princes and princesses from all over the world. It was on this visit in 1902 that he met one of the British royal family's extended relatives, Princess Alice of Battenberg. He was twenty at the time and struck an impressive figure – tall, slim, relatively handsome and reputedly very charming. Alice was just seventeen at the time and was also attractive, fairly tall and intelligent. As a child, she had overcome deafness and had learnt to lip read perfectly in many different languages. The two quickly fell passionately in love. In those days, it was exceptionally rare for two young royal people to fall in love organically; it was nearly always an arranged match by their respective fathers for political reasons. Alice and Andrew, by contrast, were passionate about each other. She compared him to a Greek god. Within a month of becoming acquainted in London as the coronation was being prepared, they were engaged despite her youth.

Alice belonged to a slightly scandalous morganatic branch of the grand-ducal family of Hesse-Darmstadt, the House of Battenberg. The House of Hesse-Darmstadt was itself a branch of the House of Hesse, sometime Prince-Electors of Hesse in the Holy Roman Empire. Alice's grandfather had been Prince Alexander of Hesse and by Rhine (1823-1888). Instead of marrying an equal (viz: a princess or royal highness), he took to wife one of his sister's ladies-in-waiting, Countess Julia Hauke, daughter of a recently ennobled Polish general (who had fought for Napoleon). Because the couple were not equals, their union was frowned upon by their families. Their marriage also had negative legal repercussions as their issue were disqualified from being part of the succession to the throne of Hesse. Despite this, Julia's in-laws were not heartless; the Grand Duke of Hesse-Darmstadt gave her the title of Countess of Battenberg then later Princess of Battenberg and the style of Serene Highness in 1858. Their children and descendants would also bear this title. Battenberg is a small town within the state of Hesse. In fact, there had been a medieval family who were Counts of Battenberg dating back to around 1200, so the title was more of a revival. However, it never completely blocked out the whiff of scandal. Julia and Prince Alexander's eldest son, Louis, was a particularly driven and ambitious man.

His Serene Highness Prince Louis of Battenberg had the advantage of being (by a whisker) a European royal, but without the funds or the kudos or the influence. His cousin, Louis (future Grand Duke of Hesse), had married Princess Alice of the United Kingdom, daughter of Queen Victoria. Through this connection, Prince Louis was able to socialise with the British royal family, particularly with some of Victoria's children and grandchildren. Like them, he enjoyed playing practical jokes, some of which may have involved putting a sleeping donkey into someone's bed or covering the future King of England in flour. He became a naturalised British subject and joined the Royal Navy, where he began a meteoric career. He entered as a cadet aboard HMS *Victory* in 1863. (It was permanently moored by then.) Being an ambitious man, Prince Louis needed a good and impressive match. What better way to further ingratiate himself with the British royal family than to join it?! In 1884, he married Queen Victoria's grand-daughter, Princess Victoria of Hesse and by Rhine (the daughter of his cousin the Grand Duke and Princess Alice). They had four children together, all of whom, in Battenberg tradition, made good marriages. Their first child in 1885 was named Princess Alice after her grandmother. Their second daughter, Princess Louise, became Queen of Sweden by marrying the future Gustav VI Adolf of Sweden. Prince Louis and Victoria's eldest son, George, went on to marry a Romanov countess (a year before the fall of the Tsar), and their second son, Louis, went on to marry an English heiress, Edwina Ashley. Today, he is more familiar to us as Louis, 1st Earl Mountbatten of Burma, who, like his father, had a glittering naval career.

His Serene Highness Prince Louis of Battenberg's undeniable closeness with the royal family certainly helped his rise through the senior levels of the Royal Navy. By 1902, he was a commodore and director of naval intelligence, and his wife's cousin, Edward (Bertie), was preparing for his coronation as King of the United Kingdom.

Marriage

The coronation of Edward VII in 1902 had to be briefly postponed owing to health problems of the king. A month later, the show was back on. The newly smitten young couple, Princess Alice of Battenberg and Prince Andrew of Greece and Denmark enjoyed a few blissful days together after the coronation. Then Andrew had to return to his reg-iment in Greece, and Alice followed her family home to Darmstadt in Germany. With Alice having a military father and George being so active in his military duties, it seemed a perfect match. Nearly a year of difficult separation followed their meeting, but the distance did not dwindle their love. They were finally married on 6 October 1903 in Darmstadt in a civil ceremony with religious ceremonies (both Greek Orthodox and Lutheran) taking place later. Their first home together was the Battenberg apartments in the Old Palace, Darmstadt, the official residence of the Grand Dukes of Hesse. George had received permission from his father to serve in the Hessian army so as to be near to his wife.

In 1904, Andrew and Alice journeyed to Greece and were officially met by his parents, King George and Queen Olga. They set up a home in the royal palace in Athens and regularly stayed at the royal palace and estate at Tatoi, where Andrew eventually had their own house built by 1907. They lived a relatively modest life for royals. They were surrounded by family and took long horse rides in the Greek countryside, and Andrew served as a Greek cavalry officer. At the time, Andrew seems to have been a very caring and dutiful husband and a great lover of their dogs (which he treated as if they were his own children). He was present at the birth of their first two daughters, Princesses Marguerite and Theodora (in 1905 and 1906, respectively).

By 1906, Andrew was a cavalry commander with the responsibility of mustering and training recruits from the surrounding hills. Both he and Alice were often abroad either in Hesse, Denmark, Sweden, Russia, Spain or Britain visiting relations or attending their weddings to other royals. Andrew and Alice attended the wedding of King Alfonso of Spain to Alice's cousin, Victoria Eugenie of Battenberg, in Madrid in 1906. They then returned to London to stay with Edward VII and Queen Alexandra – whom they had remained close with since they met at their coronation. In 1907, they also travelled to Russia and attended the royal wedding of Andrew's Romanov niece to Prince William of Sweden. They really were related to everyone!

The Army

In Greece, Andrew and his brothers were subject to scrutiny in the press. Republican sentiment often argued that, despite their involvement in the military, they were a burden on Greek taxpayers – which in reality was far from true. Furthermore, some military officers did not take it well that the young princes were given ranks and positions above them, when they may have had more experience. The Military League, which formed against the government in 1909, certainly held that as one of its many grudges. As we have seen, following the Goudi Coup, the king's brothers were required to resign all their military offices – much to Andrew's dismay. Furthermore, the Cretan politician Eleftherios Venizelos became prime minister of Greece.

Andrew had always been a military man. Now, he was barred from serving in his own country's armed forces. His sense of purpose must have been knocked, and he withdrew into himself. He could not bear the idea of appearing as a Greek royal in public without his military uniform. He remained in Greece but shunned public duties or attendances as much as possible. On Christmas Eve 1909, a fire destroyed much of the Royal Palace in Athens. The official royal residence had to switch to the crown prince's palace. In the meantime Andrew and Alice moved to Corfu. In 1910, they received a visit from Andrew's aunt, Queen Alexandra of the United Kingdom, after which Andrew and the family travelled back to London for a reunion of the Battenbergs and their families. He considered staying and settling in London, away from the precariousness of the political situation in Greece, but eventually he returned, despite the difficulties. In June 1911, Alice and Andrew's third child, Cecile, was born at Tatoi.

Other than the King and Queen of Greece and their daughter, the princess royal (Sophie), the royal family still refused to take part in public engagements unless they were allowed to be in military uniform. Though they were attempting to make a point, it began to look quite petulant. After some persuading, Andrew and his brothers eventually and reluctantly turned up to a naval ball in civilian clothes in late 1911, but they remained bitter and all regularly travelled abroad. However, with the start of the First Balkan War in 1912, it became necessary to re-enlist the help and support of the Greek princes in the military. Andrew and his brother were returned to senior ranks of the armed forces, and his eldest brother the crown prince was even made commander in chief. Andrew was a lieutenant colonel in the Hellenic cavalry. Princess Alice was involved in the setting up of field hospitals. Andrew threw himself into his duties and saw action in Macedonia, Ioannina, and Thessaloniki – getting his promotion to colonel in November 1912. The prospects for Greece and, with it, the popularity of the royal family were on the rise.

Success in war, however, was overshadowed by the assassination of Andrew's father King George on 18 March 1913 in Thessaloniki. Politically, it helped legitimise Greek control over newly won territory in Macedonia though. It seemed that hostilities were at an end with the Treaty of London in May 1913. For Andrew, there was an early inheritance. His father had left him several thousand pounds as well as the Greek palace of Mon Repos on the island of Corfu. Just a month after the peace treaty, however, war broke out in the Balkans again. Andrew took part in the battle against Bulgarian forces at Kilkis-Lachanas, where the Greek forces were victorious.

Family Politics

Despite Greece's successful national expansion and victory over her enemies, there was slight division within the royal family. A quarrel broke out between Andrew's wife, Alice, and his sister, the Princess Royal Sophie, regarding the maintenance and management of the field hospitals with which they were both involved. Andrew was surprised and enraged when his brother came down on the side of Sophie and accused Alice of having exceeded her duties. No family is without politics. Following the war, Andrew and Alice headed to London – perhaps to get away from the family. While there, their cousin King George

V decorated Alice with the Royal Red Cross in late 1913 for her services to humanity during the Balkan Wars. Also, as is custom, Andrew dutifully returned his father's British decorations to King George V. (Usually items such as mantles and collars from British chivalric orders get returned after the recipient dies.) Though they seemed to have time for shopping and having their portraits painted (by the great Philip de Laszlo MVO), Andrew was concerned about the international political situation in Europe, and they returned to Greece.

Once back in Greece, on 26 June 1914, Alice gave birth to a fourth daughter, Princess Sophie (perhaps named after her sister-in-law to heal past wounds), at their home, Mon Repos, on Corfu. Just two days later, Archduke Franz Ferdinand of Austria was assassinated together with his wife while visiting Sarajevo in Bosnia-Herzegovina – sparking the First World War. With the great and mighty powers of Europe declaring war on each other, Greece was in a difficult position. King Constantine I, Andrew's elder brother, wanted to keep Greece effectively neutral and out of the war. Meanwhile, the prime minister, Venizelos, hoped to enter the war on the side of the British and French – particularly against the Ottomans, Greece's natural enemy. Constantine had long believed that his country had been overstretched during the Balkan crisis, and the idea of fighting on two fronts (against Germany and Austria-Hungary in the north and the Ottoman Empire to the east) frightened him. He also had potential family reasons for attempting to stay neutral. He was related to the King of England and the Tsar of Russia, but the Kaiser of Germany was his brother-in-law. Greece would have to walk a tightrope if she were to remain neutral for the duration of the war. Constantine dismissed Venizelos after he allowed Allied ships to dock at Thessaloniki in 1915. This formed a great schism in Greek politics. Venizelos went north to Macedonia, where he formed his own government in 1916.

The First World War: A Difficult Neutrality

Both sides in WWI, the Allied Powers (or Entente) and the Central Powers, were concerned that Greece would choose to fight on the enemy side. Prince Andrew had been posted to Thessaloniki with his regiment. While there, both he and Alice did their best to try and persuade British officers and diplomats that Constantine was not pro-German but was merely trying to keep Greece out of the conflict. Subsequently, in 1916, Constantine sent Andrew on a diplomatic trip to do the same in London and Paris – with little success. The Entente was not convinced of Greek neutrality. Perhaps as a direct consequence, Allied troops under French command landed in Athens towards the end of 1916. This was politically awkward as, from a Greek perspective, this could easily be seen as an invasion. The disembarking Allied troops were fired upon by disgruntled Greeks, and the French navy retaliated by bombing Athens. Princess Alice took shelter in the palace cellars with her four daughters. After the Athens incident, all trust between the Allies and Greece were shattered, and the Entente navies blockaded Greece, which led to food shortages. Queen Sophia of Greece (herself a German princess and sister of the Kaiser) and the Greek princesses had to organise soup kitchens for Greek children.

Whilst the 1917 Russian Revolution may have been disastrous for the Romanovs, it also had far-reaching, negative effects for the Glücksburgs of Greece. Tsar Nicholas II had been the only true member of the Allies to have supported Greece. He was of the same family line as King Constantine I and Prince Andrew and a cousin as well. Furthermore, his wife, the Tsarina, was a cousin to Princess Alice. Because of the Tsar's abdication (and subsequent murder), Greece lost its only friend in the Allied camp. The result was that the British and French put pressure on King Constantine I to abdicate in favour of his second son, Alexander I, which he did under threat of invasion in June 1917. His eldest son, Crown Prince George, was thought of as too pro-German and so was seen by the Entente as potentially untrustworthy. Constantine

and the crown prince were forced into exile, while the politically inexperienced Alexander I of Greece (in his early twenties) had most of his
powers opportunistically stripped away by Prime Minister Venizelos.
Andrew was disappointed that he had not been considered by the
Allies as a replacement monarch, especially with his and Alice's British
connections, but he was probably considered less politically malleable.
Andrew and Alice, unlike the rest of the family, were initially permitted
to stay in Athens, perhaps owing to the old comradery Andrew had
once shared with Venizelos. However, the new regime looked to sever
all ties between the new young king and his family; Andrew and his
family were soon forced to flee to exile in Switzerland later in 1917.

Exile

Andrew managed to pawn several items, including cars, to make sure
that his family had some money while in exile. He took the family to St
Moritz and then on to Lucerne. The exiled royals entered into a state of
depression at this time. Because she was a British subject, Alice was able
to go to England to visit her parents. The Battenbergs and the Greek
royals could only look on in horror over the next year or two as many
of their Romanov cousins fled into exile or were murdered. Famously,
Tsar Nicholas II, his wife and children were all murdered in 1918. Two
of Andrew's Romanov brothers-in-law were also murdered, along with
his uncle (his mother's brother). Two of Alice's aunts (including the
Tsarina) were killed as well. Depressed and frustrated, Andrew constantly appealed to be allowed to return to his home in Greece but was
denied by the Greek government. Meanwhile, the Allies, seeing him
and his family as potential German agents, did nothing to help.

It was also around this time (earlier in 1917) that anti-German sentiment was felt in Britain, and George V changed the royal name from
Saxe-Coburg und Gotha to Windsor. Similarly, German princely families living in Britain also changed their surnames and abandoned their
German titles. Thus the Battenburgs became the Mountbattens; Alice's

father, Prince Louis of Battenberg, became merely Louis Mountbatten, 1st Marquess of Milford Haven.

Even in 1919, after the war, Andrew's continuing requests for permission to return to Greece were denied. To complicate the Greek situation, young King Alexander died suddenly in 1920. On 2 October, while walking in the gardens of the family estate at Tatoi, one of his dogs attacked (or was attacked by) a pet monkey, which belonged to one of the gardeners. The dog was a German Shepherd named Fritz, which is rather startling considering his owner was a king who had been appointed on a tidal wave of anti-German sentiment. (The monkey was a Barbary macaque.) Having inherited the family love of dogs, Alexander tried to separate the quarrelling beasts. During the scuffle, another monkey bit him multiple times on the leg and on his body. He did not consider the wounds serious, but that night the wounds got infected, which eventually led to sepsis. The king was very ill. Amputation of the leg was considered. Alexander's grandmother, Queen Olga, was given permission to return from exile to tend to the ailing king. She was delayed and arrived just hours after he died on 25 October 1920. The death of the young king, plus further ongoing conflicts with Turkey (the Greco-Turkish War of 1919-1922), lead to yet another political crisis in Greece. Venizelos was defeated in the elections held in November that year, and he too went into exile. Another referendum on the Greek monarchy was held, and King Constantine I was restored to the throne that same month.

Return to Greece

The royal family returned to Athens to much popular acclaim and cheering crowds. In December 1920, Andrew and Alice were finally able to return and settle at their home, Mon Repos, on Corfu. Andrew was able to return to the Greek army and was promoted to major general. Around this time, it was discovered that Alice was pregnant with their fifth child. At home at Mon Repos on 10 June 1921, Alice gave birth to

Prince Φίλιππος/Phílippos (Prince Philip of Greece and Denmark) on the dining table – presumably it was a convenient location at the time! At last, Andrew had a son.

Feeling a proud sense of achievement after the birth of a son and heir, Andrew was put in command of a barely-trained and undisciplined force of soldiers from Greece's new provinces. He led these units in battle at Eskisehir with success, which got him a promotion to lieutenant general. Following this, he was ordered to advance into Anatolia, the mainland peninsula of Turkey, but he was badly defeated at the battle of Sakarya in August and September 1921. This is often known as the Officers' Battle, owing to the unusually high number of officers killed or wounded – about 75%. The Greek advance into Turkey was halted, and the Greek army suffered casualties of over thirty-eight thousand during just twenty-one days of battle.

Andrew had a temper and was very strong willed. During the battle, he had openly disagreed with the general staff, acted on his own initiative and ignored orders. He even attempted to resign a number of times. Eventually, he was given leave, and he left the front just three days before the end of the battle. Subsequently, in the aftermath of the humiliating defeat, Andrew was blamed and accused of desertion. In a lapse of judgment scarily familiar to us today, Prince Andrew unwisely agreed to an interview with journalists, in which he gave perhaps too clear a picture of himself and made strong antigovernment accusations. Needless to say, this did not help his situation. Despite returning to the army, his reputation was clearly damaged. He eventually went back home to Corfu to lick his wounds. While he laid low at Mon Repos, his wife and daughters went to the wedding of their uncle, Alice's brother, Lord Louis Mountbatten, to Edwina Ashley in July 1922 at St Margaret's in Westminster. Meanwhile, Andrew had returned to his military duties with the Greek army in Turkey, where he observed that the military situation for Greece was becoming dire.

Anatolia

In mid-1922, as things got worse for the Greek army engaged in a potentially unwinnable conflict in Anatolia, Andrew decided to go to Athens to see his brother, the king, in the hope of changing the direction of the war and avoiding failure. This act, however, was seen by the people as desertion (again) by Prince Andrew. Opposition to the royal family was growing once again, and the war's setbacks and the vast numbers of wounded soldiers wandering the streets of Athens did not help. Andrew advised King Constantine I to abdicate (again) in favour of his son, Crown Prince George. This idea caused arguments between Andrew and his royal brothers who did not want to give ground to the republicans or revolutionaries. Meanwhile, in September 1922, the war came to a climax; Greek forces were pushed out of Anatolia, and the largely-Christian city of Smyrna was occupied by (mainly) Muslim Turkish forces and deliberately put to the torch in a bloody kind of reprisal. It has been estimated that between 15,000 and 125,000 Greek and Armenian Christian inhabitants of Smyrna were burned, killed or raped while trying to escape the city. It was a massacre – a genocide of monumental proportions.In the end, nearly all the Christian communities of Anatolia were wiped out, their citizens either killed or expelled and made refugees. This is known as the Great Catastrophe in Greece. The stories of these atrocities shocked the press and the Western world. Sensing that the eyes of the world were upon them and frustrated with the current situation, Greek army and naval officers took matters into their own hands. They removed the Greek government and set up a revolutionary committee in its place. Constantine I went into exile in Italy with many other Greek royals, and his son was declared King George II of Greece.

Once again, Andrew decided to stay in Greece – perhaps foolishly. He was given assurance by the government that he would not be interfered with. However, by October 1922, he was under surveillance and was questioned about his conduct in Anatolia. When he was summoned back to Athens to give testimony, he was quickly put under arrest for desertion and disobeying direct orders. If found guilty, he would face possible execution. In the wake of the coup, several key government officials of the former regime had been arrested – Andrew and eight others. These individuals (along with the now-exiled Constantine) were deemed responsible for the Great Catastrophe, and the revolutionary committee, harnessing public outrage, planned to make an example of these men and put them on trial for treason. This was soon known as the Trial of the Six (November 1922) as six were quickly sentenced to death and shot. Two others received life imprisonment sentences. Despite widespread international condemnation of such a trial, the Greek military government proceeded. Andrew's trial began in December. He defended himself and had an answer to every accusation. However, he was found guilty of desertion and disobeying orders anyway – with the implication that he had lost Greece the Battle of Sakarya. Pressure was exerted on his behalf by several foreign governments, particularly the British and possibly even his old comrade and former prime minister of Greece, Venizelos. The judges accepted, as a mitigating circumstance, Prince Andrew's lack of command experience with large forces – which in itself was humiliating. Instead of death, Andrew was stripped of his Greek citizenship and sentenced to life in exile. Having made a final trip to Mon Repos to collect their possessions, Andrew was hurriedly shipped out of Greece on board British light cruiser HMS *Calypso* after sentencing. Andrew, Alice and the children made their way to exile first in Italy and eventually Paris.

Exile (Again)

Humiliated, bitter and completely without money, Andrew, his poor family, and six servants had little to live on but their name and wealthy relations. Within days of his exile, Andrew departed for Britain. George V, who had been famously nervous about giving his cousin Tsar Nicholas II asylum for fear of public opinion, was also nervous about giving asylum to his other cousin Prince Andrew of Greece – whose colours were well and truly in the mud at this point in time. However, asylum was granted, and Andrew thanked the king personally.

Andrew had to look to members of his family to support him. A natural but surprising financial supporter was Princess Marie Bonaparte, the wife of his brother Prince George. She was the descendant and heiress of Emperor Napoleon I's younger brother, Jerome Bonaparte, 1st Prince of Canino and Musignano. She was also the heiress of her maternal grandfather, Francois Blanc, a wealthy entrepreneur and casino owner. He was the first to establish a casino in Monte Carlo, Monaco. In short, she had a lot of money. She put up Andrew and his family in a house near her own in Saint-Cloud near Paris and paid for the education of the children.

The exiled king, Constantine I, died in Palermo in January 1923. Andrew was visiting his younger brother, Prince Christopher, and his rich American wife, Nancy Stewart, in the USA at the time. While in the States, Andrew did himself no favours by making spontaneous bitter statements to the press about his treatment in his trial. Back in Greece, King George II was deposed and told to leave the country in December 1923. A few months later, during the following year, Greece was formally declared a republic. It felt like the lid was shut on a possible return to Greece for Andrew and the other Greek royals. Still the legal owner of Mon Repos on Corfu, Andrew made a tactical decision to rent it out to his brother-in-law, Lieutenant Lord Louis Mountbatten KCVO RN, to give it an air of British protection. Although not entirely poor or homeless, it seemed that Andrew and Alice would have to live off the generosity of three of their rich sisters-in-law: Princess Marie Bonaparte, Nancy Stewart, and Edwina Ashley (Lady Louis Mountbatten). As an ex-royal with expensive tastes and no money, Andrew sometimes had difficulties with his creditors. Their life in Saint-Cloud was a nice one however. Surrounded by other royal relatives exiled from Greece and Russia, they would meet at Marie Bonaparte's for Sunday lunch and take walks in the park. Throughout the 1920s, Andrew and Alice hoped to find rich husbands for their two eldest daughters among the gentry and aristocracy of Britain. However, having no fortune, husbands were not found.

In the late 1920s, Andrew attempted to exonerate himself and redeem his reputation by writing and publishing a book that was effectively his own account of what happened and went wrong in the Greco-Turkish Wars. *Towards Disaster* was written in Greek and translated into English by Princess Alice. It did not have the desired effect however and received negative critiques. Threats were made about the seizure of his home Mon Repos. Louis Mountbatten and his wife, Edwina, had to ship more than thirty crates of Andrew's possessions out of the house in order to prevent them from being stolen – or so Andrew could sell them for money. Andrew sued the Greek authorities over the ownership of the house. He won in 1934 but could not afford the upkeep and so had to give Mon Repos to his nephew George II in return for some annual income. After the fall of the Greek dictator, General Pangalos, Alice and others pushed for Andrew to get appointed as the new president of the Green republic. Andrew was reluctant, and this did not occur.

Princess Alice's Illness

Since his first and second exiles, there had been a lot of pressure on Andrew and Alice's marriage. They had been through a lot together – wars, revolutions, politics and trials, and it is easy to imagine that some bitterness and depression had developed too. Not surprisingly, cracks in the marriage began to show in the late 1920s. At one point, Alice was in love with another man (an Englishman), but she also began to soothe her depression and failing marriage with religion. After their twenty-fifth wedding anniversary, Alice converted to Greek Orthodoxy and became more and more mystical, reportedly believing herself to be a saint or even affianced to Christ himself. Andrew found it difficult to cope with his wife's strange state of mind and called for the assistance of their female family members, including Alice's mother, now the Dowager Marchioness of Milford Haven, and his sister-in-law and benefactor, Princess Marie Bonaparte.

Marie Bonaparte was a friend and sponsor of Sigmund Freud. She was interested in the new science of psychoanalysis, particularly anything to do with sex. In fact, she herself underwent two surgical operations to move her clitoris closer to her vagina so that she might experience penetrative orgasms during sexual congress. This of course did not actually work. Nevertheless, Andrew had turned to her for help. Under Freud's advice, Alice was taken to be treated by Dr Ernst Simmel at his clinic near Berlin. He diagnosed her with schizophrenia, supposedly brought on by powerful sexual urges. The treatment was to x-ray her ovaries to suppress her sex drive and bring on early menopause. After eight weeks of this torturous treatment, she discharged herself from the clinic to return to the family at Saint-Cloud in the spring of 1930. However, shortly after returning, she began preaching her outlandish beliefs again including her special relationship with Jesus. Andrew began to consider having her committed to an asylum.

Meanwhile, the couple's third daughter, Cecile, had become close to her cousin, George Donatus, heir to the Grand Duchy of Hesse. The family was to travel to Darmstadt in May 1930 to celebrate their official engagement. Andrew was therefore able to use this journey and event to have Alice forcibly hospitalised at Kreuzlingen in Switzerland shortly after the engagement party. She remained there until September 1932, receiving only one visit from Andrew in that time. Somewhat sadly, during her time in hospital, all four of Alice and Andrew's daughters were married, all to German princes in true family tradition: Sophie to Prince Christoph of Hesse in December 1930; Cecile to Georg Donatus, hereditary Grand Duke of Hesse in February 1931; Margarita to Gottfried, Prince of Hohenlohe-Langenburg in April 1931 and Theodora to Prince Berthold, Margrave of Baden in August 1931.

During Alice's treatment in Switzerland, Andrew only kept in contact with the doctors. He had largely ceased to care or worry about his 'mad' wife. In his own way, he had moved on. Andrew entrusted their youngest child and only son, Philip, to his maternal grandmother, Lady Milford Haven. It is at this point that Andrew began to live life like he had few cares. He moved to the French Riviera and travelled between there, Paris and his daughters' homes in Germany. He became a regular in Monte Carlo, and soon earned a reputation as something of a playboy. He took up with a mistress. When Alice was free from hospital or between treatments, she expressed a desire to return to married life, but Andrew was not moved by this. It is thought that they did not meet in person again until as late as 1937. That year in Bonn, she also got to meet Cecile and Philip (who was a schoolboy at Gordonstoun in Scotland by then) for the first time in years. Most family members thought, after their meeting Alice again in Bonn, that she was cured. However, her mother, Lady Milford Haven, thought it best to continue the treatments, even if only to monitor her.

The 1930s

Through the 1930s, one can imagine that Andrew became bitter and lonely. Politics in Greece were not improving, and he continually made a fool of himself in the eyes of the Greek press by behaving rashly – like taking an unofficial trip to Cyprus, which became quite official when Greek Cypriots flocked to him, thinking it signalled Greek intentions on the island. This was viewed as something of a minor diplomatic incident. He reportedly drank more than he used to, seeking solace in wine and women. His mistress was a French actress named Andrée Lafayette – the beautiful daughter of a train driver who was known to have monetary aspirations. It is thought that that is where much of Andrew's little money went. He only sent his son Philip a pound per week and sent nothing to his wife, who received an allowance from Edwina (Lady Louis Mountbatten).

On 16 November 1937, disaster struck. Cecile was known to be Andrew's favourite daughter. While traveling by plane from Munich to London, Cecile, her husband, their two sons and newborn child (another son), whom it is thought she gave birth to while the plane was in the air, were all killed when the plane crashed near Ostend in Belgium. The crew and other passengers (including Cecile's mother-in-law) also died. Cecile's fourteen-month-old daughter, Joanna, had not been on the plane and so was the only family member to survive. However, she died of meningitis two years later in 1939. In the years preceding the crash, Andrew had also lost two of his brothers, Nicholas and Christopher (in 1938 and 1940, respectively), and his sister, Maria (also in 1940).

By the outbreak of the Second World War in 1939, Andrew's son, Philip, was training as an officer in the Royal Navy. The oncoming war was sure to split the family (again) as most of Andrew's sons-in-law and several other relatives were in the German military. Andrew made his final trip to Athens in late 1939. He met Alice and other members of his family for the last time, after which he returned to the French Riviera. The invasion of France by Germany in 1940 shocked many by its speed and success. Two of Andrew's sons-in-law were injured in the process (fighting for Nazi Germany). Andrew's brother and sister-in-law, George and Marie Bonaparte, fled France for England, advising Andrew to do the same, but he did not act quickly enough and found himself stuck on the south coast of France with his expensive mistress.

Monte Carlo

Effectively trapped and cut off from family (but in one of the world's nicer parts), he acquired a yacht from a friend and from 1940 onward lived most of his days on the water, though eventually he was forced to move into the Hotel Metropole in Monte Carlo. Though still living quite extravagantly, Andrew was getting into serious debt and feeling so isolated that his health declined. He is thought by then to have been an alcoholic, suffering as he was from atherosclerosis and palpitations. He died on 3 December 1944, presumably of a heart attack in his hotel room after attending one last party. Just three years later, his son was married to the future Queen of England. In 1946, Andrew's nephew George II was restored to the Greek throne. Andrew's ashes were then repatriated from Nice to the royal burial site at Tatoi, where they remain.

Princess Alice continued to live a religious life – virtually as a nun. She devoted herself to charitable works and did not leave Athens, even during the German occupation during the war. Unlike several in her family, she was not at all antisemitic and opposed the German persecutions and roundups. She actually hid a small Jewish family in her old home at great personal risk. At the end of the German occupation, the British sent a minister to Athens in late 1944 to see if Alice, the future mother-in-law to their future sovereign, was alright or if she needed anything. It was the future prime minister, Harod MacMillan, who found her in squalid conditions yet uncomplaining and content. When asked if she had enough food, she merely exclaimed that they had enough bread but hardly any sugar, tea or tinned food. MacMillan sent a large food parcel, which was met by tears of joy as Alice's household had been deprived of meat and indeed of any proper food for months.

Alice later attended her son's wedding to Princess Elizabeth at Westminster Abbey in 1947. As part of the marriage, Philip renounced his Greek titles and rights and changed his name to Mountbatten, his mother's family's new name. In the years that followed, Alice also rekindled a closeness with her daughters, who were ostracised in many parts of the world, having all been married to active Nazis. After the restoration of the monarchy in Greece, Alice received a Greek army pension as the widow of a general. She also still had monthly allowances from the Countess Mountbatten of Burma as well as her own sister, Louise. The problem was that she constantly gave away all the money she received either to the needy or to the church, saving little or nothing for herself. Despite her increasingly monastic lifestyle, pilgrimages and eccentric behaviour, she was still related to many of the royal families of Europe and played a small visiting role in those courts.

Princess Alice of Battenberg (Princess Andrew of Greece and Denmark) died on 5 December 1969 while staying at her son's family's home in Buckingham Palace. She was initially buried in the royal crypt at St George's Chapel in Windsor, which seemed somehow appropriate given she was born at Windsor Castles. However, according to her wishes, her remains were eventually moved to the convent church of St Mary Magdalene in Gethsemane, Jerusalem, in 1988. A few years later, in 1994, Prince Philip and his sister Sophie visited Jerusalem and attended a ceremony in which the State of Israel honoured their mother as one of the Righteous Among the Nations for having hidden a Jewish family during WWII. In 2010, Alice was honored as a British Hero of the Holocaust.

Figure 25: A photograph of assembled Mountbatten family members taken c. 2 November 1923.

Top Row Left to Right: The Crown Prince of Sweden (future King Gustav VI Adolf), Lord Louis Mountbatten (formerly Prince Louis of Battenberg, future 1st Earl Mountbatten of Burma), George Mountbatten (2nd Marquess of Milford Haven, formerly Prince George of Battenberg), Prince Andrew of Greece and Denmark.
Middle Row Left to Right: Louise Mountbatten (later Queen of Sweden), Lady Louis Mountbatten (née Edwina Ashley), The Marchioness of Milford Haven (née Countess Nadejda Mikhailovna de Torby), Princess Andrew of Greece and Denmark
(née Princess Alice of Battenberg).
Bottom Centre: The Dowager Marchioness of Milford Haven
(formerly Princess Victoria of Hesse and by Rhine).
Photo used by Central News, 1923, appearing in Beagle Postcards.

7 – *The House of Mountbatten-Windsor*

To BELIEVE THAT human history is the product of a shifting of the great geopolitical tectonic plates of civilisation or that it is somehow changed by slow collective undercurrents of the masses is unwise and borderline wrong. The fate of a nation's history can be turned by the decision of a handful of people or by even the tastes and preferences of just one person. Therefore, there is an element of individual choice, chance and luck to all aspects of history from the siege of Troy to the recent conflict in Ukraine. We will find this true in our own individual lives if we really ponder them; so much has hinged on individual decisions. Our prosperity or misfortune has come about by means of the choices we have made, the lucky or unlucky happenstances we've encountered and the opportunities that we have been able to grab.

The twentieth century was momentous for the fate of the world for innumerable reasons. Many of the wars, revolutions, assassinations, genocides and peace deals might have gone very differently if one or two people had made a slightly different decision or were out of the equation altogether. In the case of the British royal family, the abdication of Edward the VIII in 1936 stands out as the single most impactful decision of the modern era. It changed everything. When he stepped down, in favour of his younger brother, George VI, so that he might marry his twice divorced lover, Wallis Simpson, this also meant that George's eldest daughter and heir, Elizabeth, would one day be queen.

Arguably, Elizabeth's choice of husband was the second most influential decision for the royal family in the twentieth century. In 1936, this

Figure 26: Princess Elizabeth and Princess Margaret being 'taught' croquet on a visit to Britannia Royal Naval College, Dartmouth, in Devon in July 1939. Prince Philip is on the far right. Princess Elizabeth is the girl in the foreground. They were 18 and 13, respectively. From the collection of Britannia Royal Naval College.

was not a question that needed an immediate answer as she was still quite young when Edward abdicated. Nevertheless, it was an important question that loomed on the near horizon as Elizabeth would come of age in 1944. When George VI took the throne, however, there were more concerning matters facing Britain. War was coming again.

By 1945, Britain had fought two world wars against Germany. During the first of these, the royal family had changed their name from Saxe-Coburg und Gotha to Windsor in order to sound less German. The majority of British people, having been bruised by Germany twice inside twenty-five years and still clearing the rubble from blitzed cities all over the kingdom, were decidedly anti-German in their attitudes. It is surprising therefore that the future head of the British monarchy should have ended up marrying someone with such prevalent German roots and family connections.

Princess Elizabth's mother was known to favour the idea of Elizabth marrying a wealthy English aristocrat from the existing blood stock of them in the English countryside. Netflix's *The Crown* has popularised the theory that a family friend and fellow racehorse enthusiast, Henry

Herbert, Lord Porchester, a childhood friend and the future 7th Earl of Carnarvon, was the favorite. Almost certainly, a Greek prince was not part of the initial plan. However, it is clear to most that, from the beginning, Princess Elizabeth only had eyes for one man. In 1939, the king and queen, together with their young daughters, were there to perform a royal inspection at Dartmouth Royal Naval College. Prince Philip's maternal uncle, Lord Louis Mountbatten, a senior naval officer and distant cousin to King George VI, engineered things so that his nephew would be put in charge of looking after the princesses. Philip was eighteen; Elizabeth was a mere thirteen. The royal group played croquet on the lawns. This famous moment is thought to have been a turning point in their relationship – the moment when Princess Elizabeth began to cast her eye on the tall, blonde and handsome young naval officer, Philip. Contrary to popular belief, this was not their first encounter. That had been years earlier as children at the royal wedding between Prince George, Duke of Kent (Elizabth's paternal uncle), and Princess Marina of Greece and Denmark (Philip's first cousin) in 1934 at Westminster Abbey. Little could the two children have known then that they would return to the same church together just thirteen years later. After their famous encounter among the croquet wickets, Elizabeth and Philip began corresponding by letter. At some point during their correspondence in the early part of the Second World War, Princess Elizabeth determined that there would be no other contender for her hand than Philip. After meeting the Greek prince, the socialite and politician Sir Henry (Chips) Channon, who was close to Elizabeth's uncle, wrote in his diary as early as 1941 that Philip was earmarked to be her prince consort one day and that his serving in the navy was part of that too. However, Channon privately objected to the match. He thought the two were too closely related, as the couple were third cousins via descent from Queen Victoria and second cousins via descent from Christian IX of Denmark. He also thought that Philip's maternal family had strains of madness and bad luck.

We have already seen how there was difficulty with Philip's name: Schleswig-Holstein-Sonderburg-Glücksburg. This difficulty was initially overcome by his adopting of his mother's family's name: Mountbatten (which was originally Battenberg). Philip Mountbatten was a more palatable name for the intended of the future queen. Of course, later in their marriage, the question of the family name or surname of the new royal family was called into question – the name usually coming from the father's side. As we have seen, a compromise was eventually landed upon in 1960, that of Mountbatten-Windsor.

Because of the decision and strong will of one teenage girl, the fate of the British Crown and royal family was set. Prince Philip of Greece and Denmark was carefully rebranded for the British anti-foreigner public as Lieutenant Philip Mountbatten RN – which was more digestible to a war-torn population. This fortunate naval lieutenant married the most eligible and famous woman of the twentieth century. To date, they have twenty-five living descendants. It is therefore highly unlikely that any future British monarchs would not be descended from Philip and Elizabeth.

continues from p.275

PRINCE PHILIP, Duke of Edinburgh   =   Elizabeth II of the United Kingdom
                        1921-2021   1926-2022

Lady Diana Spencer   =   CHARLES III   =   Camilla Shand
          1961-1997   of the United Kingdom   Born 1947
                                        Born 1948

ends on p.360

Figure 27: Photograph of Prince Philip of Greece and Denmark, later Prince Philip, Duke of Edinburgh, in the Chinese Room, Buckingham Palace, in 1992 by Allan Warren.

Prince Philip of Greece and Denmark, latterly Prince Philip, Duke of Edinburgh

(father)

| c. 1921–1947 | 1947–1949 | 1949–2021 |

Born: 10 June 1921 at Mon Repos, Corfu, Greece

Died: 9 April 2021 at Windsor Castle

Spouse: Princess Elizabeth, later Queen Elizabeth II of the United Kingdom

Concurrent British monarchs: *George V, Edward VIII, George VI and Elizabeth II*

PRINCE PHILIP ANDREW (Φίλιππος Ανδρέου or Phílippos Andréou) of Greece and Denmark was born on the dining room table at Mon Repos, Corfu, in 1921. Just months after he was born, his maternal grandfather, Admiral the Marquess of Milford Haven (formerly Prince Louis of Battenberg), died. He had been a naturalised British subject and was the first to anglicise his name from Battenberg to Mountbatten in 1917, owing to the anti-German sentiment felt in Britain at the time. Louis and his family had been steadily becoming closer and closer to the British Crown throughout the mid-nineteenth century onwards. When he died, he could not have known just how close his newest grandson would take the family. Philip was not however a Battenberg or Mountbatten when he was born. He was a Prince of Greece first and foremost. Simultaneously, he was also a Prince of Denmark. Therefore, he was a member of the House of Schleswig-Holstein-Sonderburg-Glücksburg like his fathers before him, descended from medieval Kings of Denmark and one King of Greece – his grandfather.

Childhood

Prince Philip was baptised at St George's Church in the old Venetian fortress on the island of Corfu. Amongst his godparents were members of the Greek royal family, the mayor of Corfu, and his maternal uncle, Lord Louis Mountbatten (then just a lieutenant in the Royal Navy). Philip was born into turmoil and is rightly said to have been something of a lost boy as a child, having to move from home to home among different relatives and friends. Two years after Philip's birth, his uncle, King Constantine I of Greece, was forced to abdicate and flee into exile. Amid the turmoil and political executions, Philip's parents were put under surveillance. Prince Andrew was arrested for desertion and in danger for his life in a public show trial in the Trial of the Six in 1922. Following his release, he too was banished and moved the family to France with the help of the Royal Navy ship *Calypso*. The crew of the *Calypso*, which had seen action in WWI, could not have known that the eighteen-month-old Greek royal would one day be Lord High Admiral of the United Kingdom. Sadly, *Calypso* had the distinction of being the first British ship to be sunk by the Italian navy in WWII, having been torpedoed by submarine (*Alphino Bagonlini)* in 1940.

For the rest of the 1920s, Philip spent his childhood on the outskirts of Paris. His parents had lost funds and possessions in their flight from Greece and had little way of making money, even as ex-royals, and were therefore reliant on the support and generosity of their wider family. Philip's aunt, Princess Marie Bonaparte (Princess George of Greece and Denmark), was an heiress twice over and therefore very well-off, so she paid for the family to stay in a house next to her own. She likely also sponsored Philip's initial schooling at an American private school in Paris, The Elms, where he became fluent in French. Owing to his parent's financial situation, he was only a half-board student. Interestingly, the school building had once been the home of the French writer Jules Verne.

In 1930, the now nine-years-old Philip was old enough to be sent to British prep school, a common practice among European royals. He was sent to Cheam School in Surrey and watched over by his maternal grandmother, Princess Victoria (Marchioness of Milford Haven), from Kensington Palace. His legal guardian was his uncle, George, 2nd Marquess of Milford Haven. During his few years at Cheam, all of Philip's sisters married German princes and moved to Germany, his mother was committed into clinics and asylums, and his father began to spend more time in Monte Carlo with his mistress. Philip did not see his mother for several years. In late 1933, he was sent to a boarding school in Switzerland known as Schule Schloss Salem, mostly because his sister's husband's family owned the building, and Philip's fees were therefore waived. The school's founder, Kurt Hahn, famously decided to leave the Continent, feeling the increase in persecution of the Jews from the Nazis. He refounded the school at Gordonstoun in Scotland. After just a few terms in Switzerland, Philip also moved to Gordonstoun. Hahn's philosophy for the school was that the boys should be taught to become community leaders through a lot of physical learning – outdoor pursuits, manual labour and building things. This philosophy certainly left an imprint on the mind of the young Prince Philip.

The sixteen-year-old prince was particularly affected by the death of his sister, brother-in-law and their children in a plane crash on their way to England from Germany in 1937. Philip attended the funeral in Darmstadt together with other family members, but as the couple had both been members of the Nazi Party, there were many prominent Nazis present as well. In a scene made famous by its dramatic portrayal in *The Crown* on Netflix, young Philip had to march behind the coffin of his sister flanked by men and relatives in Nazi uniform. His uncle, Lord Louis Mountbatten, walked behind him – in Royal Naval uniform. Photos of the event have also been slipped into modern-day tabloids.

In the Navy

Leaving Gordonstoun in 1939, Philip was ushered into the Britannia Royal Naval College at Dartmouth by his watchful uncle, Lord Louis Mountbatten. Of course, something of a naval tradition had been formed in Philip's family beginning with his maternal grandfather. Initially, Philip only did a term at Dartmouth (as is often the case with foreign royals) and then returned to Athens to be with his mother. However, his Greek royal family and his Battenberg family all suggested that it would be better for him to return and finish his naval training. It is during his time at Dartmouth that the famous meeting between him and Princess Elizabeth occurred.

As the Second World War began, Philip was in the odd position of serving in the British Royal Navy whilst two of his brothers-in-law were in the German army. By the beginning of 1940, Philip was a midshipman serving on battleships protecting convoys in the Indian Ocean.

Italy invaded Philip's homeland of Greece in October 1940, and Philip found himself transferred to the Mediterranean fleet. He was a fully commissioned officer, coming top of his class in many areas, by the time of the Battle of Crete (May-June 1941), which was a costly defeat for the Royal Navy. However, Philip had earlier been mentioned in dispatches during the Battle of Cape Matapan (just off the coast of mainland Greece) for commanding the searchlights on HMS *Valiant* as they illuminated an Italian battleship, which the British were then able to fire upon at point-blank range. The Greeks also awarded Philip a decoration in recognition for this action. In late 1942 on HMS *Wallace*, he became the youngest first lieutenant (the second-in-command officer of a ship) in the Royal Navy. He was later transferred to the Pacific on HMS *Whelp* (a W-class destroyer). On 2 September 1945, Philip was on the *Whelp* in Tokyo Bay in sight of USS *Missouri*, aboard which the Japanese surrender took place.

Courtship and Surnames

Following the end of the war, Philip returned to Britain and stayed in the navy. He became a training instructor at a naval base at Corsham – HMS *Royal Arthur* – at the start of 1946. He and Princess Elizabeth had been corresponding by letter throughout the war. In the summer of 1946, he proposed and asked King George VI for permission to wed Elizabeth. Permission was granted, but the engagement would have to be kept quiet until she reached her twenty-first birthday, which was a little less than a year away. Elizabeth's one condition was that Philip had to give up smoking – which he did from their wedding day onwards. It was during this time that his name was also 'tidied up', and he dropped his Greek and Danish princely titles. It was considered that his real surname of Schleswig-Holstein-Sonderburg-Glucksberg would be unpalatable to the British public in the wake of two world wars against Germany. Philip's uncle, Lord Mountbatten, was all too keen to provide the alternative.

Philip became Philip Mountbatten, adopting the recently-anglicised name of his maternal uncle. Lord Mountbatten was a well-known and respected man in British society, having been a commander in chief in Burma during the war and more recently a statesman as the last Viceroy of India. The invention, if you will, of Philip Mountbatten was intended to cover over the fact that he was a foreign-born prince with Germanic origins, several close family members who had fought for the Nazis, hardly any money and no actual home. Politicians, press, and even the queen had initial reservations. Generally, though, the public were eventually won over with little fuss. Philip was baptised as an Anglican by the Archbishop of Canterbury and, the day before his wedding, was made royal highness. On the day of the wedding, 20 November 1947, he was granted the title Duke of Edinburgh, and the couple were married at Westminster Abbey to cheering crowds. In keeping with his keen interest in sport, Philip's very first solo royal engagement was to present the prizes at the boxing finals of the London Federation of Boys' Clubs in the Royal Albert Hall in 1948.

The young couple enjoyed their life together both at Clarence House and later in Malta, where Philip was still a serving Royal Naval officer. Their first two children, Prince Charles and Princess Anne, were born in 1948 and 1950, respectively. King George VI died unexpectedly early in 1952. Elizabth and Philip were on a trip to Kenya on a Commonwealth Tour at the time. Philip was now consort to his wife who was his sovereign. Following the state funeral and the preparations leading up to the coronation, the problem of Philip's family name reared its less-than-attractive head again. Lord Mountbatten had (perhaps self-indulgently) promoted the idea of the Royal House of Mountbatten; Philip offered as a palatable alternative the House of Edinburgh. Sir Winston Churchill (as well as the Queen Mother) asserted that there should be a royal proclamation declaring that the royal house would continue to be known as the House of Windsor. Philip was privately furious that he could not pass his name (albeit adopted) to his children. This was partially corrected by Elizabeth II in 1960; a compromise was reached whereby any nonroyal or non-title-holding male-line descendants that Elizabeth and Philip may have (and they may well have many) would be able to use the name Mountbatten-Windsor. Shortly after this declaration, Philip and Elizabeth produced their other two children, Andrew in 1960 and Edward in 1964.

Consort, Husband, Father

Philip's life and his undeniably strong marriage to the British sovereign are worthy of so many good and long books, many of which are already written or will certainly be written in the future. However, we can only allow ourselves a short overview in this work. This is regrettably unworthy of the man – although he likely would have said, "Just get on with it!" With that in mind, here is an attempt to summarise Prince Philip's vast and well-documented career, in which he constantly served the nation as prince consort.

Philip hoped to continue his career in the navy. However, in his position as consort after his wife's accession, this was no longer possible, although he of course retained commissions and honorary commissions in a variety of British armed forces units, regiments, ships and squadrons. Philip saw his role first and foremost as supporting the sovereign wherever she was and whatever she was doing all over the world. He also threw himself into useful hobbies, such as flying planes and helicopters, and less useful ones, like polo and later carriage driving. Having become Ranger of Windsor Great Park, he turned an old RAF field from WWII days into a polo pitch – as it was already flat. There he founded Guards Polo Club in 1955, starting a family keenness for the sport which has lasted generations.

In 1956, together with his old headmaster, Kurt Hahn, Philip established the Duke of Edinburgh's Award – a legacy that will likely live on for generations. This programme was and is designed to encourage young people who might not already be involved in other youth groups, like the scouts or the cadets, to complete a range of challenging (often outdoor) activities in four key areas: expedition, physical activity, skills and volunteering.

From 1956 to 1957, the Duke of Edinburgh travelled on the newly-commissioned royal yacht, HMY *Britannia*, on a huge worldwide trip. On the trip, he opened the Olympic Games in Melbourne (as a Greek prince, who better?) as well as visited Antarctica.

At some point in the 1950s and 1960s, a religious sect of the Kastom people of the Yaohnanen tribe island of Tanna in the South Pacific began to believe that Prince Philip was a kind of god and began to worship him as such. Since his death, their veneration has slowly transferred to King Charles.

Also, in 1957, Philip was created a Prince of the United Kingdom (instead of just merely being a duke). This made him HRH The Prince Philip, Duke of Edinburgh.

According to the Royal Collection Trust, Prince Philip accompanied his wife, the queen, on every Commonwealth Tour and state visit that she made overseas. In addition to this, he himself made over 620 separate solo visits to 143 countries across the world. (At the time of this writing, there are a total of 195 countries in the world.) The list of Prince Philip's honours, decorations, presidencies, patronages, memberships, awards and honorary appointments is staggering. He was patron of over eight hundred organisations. Many of these involved charity work, engineering and especially sports – from football and cricket to shooting and carriage driving. (He and the queen went on a tiger hunt during a royal tour of India in 1961, and the tiger's skin is at Windsor Castle.) Through the Duke of Edinburgh Award, the prince took a keen interest in education and was made Chancellor of the University of Cambridge in 1976, the year after his eldest son, the Prince of Wales, had his degree from Trinity College promoted to a Master of Arts degree.

A Life of Service

By 2009, Philip had become the longest-serving royal consort to a British sovereign. He had overtaken the lengthy service of the wife of George III, Queen Charlotte of Mecklenburg-Strelitz, who was queen consort for over fifty-seven years. Four years later in 2013, Philip became the oldest royal ever on record. Something he was himself not altogether impressed by. In a display of his acid wit, when asked if he thought he would make it to be a centenarian, he explained that he could not think of anything worse, partly because bits of him were already falling off. If his stated goal was not to reach the age of one hundred, he lived up to his word.

After his ninetieth birthday, the Duke of Edinburgh gradually began to slow down and pass on his duties to other members of the royal family. His colonelcies and patronages were returned to the sovereign and passed on to others. It was rather like a slow winding up. One of the duke's last awards was the Naval Long Service Good Conduct Medal. This had originally been a medal given in recognition of fifteen years of service, with clasps for every further ten years. In 2016, however, some back-room boys at the Ministry of Defence thought it was a good idea to make officers eligible for the award too. No one had considered that Prince Philip had technically been serving as an Royal Naval officer since the 1930s and was now Lord High Admiral. It was found that the Duke of Edinburgh was eligible for six clasps on his medal. The author of this book was personally responsible for mounting the duke's last set of medals, which included his new Naval Long Service Good Conduct Medal and all six clasps, the last to be added to his rack. It looked as impressive as it did comical, but it was nonetheless a worthy way to recognise a staggering career of duty and service.

Prince Philip, Duke of Edinburgh, died on the morning of 9 April 2021 at Windsor Castle at the age of ninety-nine; he was two months and a day away from his one-hundredth birthday. Queen Elizabeth was reportedly at his side. In keeping with his style and wit, when it came to his funeral arrangements, he had always joked that they should just chuck him in the back of a Land Rover. At the funeral procession from Windsor Castle, his coffin was indeed placed on the back of a specially-built Defender and driven to St George's Chapel where he is buried. His life was a surprising and remarkable journey from impoverished Greek prince to naval officer and veteran to the husband of the British sovereign and father, grandfather and great-grandfather of the kings to come.

*Figure 28: HM The King at his coronation in Westminster Abbey, 6 May 2023.
(British Broadcasting Corporation.)*

Charles III, King of the United Kingdom of Great Britain and Northern Ireland

Also King of:

Antigua and Barbuda

Australia

The Bahamas

Belize

Canada

Grenada

Jamaica

New Zealand

Papua New Guinea

Saint Kitts and Nevis

Saint Lucia

Saint Vincent and the Grenadines

The Solomon Islands

and Tuvalu

Born: *14 November 1948 at Buckingham Palace*

Spouses: 1ˢᵗ: *Lady Diana Spencer*

2ⁿᵈ: *Camilla Rosemary Shand*

As we have seen, His Majesty King Charles III's male-line ancestry is a line of monarchs, minor royals, aristocrats and, going further back, tribal leaders. The public consciousness is very well aware and educated on the ancestry of his long-lived predecessor, his mother, Elizabeth II. Few, however, are as knowledgeable about the ancestry of the King's father's family. The Mountbatten family are perhaps the exception to that, but they are technically of a different line and house altogether. Charles III descends in the male line from the House of Schleswig-Holstein-Sonderburg-Glücksburg, which is itself a cadet branch of the older House of Oldenburg. The King comes from a military family – a long line of generals, admirals and military commanders. However, this type of military career is not wholly possible if one is born a direct heir to the throne.

Via his maternal grandmother, Queen Elizabeth The Queen Mother (1900-2002), the King is arguably the first king since William III to have a sizable portion of his ancestry be British. Lady Elizabeth Bowes-Lyon, as she was born, was a Scottish aristocrat with an ancestry stemming back to England and Scotland's medieval past. Highly simplified, one could argue that The King is, at the very least, one-quarter Scottish. The King was the longest-serving Prince of Wales and heir apparent to the throne (from 1952 to 2022) and may be the first Prince of Wales to have studied the Welsh language and have a fair ability in it.

On 29 July 1981 at St Paul's Cathedral, while Prince of Wales, Charles took as his wife Lady Diana Spencer, daughter of John Spencer, 8th Earl Spencer. She was twenty; he was thirty-two. Their marriage neatly mirrored the wedding of his grandparents, King George VI and Queen Elizabeth, the latter of which had herself been the daughter of an earl. Queen Elizabeth The Queen Mother (Lady Elizabeth Bowes-Lyon) had been the first British consort in centuries not to already be a royal princess. Before her, one has to go back as far as Catherine Parr (who became Henry VIII's queen in 1543) to find the nearest nonroyal consort. (Her father was Sir Thomas Parr from Westmorland.) One could argue, however, that a more recent nonroyal consort would be Lord Guildford Dudley, the husband of Lady Jane Grey, who may be considered to have been queen for nine days in 1553, but that is debatable.

King Charles's marriage to Lady Diana produced two sons, William and Henry (known as Harry), in 1982 and 1984, respectively. Famously, the marriage ended in divorce in 1996, and the following year Diana died tragically in a car accident in Paris.

In 2005, King Charles married his long-time confidante, Camilla Shand at Windsor. She had previously been divorced from her first husband, Andrew Parker-Bowles, in 1995. On the accession of King

Charles III in 2022, she became Queen Camilla of the United Kingdom. She is the daughter of Major Bruce Shand MC & Bar DL who served in the Second World War in the Twelfth Lancers and in other units with distinction. He was awarded his first Military Cross in 1940 for covering the retreat at Dunkirk. He earned his second Military Cross for covering another retreat in North Africa in 1942. He was captured and was a prisoner of war in Germany until he escaped. He married the Honourable Rosalind Cubitt, daughter of Roland Cubitt, 3rd Baron Ashcombe. The Cubitts had originally been a family of architects and builders. Thomas Cubitt (1788-1855) was responsible for many of the buildings in Belgravia and modern-day Pimlico. He was also responsible for the East Front (the main front) of Buckingham Palace which was commissioned by Victoria and Albert. Put simply, Queen Camilla's own family designed and built the famous balcony she now waves from! Interestingly, Queen Camilla is not the first commoner to become queen; there have already been several. That said, she may be the first queen whose father did not have a peerage, knighthood or similar title.

It would be unfair to write a short biography of King Charles while the most important part of his life has only recently begun (since his accession in late 2022). Besides, this is a work about all of his fathers, not about him. HM The King has at times shown a great interest in his ancestry, particularly the lesser-known parts. He has ancestors from Central but also Eastern Europe, specifically, Transylvania. The King's interest in Transylvania stems not just from his having read Bram Stoker's *Dracula* when he was young but from the fact that he has important ancestors from that province. In fact, he is the sixteenth great-grandson of Prince Vlad III – known as Vlad Dracula or Vlad the Impaler (1431-1476) – the inspiration for Count Dracula. The King, while Prince of Wales, has subsequently bought and restored several old properties in Transylvania and turned them into holiday lets.

It is fair to note that His Majesty is perhaps the most academic monarch the UK has had for some time. Before him, all monarchs had been educated by private tutors. Queen Elizabeth and Prince Philip, the latter in particular, thought it best that Charles receive a traditional boarding school education such as Philip had. Charles attended his father's prep school, Cheam, and then his public school, Gordonstoun. Unlike his father, Charles wanted to go to university and gain a degree. He is the first UK monarch to have done so. Charles was admitted as a student to Trinity College, Cambridge, in 1967 and studied archaeology, anthropology and history. His second year of study was spent in Aberystwyth at the University College of Wales studying Welsh history and language. He graduated from Cambridge in 1970.

In his patrilineal line, Charles III is not the first to be a king. His great-grandfather and his great-great-grandfather were both kings – Christian IX of Denmark and George I of Greece, respectively. Before them, one has to go back nearly five hundred years to Christian III of Denmark and Norway in 1534. As we have seen, the earliest king in Charles III's line was Christian I of Denmark, Sweden and Norway in 1448. Before that, the family were merely Counts of Oldenburg, a town in north-western Germany. Currently, Charles will not be the last in his line to be a king. With a son and a grandson to succeed Charles III, the House of Schleswig-Holstein-Sonderburg-Glücksburg and that of Oldenburg will continue on the throne.

Figure 29: HM King Charles III, his son (HRH The Prince of Wales), and grandson (HRH Prince George of Wales). Official coronation photograph taken in the Throne Room, Buckingham Palace, 6 May 2023, by Hugo Burnand.

8 – The Kings to Come

THE FUTURE OF THE DYNASTY

WITH THE SLIGHT change to the laws of succession and His Majesty King Charles already having three grandsons and two granddaughters, it is likely that all successors to his throne will be his descendants, or if not his own then certainly those of his father, for centuries to come. Of course, due to the 2013 Act of Succession, these successors may not always be of the House of Glücksburg, as there will always be a fifty-percent chance in each subsequent generation that a daughter will be the eldest child and therefore succeed.

The 2013 Act highlighted an important turning point in the way British society views gender in hereditary titles, roles or offices. The Act allows the crown to be passed by absolute primogeniture – as opposed to male-preference primogeniture – meaning the eldest child succeeds as monarch, regardless of gender. The Act was passed in anticipation of the birth of the King's first grandchild, HRH Prince George of Cambridge (now Wales), later that year. Obviously, as the King's first grandchild turned out to be a male, the Act did little to change recent events. However, it may have a profound impact on future generations of British monarchs in the decades and centuries to come. The change from male-preference to absolute primogeniture is hardly surprising in a country that has changed so much in the last century or so with women's suffrage, increasing equality in pay and rights between men and women, three female prime ministers, numerous female priests and bishops in the Anglican church and innumerable women in high positions in the armed forces, police, judiciary and business sectors. To top that, the United Kingdom's longest reigning monarch, who ruled over most of the aforementioned developments, was female.

That said, for the next two generations at least, it is likely that the British monarch will remain male. While technically the House of Glücksburg, the royal house will doubtlessly continue to be officially known as the House of Windsor in perpetuity, regardless of the gender of future monarchs or their 'real surnames'. Whatever its official name however, for the time being, one of the oldest dynasties in Europe, an unbroken line of kings, dukes and counts dating back to the eleventh century, will continue to reign in Britain, its realms, territories and dominions.

continues from p.341

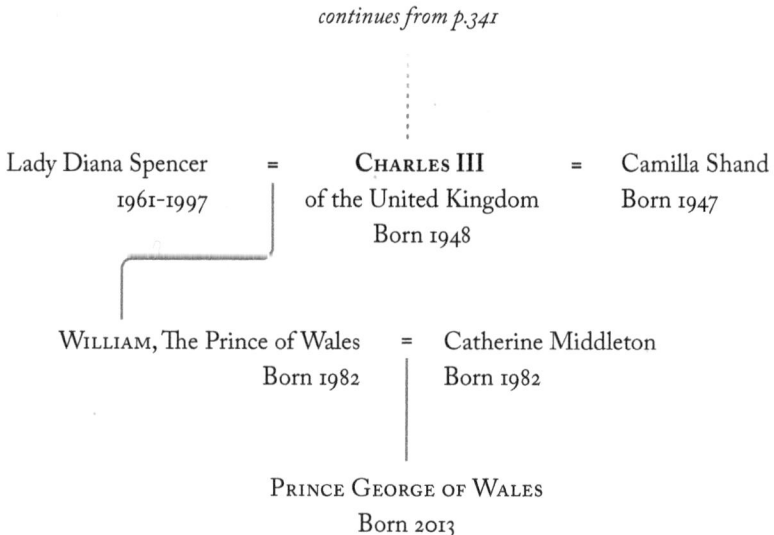

Lady Diana Spencer   =   **Charles III**   =   Camilla Shand
1961-1997   of the United Kingdom   Born 1947
Born 1948

William, The Prince of Wales   =   Catherine Middleton
Born 1982   Born 1982

Prince George of Wales
Born 2013

EDWARD HILARY DAVIS

Figure 30: Photograph of The Prince of Wales at D–Day Commemorations in Normandy in 2024. (European Union.)

WILLIAM, PRINCE OF WALES

(son)

Born: *21 June 1982 at St Mary's Hospital, City of Westminster*
Spouse: *Catherine Elizabeth Middleton*

HRH PRINCE WILLIAM of Wales (as he was then) was born in 1982 at St May's, Westminster to a then thirty-three-year-old Charles, Prince of Wales, and a twenty-one-year-old Diana, Princess of Wales. The couple had married the previous year at St Paul's Cathedral. William was the first child born to a Prince and Princess of Wales since Prince John, son of George V and Queen Mary, in 1905. The baby prince was also the first royal direct heir to be born in a hospital as previous royal births had traditionally taken place at home in a palace or castle.

As the heir apparent's heir apparent, Prince William was, at his mother's insistence, given as 'normal' an upbringing as could be achieved given his status. This meant that he may one day be the first British monarch to have actively used public transport and eaten (and enjoyed) fast food such as McDonald's or Pizza Hut as a child. More importantly, William will also be a first in terms of his matrilineal ancestry.

The Honourable Diana Spencer was born in 1961, the third daughter of John, Viscount Althorp (as he was then), and the Honourable Frances Roche. Diana's father succeeded to the title of 8th Earl Spencer when his father (the 7th Earl Spencer) died in 1975. From then on, as a daughter of an earl, Diana was entitled to the style Lady Diana Spencer. One might describe her as an English aristocratic thoroughbred.

The Spencer family has a long and illustrious history. The title of Earl Spencer was created for Diana's ancestor John Spencer, a politician and MP, in 1765. His paternal grandparents were Charles Spenser, 3rd Earl of Sunderland (First Lord of the Treasury under George I), and Lady Anne Churchill – daughter of the famous General John Churchill, 1st Duke of Marlborough. In fact, it was one of John Spencer's uncles, the 5th Earl of Sunderland (another Charles Spenser), who eventually succeeded as the 3rd Duke of Marlborough in 1733. It is for this reason that many Marlboroughs bear the double surname of Spencer and Churchill – such as Sir Winston Spencer-Churchill (although Winston preferred to drop the Spencer part)!

The Spencers had been Earls of Sunderland since 1643 (a reward for services in the Civil War, specifically the Battle of Edgehill) and Barons Spencer of Wormleighton since 1603 (a title given shortly after entertaining the queen and the then Prince of Wales at the family seat at Althorp). During the Tudor century and earlier, the Spencers were of the knightly class, with several serving as sheriffs of their native Northamptonshire. Indeed, Althorp has been their seat for around five hundred years. The earliest known founder of the dynasty, Henry Spencer, died around 1478. The family made a steady rise to wealth and fortune. By approximately the 1590s, however, the family had begun to claim descent from the then far grander and older medieval family of Le Despencer – who had been lords close to the Plantagenet kings. A descent from this family to the Spencers was likely fabricated, however, either by the family or a corrupt herald of the College of Arms, and today the theory is widely debunked as fantasy. Ironically, the family need not have fantasised about their ancestry, as in many ways it surpassed the grandeur of the Le Despencer family, providing us with the Dukes of Marlborough, Winston Churchill, Princess Diana herself and (half of) the future king!

William's dynastic status as a royal first, however, stems from the fact that Lady Diana's ancestry descends, through various lines, from two illegitimate sons of King Charles II – the Duke of Richmond and the Duke of Grafton. This means that, as king, William would be the first British monarch in history to descend from Charles II. Further to this, he would also be the first undisputed monarch to descend from Charles I (since Queen Anne in 1714).

In 2011, HRH The Duke of Cambridge (as he was then) married his university girlfriend, Catherine Middleton, daughter of Michael Middleton and Carole Goldsmith. The now Prince and Princess of Wales have three children: Prince George (b. 2013), Princess Charlotte (b. 2015) and Prince Louis (b. 2018). The House of Glücksburg (and the House of Windsor) will ostensibly continue.

Figure 31: Photograph of Prince George of Wales at Trooping the Colour in 2023 by Simon Dawson. (No. 10 Downing Street.)

Prince George of Wales

(grandson)

Born: 22 July 2013 at St Mary's Hospital, City of Westminster

PRINCE GEORGE ALEXANDER Louis of Cambridge (now Wales) may one day succeed as George VII – assuming he does not change to a different regnal name. This would make George the third most 'popular' kingly name in England, behind Henry (of which there have been eight) and Edward (of which there have been eight, plus three further Anglo-Saxon kings). Prince George may also become the first king to have a truly nonaristocratic mother, that is to say, with no immediate relations possessing titles of nobility or grand country estates.

That said, his mother, the Princess of Wales, does have a family ancestry with some royal roots and connections. This only goes to demonstrate the theory that most people in the UK, particularly those with English grandparents, are descended from an English monarch such as Edward III or William the Conqueror – in some cases it is a mathematical certainty.

Catherine Middleton's paternal ancestors include Sir Thomas Fairfax (died 1520), who was knighted by Henry VIII, and his wife, Anne Gascoigne. She actually shares these two ancestors with her husband. Anne Gascoigne was a descendant of Lionel, Duke of Clarence, the third (but second surviving) son of Edward III of England. Catherine also reportedly shares some of her ancestry with that of famed filmmaker Guy Ritchie!

The House of Glücksburg (and of Windsor) will continue with Prince George. One can only speculate what will happen when he is one day king, but that is not the purpose of this book.

FAMILY TREE – PEDIGREE OF ALL THE KING'S FATHERS

The paternal ancestry of Charles III, officially, **CHARLES THE THIRD,**

by the Grace of God of the United Kingdom of Great Britain and Northern Ireland and of His other Realms and Territories, King, Head of the Commonwealth, Defender of the Faith.

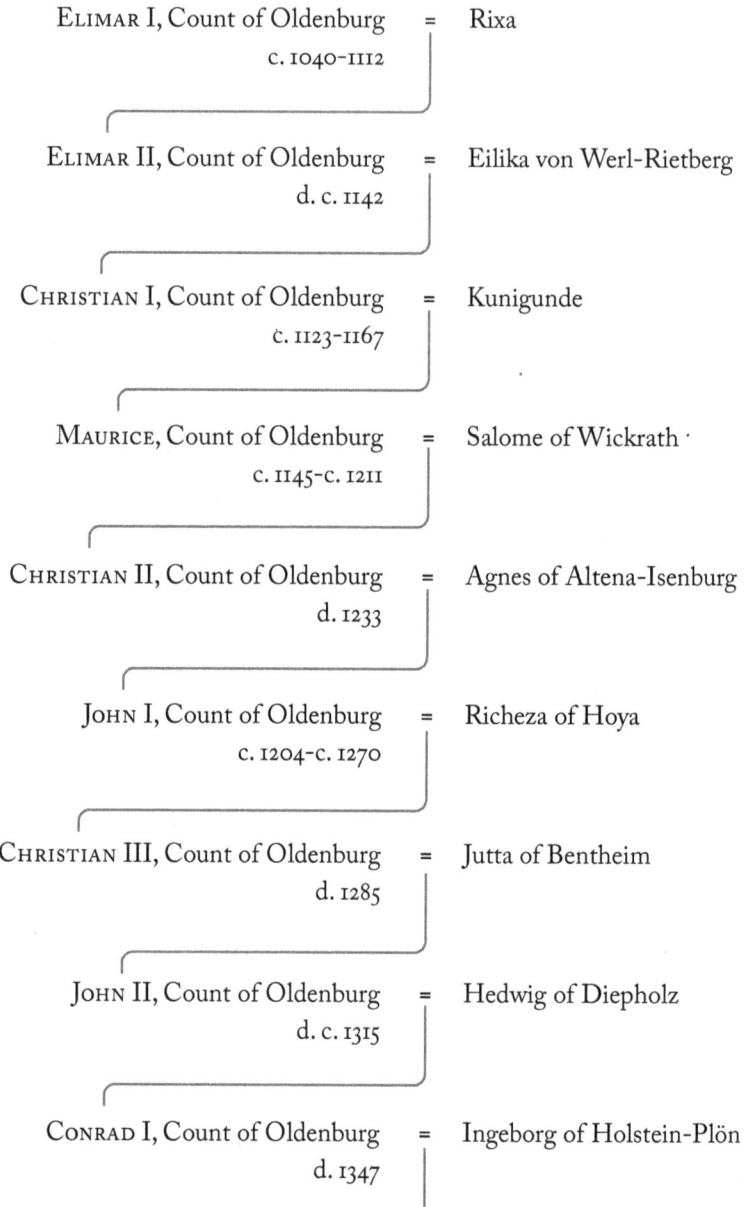

ELIMAR I, Count of Oldenburg = Rixa
c. 1040-1112

ELIMAR II, Count of Oldenburg = Eilika von Werl-Rietberg
d. c. 1142

CHRISTIAN I, Count of Oldenburg = Kunigunde
c. 1123-1167

MAURICE, Count of Oldenburg = Salome of Wickrath ·
c. 1145-c. 1211

CHRISTIAN II, Count of Oldenburg = Agnes of Altena-Isenburg
d. 1233

JOHN I, Count of Oldenburg = Richeza of Hoya
c. 1204-c. 1270

CHRISTIAN III, Count of Oldenburg = Jutta of Bentheim
d. 1285

JOHN II, Count of Oldenburg = Hedwig of Diepholz
d. c. 1315

CONRAD I, Count of Oldenburg = Ingeborg of Holstein-Plön
d. 1347

EDWARD HILARY DAVIS

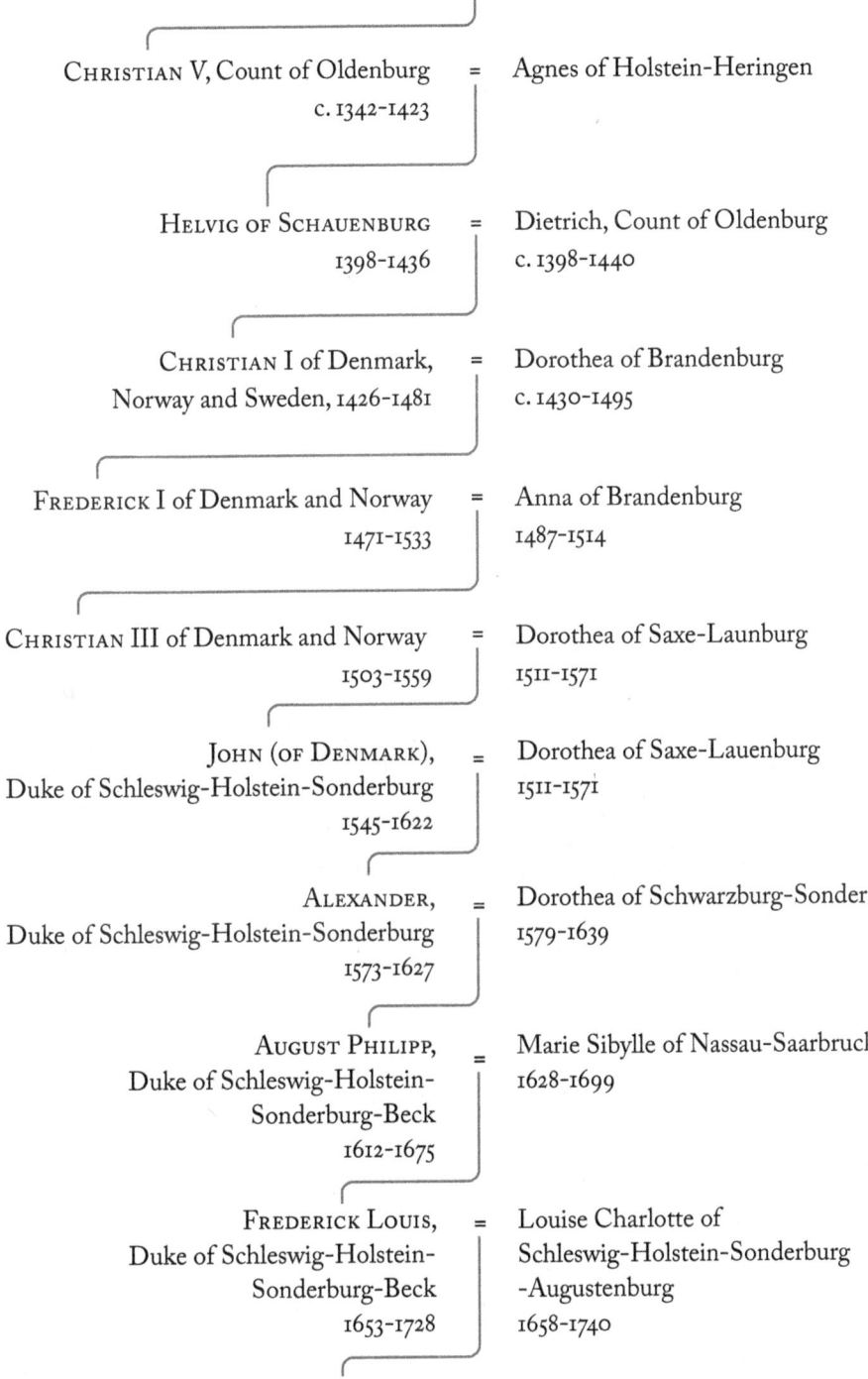

CHRISTIAN V, Count of Oldenburg = Agnes of Holstein-Heringen
c. 1342-1423

HELVIG OF SCHAUENBURG = Dietrich, Count of Oldenburg
1398-1436 c. 1398-1440

CHRISTIAN I of Denmark, = Dorothea of Brandenburg
Norway and Sweden, 1426-1481 c. 1430-1495

FREDERICK I of Denmark and Norway = Anna of Brandenburg
1471-1533 1487-1514

CHRISTIAN III of Denmark and Norway = Dorothea of Saxe-Launburg
1503-1559 1511-1571

JOHN (OF DENMARK), = Dorothea of Saxe-Lauenburg
Duke of Schleswig-Holstein-Sonderburg 1511-1571
1545-1622

ALEXANDER, = Dorothea of Schwarzburg-Sonder
Duke of Schleswig-Holstein-Sonderburg 1579-1639
1573-1627

AUGUST PHILIPP, = Marie Sibylle of Nassau-Saarbrucl
Duke of Schleswig-Holstein- 1628-1699
Sonderburg-Beck
1612-1675

FREDERICK LOUIS, = Louise Charlotte of
Duke of Schleswig-Holstein- Schleswig-Holstein-Sonderburg
Sonderburg-Beck -Augustenburg
1653-1728 1658-1740

PETER AUGUST,
Duke of Schleswig-Holstein-
Sonderburg-Beck
1697-1775

=

Princess Sophie of
Hesse-Philippsthal
1695-1728

PRINCE KARL ANTON AUGUST
of Schleswig-Holstein-
Sonderburg-Beck
1727-1759

=

Countess Charlotte of
Dohna-Leistenau
1738-1785

FRIEDRICH KARL LUDWIG,
Duke of Schleswig-Holstein-
Sonderburg-Beck
1757-1816

=

Countess Friederike Amalie
of Schlieben
1757-1827

FRIEDRICH WILHELM,
Duke of Schleswig-Holstein-
Sonderburg-Glücksburg
1785-1831

=

Princess Louise Caroline
of Hesse-Kassel
1789-1867

CHRISTIAN IX of Denmark
1818-1906

=

Princess Louise Caroline of Hesse-Kassel
1789-1867

GEORGE I of Greece
1845-1913

=

Grand Duchess Olga of Russia
1851-1926

PRINCE ANDREW
of Greece and Denmark
1882-1944

=

Princess Alice of Battenberg
1885-1969

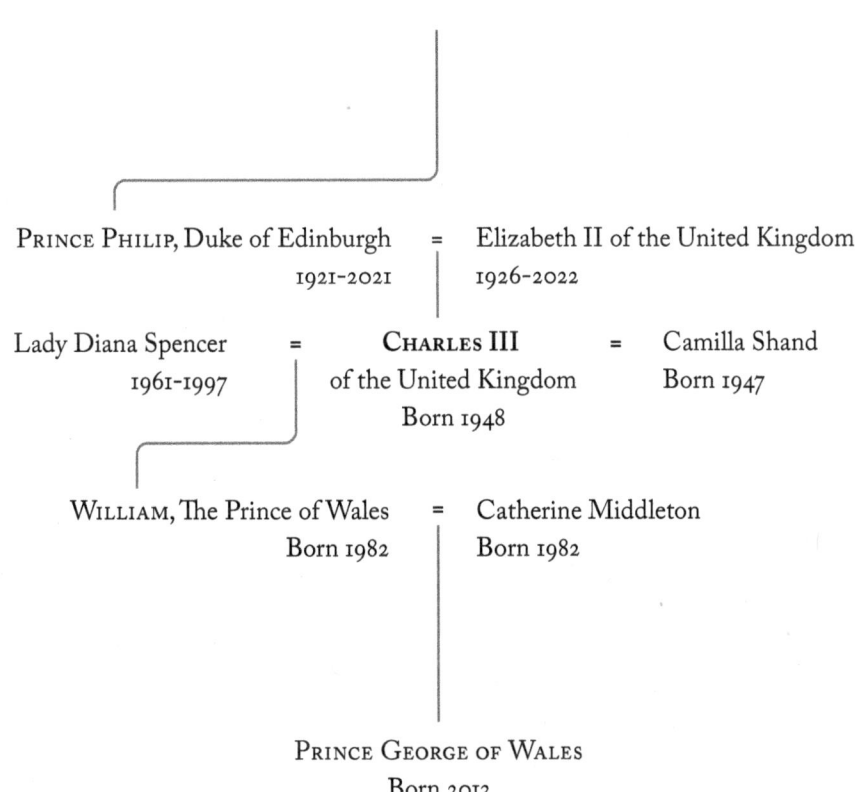

PRINCE PHILIP, Duke of Edinburgh   =   Elizabeth II of the United Kingdom
                      1921-2021   1926-2022

Lady Diana Spencer   =   CHARLES III   =   Camilla Shand
        1961-1997   of the United Kingdom   Born 1947
                                   Born 1948

WILLIAM, The Prince of Wales   =   Catherine Middleton
                      Born 1982   Born 1982

PRINCE GEORGE OF WALES
            Born 2013

Pedigree combining the House of Glücksburg/Oldenburg with the previous ruling houses of England

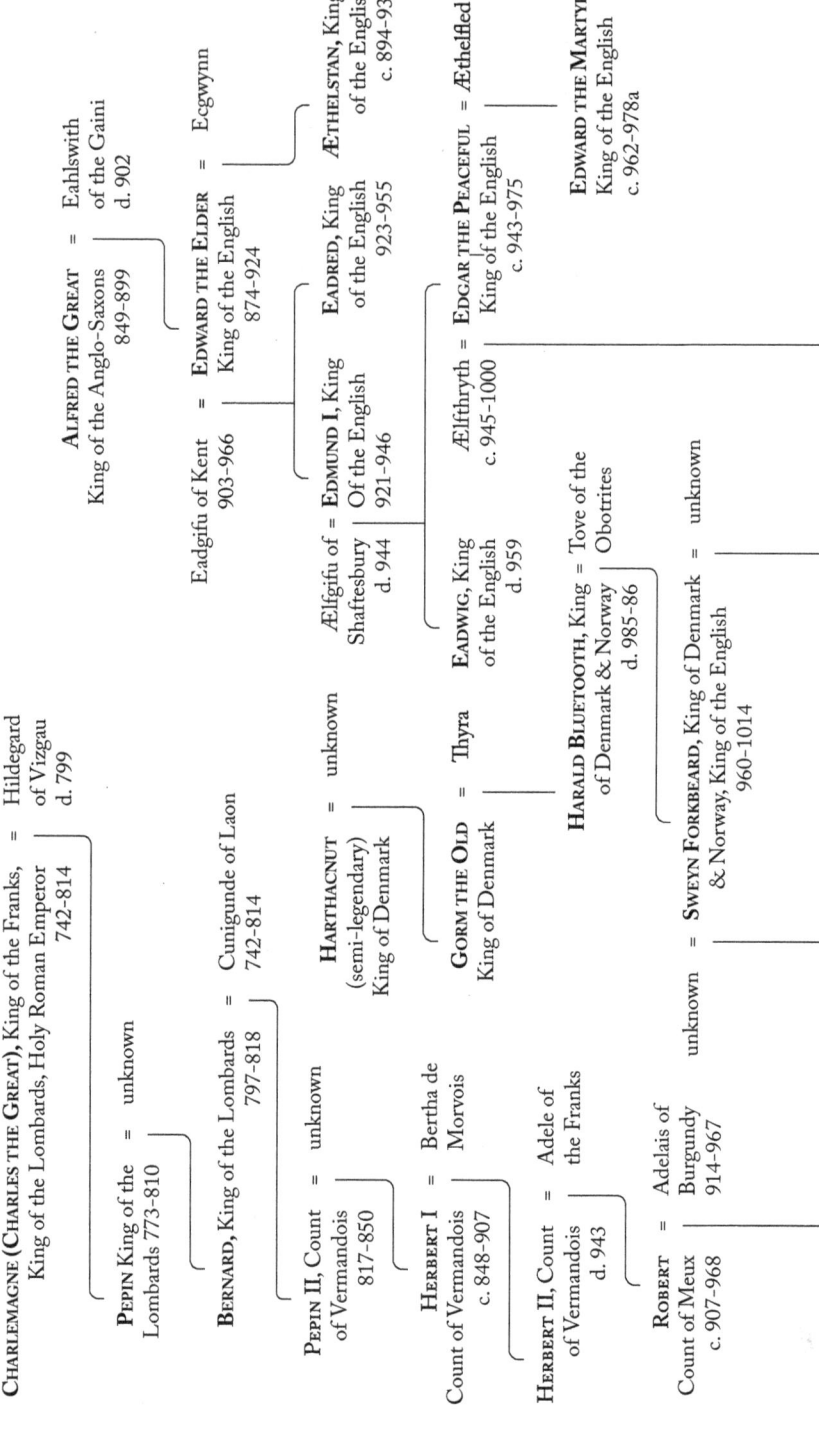

CHARLEMAGNE (**CHARLES THE GREAT**), King of the Franks, = Hildegard
King of the Lombards, Holy Roman Emperor   of Vizgau
742-814   d. 799

PEPIN King of the = unknown
Lombards 773-810

BERNARD, King of the Lombards = Cunigunde of Laon
797-818   742-814

PEPIN II, Count = unknown
of Vermandois
817-850

HERBERT I = Bertha de
Count of Vermandois   Morvois
c. 848-907

HERBERT II, Count = Adele of
of Vermandois   the Franks
d. 943

ROBERT = Adelais of
Count of Meux   Burgundy
c. 907-968   914-967

ALFRED THE GREAT = Eahlswith
King of the Anglo-Saxons   of the Gaini
849-899   d. 902

Eadgifu of Kent = **EDWARD THE ELDER** = Ecgwynn
903-966   King of the English
874-924

Ælfgifu of = **EDMUND I**, King   **EADRED**, King   **ÆTHELSTAN**, King
Shaftesbury   Of the English   of the English   of the English
d. 944   921-946   923-955   c. 894-939

HARTHACNUT = unknown
(semi-legendary)
King of Denmark

EADWIG, King   Ælfthryth = **EDGAR THE PEACEFUL** = Æthelflæd
of the English   c. 945-1000   King of the English
d. 959   c. 943-975

GORM THE OLD = Thyra
King of Denmark

EDWARD THE MARTYR
King of the English
c. 962-978a

HARALD BLUETOOTH, King = Tove of the
of Denmark & Norway   Obotrites
d. 985-86

unknown = **SWEYN FORKBEARD**, King of Denmark = unknown
& Norway, King of the English
960-1014

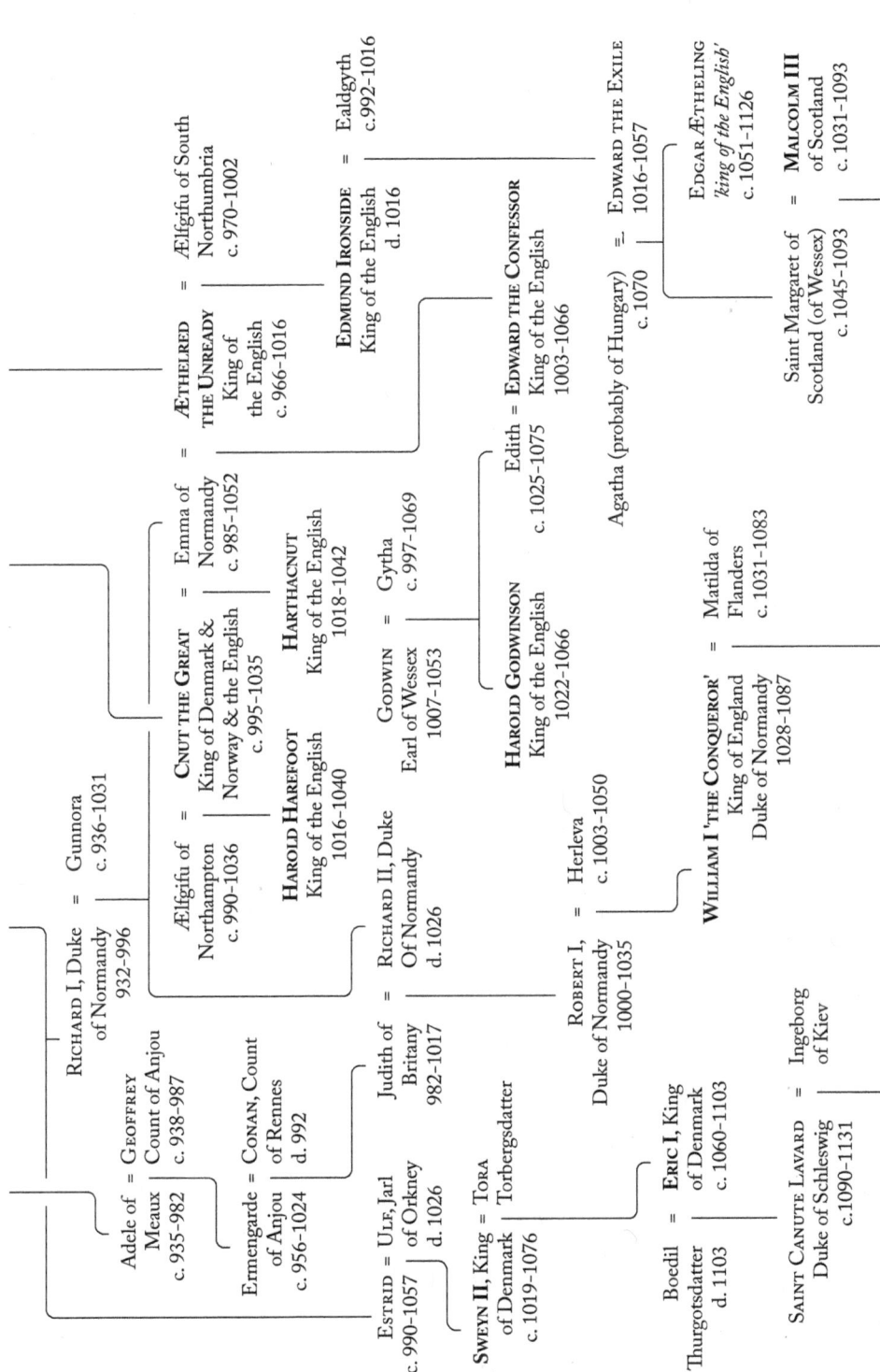

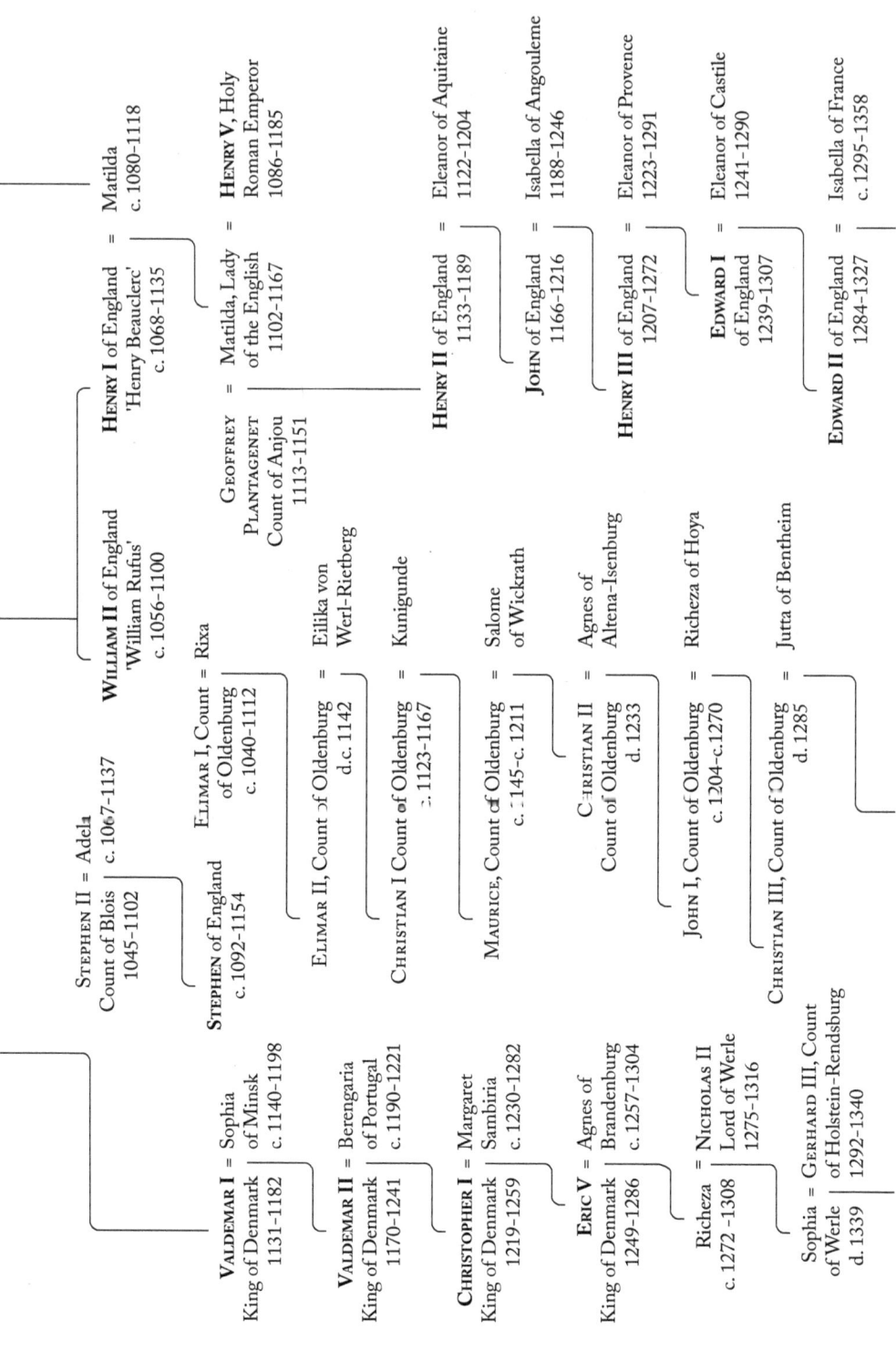

STEPHEN II = Adela
Count of Blois   c. 1067–1137
1045–1102

HENRY I of England = Matilda
'Henry Beauclerc'   c. 1080–1118
c. 1068–1135

WILLIAM II of England
'William Rufus'
c. 1056–1100

ELIMAR I, Count = Rixa
of Oldenburg
c. 1040–1112

STEPHEN of England
c. 1092–1154

GEOFFREY = Matilda, Lady = HENRY V, Holy
PLANTAGENET   of the English   Roman Emperor
Count of Anjou   1102–1167   1086–1185
1113–1151

ELIMAR II, Count of Oldenburg = Eilika von
d.c. 1142   Werl-Rietberg

CHRISTIAN I Count of Oldenburg = Kunigunde
c. 1123–1167

HENRY II of England = Eleanor of Aquitaine
1133–1189   1122–1204

MAURICE, Count of Oldenburg = Salome
c. 145–c. 1211   of Wickrath

VALDEMAR I = Sophia
King of Denmark   of Minsk
1131–1182   c. 1140–1198

JOHN of England = Isabella of Angouleme
1166–1216   1188–1246

CHRISTIAN II = Agnes of
Count of Oldenburg   Altena-Isenburg
d. 1233

VALDEMAR II = Berengaria
King of Denmark   of Portugal
1170–1241   c. 1190–1221

HENRY III of England = Eleanor of Provence
1207–1272   1223–1291

JOHN I, Count of Oldenburg = Richeza of Hoya
c. 1204–c. 1270

CHRISTOPHER I = Margaret
King of Denmark   Sambiria
1219–1259   c. 1230–1282

EDWARD I = Eleanor of Castile
of England   1241–1290
1239–1307

CHRISTIAN III, Count of Oldenburg = Jutta of Bentheim
d. 1285

ERIC V = Agnes of
King of Denmark   Brandenburg
1249–1286   c. 1257–1304

EDWARD II of England = Isabella of France
1284–1327   c. 1295–1358

Richeza = NICHOLAS II
c. 1272 –1308   Lord of Werle
1275–1316

Sophia = GERHARD III, Count
of Werle   of Holstein-Rendsburg
d. 1339   1292–1340

374

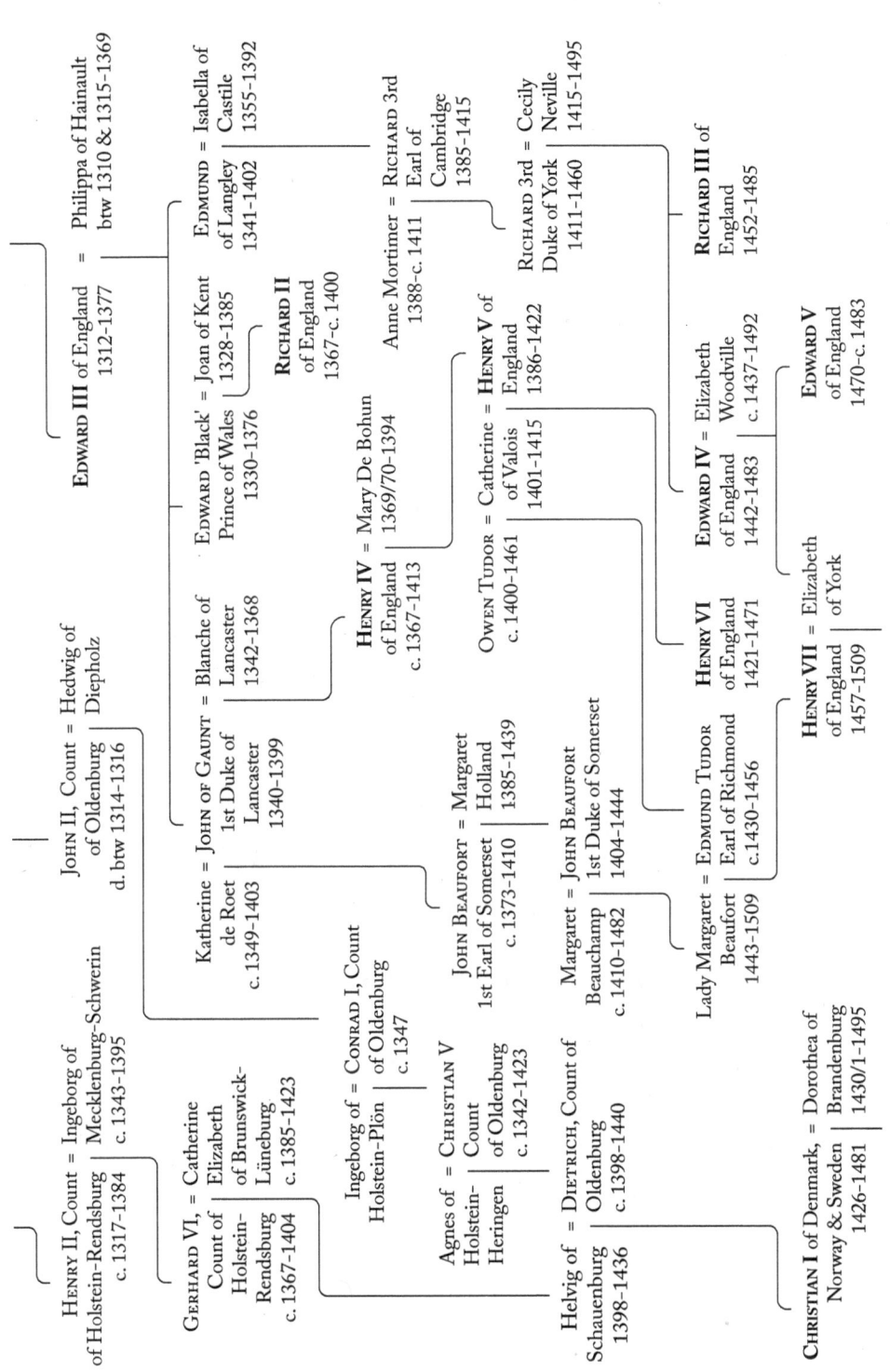

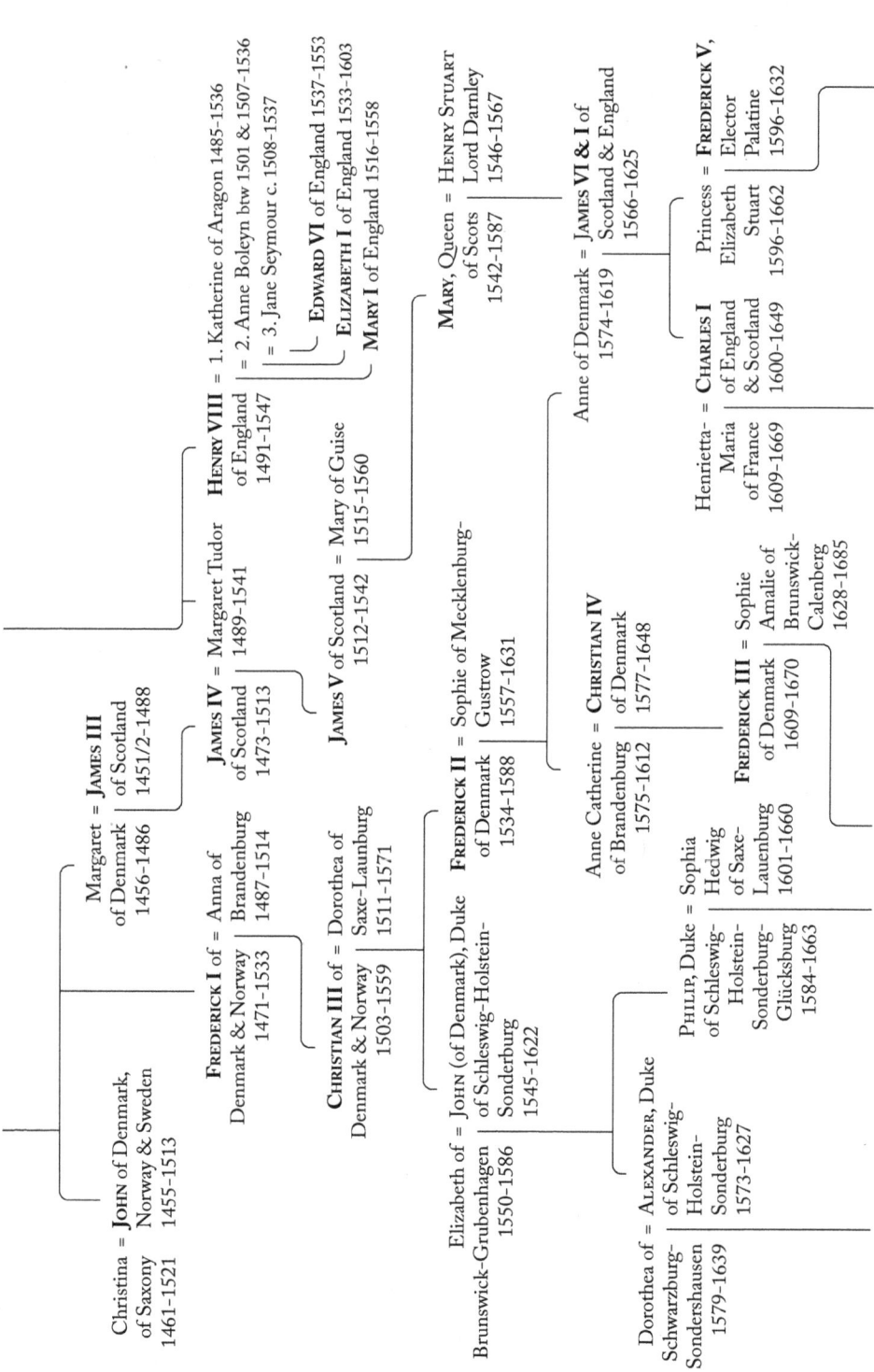

Christina = **John** of Denmark,
of Saxony   Norway & Sweden
1461-1521   1455-1513

Margaret = **James III**
of Denmark   of Scotland
1456-1486   1451/2-1488

Henry VIII = 1. Katherine of Aragon 1485-1536
of England = 2. Anne Boleyn btw 1501 & 1507-1536
1491-1547   = 3. Jane Seymour c. 1508-1537

Edward VI of England 1537-1553
Elizabeth I of England 1533-1603
Mary I of England 1516-1558

Mary, Queen = **Henry Stuart**
of Scots   Lord Darnley
1542-1587   1546-1567

Anne of Denmark = **James VI & I** of
1574-1619   Scotland & England
                1566-1625

Princess = **Frederick V**,
Elizabeth   Elector
Stuart   Palatine
1596-1662   1596-1632

Frederick I of = Anna of
Denmark & Norway   Brandenburg
1471-1533   1487-1514

James IV = Margaret Tudor
of Scotland   1489-1541
1473-1513

James V of Scotland = Mary of Guise
1512-1542   1515-1560

Frederick II = Sophie of Mecklenburg-
of Denmark   Gustrow
1534-1588   1557-1631

Henrietta- = **Charles I**
Maria   of England
of France   & Scotland
1609-1669   1600-1649

Christian III of = Dorothea of
Denmark & Norway   Saxe-Launburg
1503-1559   1511-1571

Anne Catherine = **Christian IV**
of Brandenburg   of Denmark
— 1575-1612   1577-1648

Frederick III = Sophie
of Denmark   Amalie of
1609-1670   Brunswick-
                  Calenberg
                  1628-1685

Elizabeth of = **John** (of Denmark), Duke
Brunswick-Grubenhagen of Schleswig-Holstein-
1550-1586   Sonderburg
                       1545-1622

Philip, Duke = Sophia
of Schleswig-   Hedwig
Holstein-   of Saxe-
Sonderburg-   Lauenburg
Glücksburg   1601-1660
1584-1663

Dorothea of = **Alexander**, Duke
Schwarzburg-   of Schleswig-
Sondershausen Holstein-
1579-1639   Sonderburg
               1573-1627

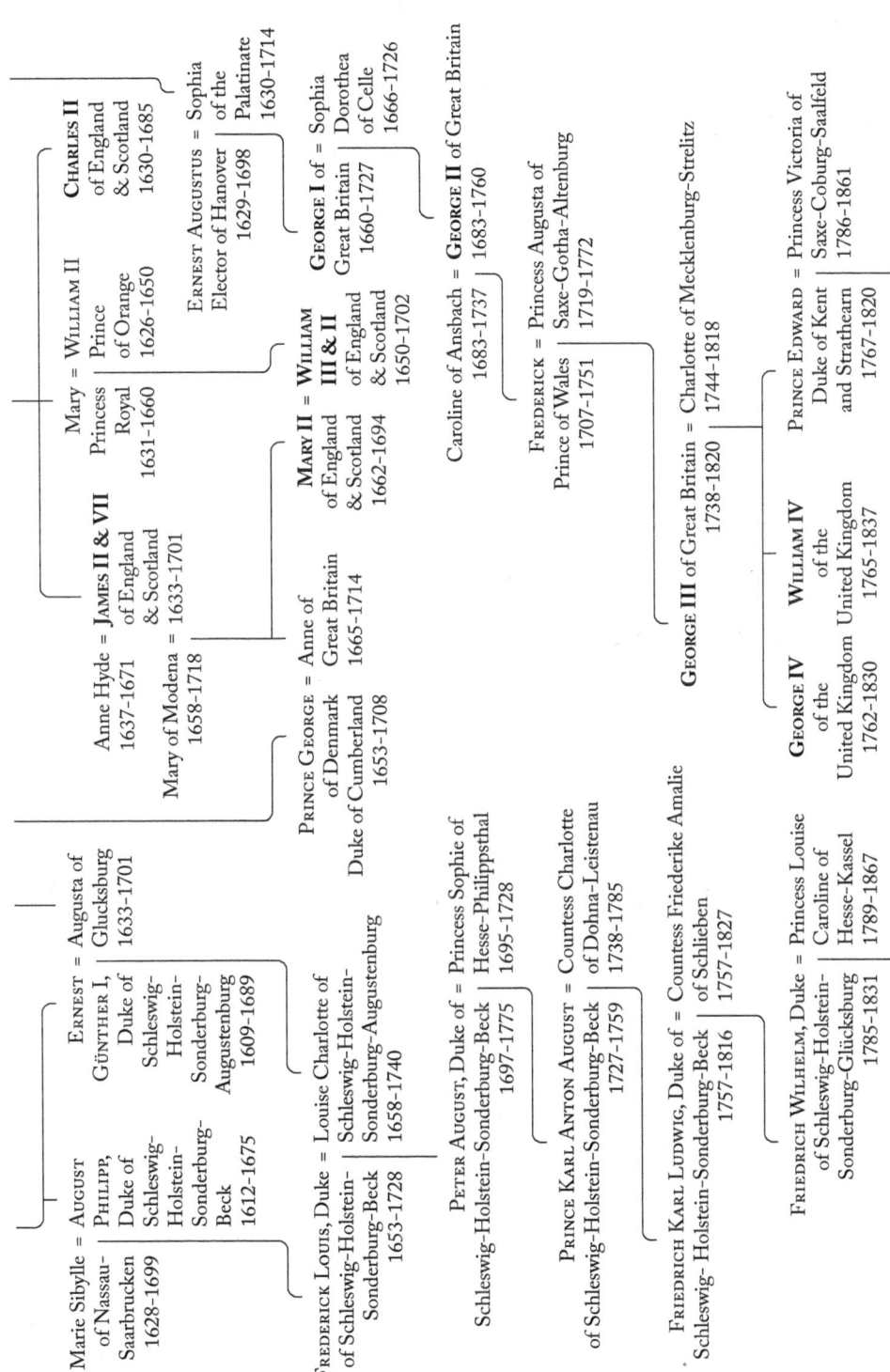

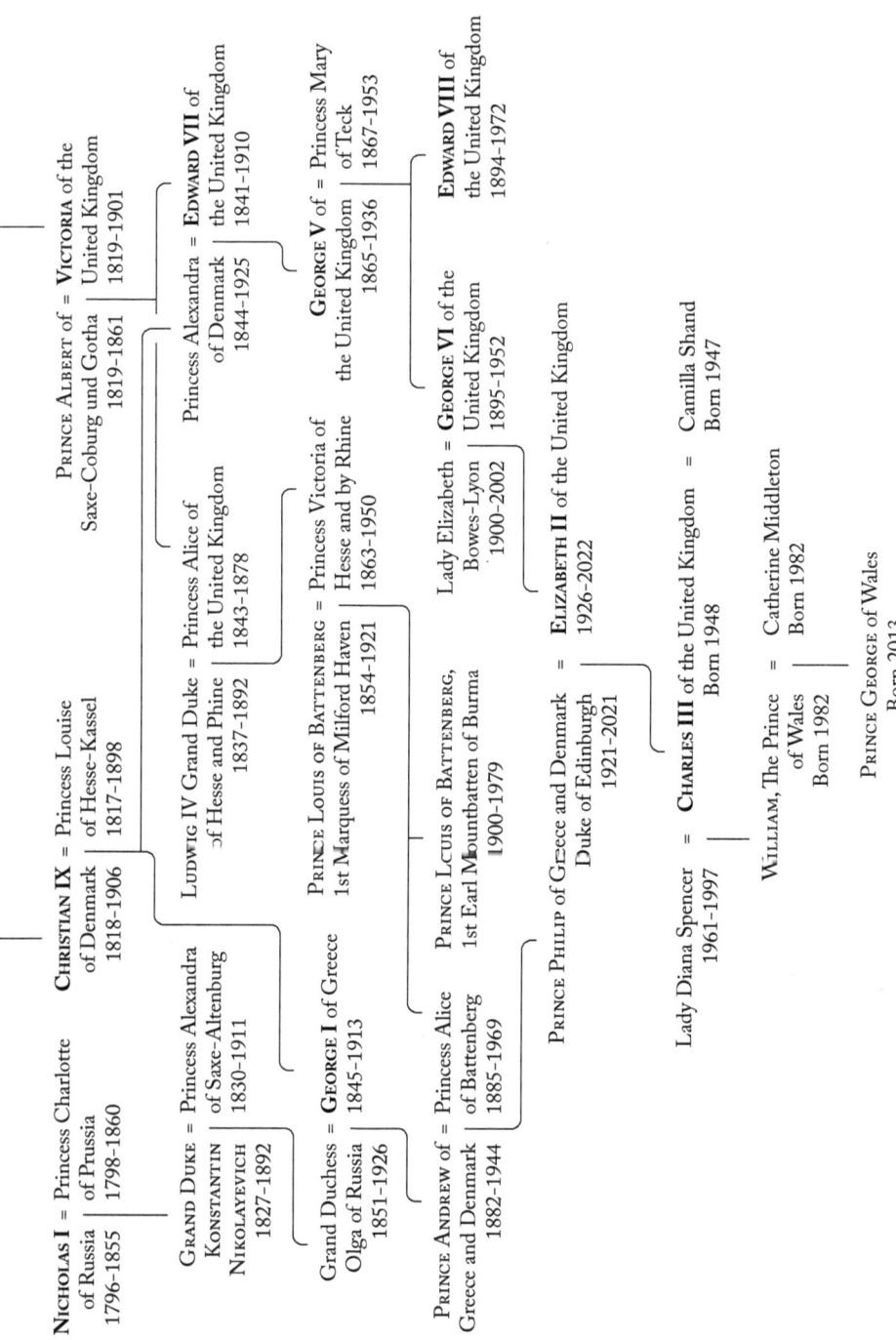

NICHOLAS I = Princess Charlotte
of Russia   of Prussia
1796–1855   1798–1860

CHRISTIAN IX = Princess Louise
of Denmark   of Hesse-Kassel
1818–1906   1817–1898

PRINCE ALBERT of = VICTORIA of the
Saxe-Coburg und Gotha   United Kingdom
1819–1861   1819–1901

Princess Alexandra = EDWARD VII of
of Denmark   the United Kingdom
1844–1925   1841–1910

GEORGE V of = Princess Mary
the United Kingdom   of Teck
1865–1936   1867–1953

EDWARD VIII of
the United Kingdom
1894–1972

GRAND DUKE = Princess Alexandra
KONSTANTIN   of Saxe-Altenburg
NIKOLAYEVICH   1830–1911
1827–1892

LUDWIG IV Grand Duke = Princess Alice of
of Hesse and Phine   the United Kingdom
1837–1892   1843–1878

Grand Duchess = GEORGE I of Greece
Olga of Russia   1845–1913
1851–1926

PRINCE LOUIS OF BATTENBERG = Princess Victoria of
1st Marquess of Milford Haven   Hesse and by Rhine
1854–1921   1863–1950

Lady Elizabeth = GEORGE VI of the
Bowes-Lyon   United Kingdom
1900–2002   1895–1952

PRINCE ANDREW of = Princess Alice
Greece and Denmark   of Battenberg
1882–1944   1885–1969

PRINCE LCUIS OF BATTENBERG,
1st Earl Mcuntbatten of Burma
1900–1979

ELIZABETH II of the United Kingdom
1926–2022

Camilla Shand
Born 1947

PRINCE PHILIP of Greece and Denmark =
Duke of Edinburgh
1921–2021

CHARLES III of the United Kingdom =
Born 1948

Lady Diana Spencer =
1961–1997

WILLIAM, The Prince =
of Wales
Born 1982

Catherine Middleton
Born 1982

PRINCE GEORGE of Wales
Born 2013

378

LIST OF ILLUSTRATIONS

Figure 1: An early page from the Winchester Chronicle giving the genealogical preface of King Alfred the Great. It was begun during Alfred's reign (871-899) and forms part of the Anglo-Saxon Chronicle. Parker Library, Corpus Christi College, Cambridge.

Figure 2: The Emperor Charlemagne receiving the submission of Widukind at Paderborn in 785AD, by Ary Scheffer (1795-1858). Galerie des Battailes, Palais de Versailles.

Figure 3: Christian V. Section of a large illustrated Oldenburg family tree depicting Christian V, Gavno Castle Collection, copied and 'restored' from a damaged painted panel at Nyborg Castle, Funen, Denmark made in the reign of King Christian III of Denmark (1534-1559). (See Figure: 8).

Figure 4: Drawing of a Count of Oldenburg in fifteenth century armour by Gustav Adolf Closs (1864-1938) in his "Deutschen Wappenkalenders" (c. 1938).

Figure 5: Dietrich, Count of Oldenburg. From a family tree painting at Rosenborg Castle, Copenhagen.

Figure 6: Christian I, King of Denmark, Norway and Sweden. 15th century portrait held at Frederiksborg Castle.

Figure 7: Frederick I, King of Denmark, Norway and Sweden. 1539 portrait attributed to Jacob Binck. Fredericksborg Castle.

Figure 8: Christian III, King of Denmark and Norway. 1550 portrait by Jacob Binck, Fredericksborg Castle.

Figure 9: A fan pedigree of King Christian III of Denmark & Norway (1503-1599), showing all sixteen of his great-great-grandparents painted onto a panel at Nyborg Castle, Funen, Denmark.

Figure 10: A recent photo of Sønderborg Castle, South Jutland by Kim Toft Jørgensen, Museum of Sønderjylland.

Figure 11: Hans/John (II), Duke of Schleswig-Holstein-Sonderburg, by an unknown painter. Frederiksborg Hillerod Museum, Denmark.

Figure 12: Woodcut of Alexander, Duke of Schleswig-Holstein-Sonderburg. Sonderburg Castle, Denmark.

Figure 13: A 1791 family portrait of Princess Katharina (of Holstein-Beck) seated next to a bust of her father, Peter August, Duke of Schleswig-Holstein-Sonderburg-Beck (carved by Alexander Trippel). To her right: her son Prince Ivan Baryatinsky, her daughter Anna with the latter's husband Count Nikolai Alexandrovich Tolstoy. Charlotte holds a miniature of her late husband, Prince Ivan Sergeevich Baryatinsky. By Angelika Kauffman RA (1741-1807). Pushkin Museum of Fine Arts.

Figure 14: August Philipp, Duke of Schleswig-Holstein-Sonderburg-Beck. Unknown artist. English school.

Figure 15: Miniature portrait of Frederick Louis, Duke of Schleswig-Holstein-Sonderburg-Beck (1653-1728). Painter unknown. Pushkin Museum of Fine Arts.

Figure 16: Peter August, Duke of Schleswig-Holstein-Sonderburg-Beck. Painter unknown.

Figure 17: Miniature portrait of Charles/Karl Anton August, Prince of Schleswig-Holstein-Sonderburg-Beck (1727-1759). Painter unknown. Pushkin Museum of Fine Arts.

Figure 18: Frederick Charles, Duke of Schleswig-Holstein-Sonderburg-Beck, circa. 1800, by Johan Friederich August Tischbein (1750-1812). State Tretyakov Gallery, Moscow.

Figure 19: A Photograph of Glücksburg Castle taken in 2018 by Matthias Süßen.

Figure 20: A print of Frederick William, Duke of Schleswig-Holstein-Sonderburg-Glücksburg. Possibly by Albert Emil Kirchner in 1830-1831. Royal Danish Library.

Figure 21: Photograph of King Christian IX of Denmark. Royal Danish Library.

Figure 22: 'The Family of Christian IX of Denmark' – by Laurits Tuxen – depicting the family group in the Garden Hall of the Fredensborg Palace, 1886. Now on display at the Christianborg Palace, Denmark. The thirty-two individuals depicted are (from left to right): Prince Albert Victor Duke of Clarence and Avondale (Charles III's great-great-uncle), Edward VII then Prince of Wales (Charles III's great-great-grandfather), Queen Alexandra then Princess of Wales (Charles III's great-great-grandmother), Princess Ingeborg of Denmark, Prince Harald of Denmark, Prince George of Cumberland, Princess Marie of Cumberland, Princess Thyra Duchess of Cumberland, Princess Alexandra of Cumberland, Queen Louise of Denmark, Prince Valdemar of Denmark, King Christian IX of Denmark, Prince Christian of Denmark (later Christian X), The Tsarevich of Russia (later Tsar Nicholas II), Grand Duke Michael Alexandrovich of Russia, Tsarina Maria Feodorovna of Russia, Grand Duchess Olga Alexandrovna of Russia, Tsar Alexander III of Russia, The Crown Prince of Denmark (later Frederick VIII), The Crown Princess of Denmark (later Queen Louise), King George I of Greece, Princess Thyra of Denmark, Princess Alexandra of Greece, Queen Olga of Greece, Princess Marie of Greece, Princess Louise of Wales (later Princess Royal), Prince Carl of Denmark (later King Haakon VII of Norway), Grand Duke George Alexandrovich of Russia, Princess Victoria of Wales, Princess Maud of Wales (later Queen Maud of Norway), Grand Duchess Xenia Alexandrovna of Russia, Princess Louise of Denmark.

Figure 23: Photograph of King George I of the Hellenes/Greece circa. 1912. National Portrait Gallery.

Figure 24: Photograph of Prince Andrew of Greece and Denmark in 1935 by Bassano Ltd. National Portrait Gallery.

Figure 25: A photograph of assembled Mountbatten family members taken c.2 November 1923.

Figure 26: Princess Elizabeth and Princess Margaret being 'taught' croquet on a visit to Britannia Royal Naval College, Dartmouth, in Devon in July 1939. Prince Philip is on the far right. Princess Elizabeth is the girl in the foreground. They were 18 and 13 respectively. From the collection of Britannia Royal Naval College.

Figure 27: Photograph of Prince Philip of Greece and Denmark, later Prince Philip, Duke of Edinburgh, in the Chinese Room, Buckingham Palace in 1992 by Allan Warren.

Figure 28: HM The King at his Coronation in Westminster Abbey, 6 May 2023. (British Broadcasting Corporation).

Figure 29: HM King Charles III, his son HRH The Prince of Wales, and grandson, HRH Prince George of Wales. Official Coronation photograph taken in the Throne Room, Buckingham Palace, 6 May 2023, by Hugo Burnand.

Figure 30: Photograph of The Prince of Wales at D-Day Commemorations in Normandy in 2024. (European Union).

Figure 31: Photograph of Prince George of Wales at Trooping the Colour in 2023 by Simon Dawson. (No. 10 Downing Street).

BIBLIOGRAPHY

Addington, A.C. *'The Royal House of Stuart: The Descendants of King James VI of Scotland (James I of England)'* Vol. 2. (Charles Skilton, 1971).

Alexandra of Yugoslavia, Queen. *'Prince Philip: A Family Portrait'* (Hodder and Stoughton, 1959).

Amin, N. *'The House of Beaufort: The Bastard Line that Captured the Crown'* (Amberley, 2017).

Anderson, J. *'Royal Genealogies, Or the Genealogical Tables of Emperors, Kings and Princes'* (James Anderson, 1732).

Andrew of Greece and Denmark, Prince. *'Towards Disaster: The Greek Army in Asia Minor in 1921'* (Alan Sutton, 2025).

Aronson, T. *'A Family of Kings: The descendants of Christian IX of Denmark'* 2nd ed. (Thistle Publishing, 2014).

Ashdown, D. *'The Royal Line of Succession'* (Pitkin, 2023).

Bain, R.N. *'Christian III'* in Chisholm, H. *(ed.)*. *'Encyclopædia Britannica'* Vol. 6, 11th edition (Cambridge University Press, 1911).

Baldwin, S. *'The Henry Project: The Ancestors of King Henry II of England'* (The American Society of Genealogists, 2002).

Barlow, F. *'Edward the Confessor'* (Yale University Press, 2011).

Barlow, F. *'The Feudal Kingdom of England, 1042–1216'* (5th ed.) (Pearson Education, 1999).

Barrow, G. W. S. *'The Kingdom of the Scots'* (Edinburgh University Press, 2003).

Beeche, A.E., Greece, Prince Michael of., and Hemis-Markesinis, H. *'The Royal Hellenic dynasty'* (Eurohistory, 2007).

Bertin, C. *'Marie Bonaparte'* (Perrin ,1999).

Black, J. *'The Hanoverians: The History of a Dynasty'* (Hambledon Continuum, 2004).

Boothroyd, B. *'Prince Philip: An Informal Biography'* (McCall, 1971).

Bousfield, A. and Toffoli, G. *'Fifty Years the Queen'* (Dundurn Press, 2002).

Boutell, C. and Brooke-Little, J.P. *'Boutell's Heraldry'* (F. Warne Publishers, 1973).

Boutell, C. and Fox-Davies, A.C. *'English Heraldry'* (Kessinger, 2003).

Bramsen, B. *'The House of Glücksburg. The Father-in-law of Europe and his descendants'* (in Danish) (2nd ed.) (Forlaget Forum 1992).

Brandreth, G. *'Philip and Elizabeth: Portrait of a Marriage'* (Century, 2004).

Brault, G.J. *'Early Blazon' (2nd ed.)* (Boydell Press, 1997).

Bridgen, S. *'New Worlds, Lost Worlds: The Rule of the Tudors, 1485–1603'* (Penguin, 2001).

Brooke-Little, J. *'Royal Heraldry: Beasts and Badges of Britain'* (Blandford, 1976).

Burke's Peerage, *'Burke's Guide to the Royal Family'* (Burke's Peerage, 1973).

Campbell, J. and Sherrard, P. *'Modern Greece'* (Ernest Benn, 1968).

Carlton, C. *'Charles I: The Personal Monarch'* (2nd edition) (Routledge, 1995).

Cassavetti, E. *'The Lion & the Lilies: The Stuarts and France'* (Macdonald & Jane's, 1977).

Castor, H. *'The King, the Crown, and the Duchy of Lancaster: Public Authority and Private Power, 1399–1461'* (Oxford University Press, 2000).

Christmas, W. *'King George of Greece'* Trans.by Chater, A. G. (McBride, Nast & Co., 1914).

Clarke, J. and Ridley, J.G. with Fraser, A. (editor) *'The Houses of Hanover and Saxe-Coburg-Gotha'* (University of California Press).

Clay, C. *'King, Kaiser, Tsar: Three Royal Cousins Who Led the World to War'* (John Murray, 2006).

Clogg, R. *'A Short History of Modern Greece'* (Cambridge University Press, 1979).

Clogg, R. *'A Concise History of Greece'* (Cambridge University Press, 2010).

Crawford, M. *'The Little Princesses'* (Cassell & Co., 1950).

Crofton, I. *'The Kings and Queens of England'* **(Quercus, 2007).**

Crouch, D. *'The Normans: The History of a Dynasty'* (Hambledon Continuum, 2002).

Crouch, D. *'The Reign of King Stephen, 1135-1154'* (Pearson Education, 2000).

Davies, C.S.L. *'Peace, Print and Protestantism 1450-1558'* (Fontana Press, 1995).

Davies, N. *'Europe – A History'* (Pimlico, 1997).

Davies, N. *'The Isles – A History'* (MacMillan, 1999).

Davis, E.H. *'The British Bonapartes – Napoleon's Family in Britain'* (Pen & Sword, 2022).

Dean, K. *'On the Trail of the Yorks'* (Amberley, 2016).

Dennys, R. *'The Heraldic Imagination'* (Barrie & Jenkins, 1975).

Dolby, K. *'The Wicked Wit of Queen Elizabeth II'* (Michael O'Mara Books, 2015).

Eade, P. *'Prince Philip: The Turbulent Early Life of the Man Who Married Queen Elizabeth II'* (Henry Holt & Co., 2011).

Edwards, A. '*Matriarch: Queen Mary and the House of Windsor*' (Rowman & Littlefield, 2014),

Feuchtwanger, E.J. '*Albert and Victoria – The Rise and Fall of the House of Saxe-Coburg-Gotha*' (Hambledon Contunuum, 2006).

Forster, E.S. '*A Short History of Modern Greece 1821–1956*' (Methuen & Co., 1958).

Fraser, A. '*The Lives of the Kings & Queens of England. Queens*' (Phoenix, 2000).

Freeman, E.A. '*The History of the Norman Conquest of England: The Reign of Harold and the Interegnum*' First published, 1869 (Nabu Press, 2010).

Friedl, H. Günther, W. Günther-Arndt, H. and Schmidt, H. '*Biographisches Handbuch zur Geschichte des Landes Oldenburg*' (Isensee, 1992).

Geyl, P. '*Orange and Stuart 1641–1672*' (Phoenix Press, 2002).

Gillingham, J. '*The Angevin Empire*' (2nd Edition) (Bloomsbury, 2001).

Green, J. '*Henry I: King of England and Duke of Normandy*' (Cambridge University Press, 2009).

Grell, O.P. '*The Scandinavian Reformation. From evangelical movement to institutionalisation of reform*' (Cambridge University Press, 1995).

Guy, J. '*Tudor England*' (Oxford University Press, 1990).

Hamilton, A. *'The Royal Handbook'* (Mitchell Beazley, 1985).

Hamilton, J. *'The Plantagenets – History of a Dynasty'* (Bloomsbury, 2010).

Harper-Hill, C. and Vincent, N. *'Henry II: New Interpretations'* (Boydell Press, 2007).

Heald, T. *'The Duke: A Portrait of Prince Philip'* (Hodder and Stoughton, 1991).

Hermansen, V. *'The Height of Christian the First'* (National Museum of Denmark, 1950).

Huberty, M., Giraud, A., Magdelaine, B., and Magdelaine, F. *"Allemagne dynastique : les quinze familles qui ont fait l'empire' ('Dynastic Germany: The Fifteen Families Who Made the Empire')* Vol.1-7 (Alain Giraud 1976-1991).

Jones, D. *'The Plantagenets – The Kings who made England'* (William Collins, 2013).

Key, Michael John (2022). *The House of Godwin : The Rise and Fall of an Anglo-Saxon Dynasty.* Gloucestershire: Amberley Publishing.

Lerche, A. and Mandal, M. *'A royal family: the story of Christian IX and his European descendants'* (Aschehoug, 2003).

Levine, M. *'Tudor England 1485–1603'* (Cambridge University Press, 1968).

Lockhart, P.D. *'Denmark, 1513–1660. The rise and decline of a Renaissance monarchy'* (Oxford University Press, 2007).

Longford, (E.) Countess of. *'The Royal House of Windsor'* (Knopf, 1974).

Loomis, R.S. *'Arthurian Legend in Medieval Art'* (Modern Language Association of *America 1938*).

Louda, J. and Maclagan, M. *'Lines of Succession: Heraldry of the Royal Families of Europe'* *(2nd ed.)*, (Little, Brown, 1991).

Lübbing, H. *'Die Rasteder Chronik 1059-1477'* (Holzberg, 1976).

Mackie, J. D. *'The Earlier Tudors, 1485–1558'* (Oxford University Press, 1952).

Mason, Emma (2004). *The House of Godwine: The History of a Dynasty.* London: Hambledon and London.

Massie, A. *'The Royal Stuarts – A History of the Family that Shaped Britain'* (Random House, 2010).

Montgomery-Massingberd, H. 'Burke's Royal Families of the World' (1st ed.), (Burke's Peerage, 1977).

Montgomery-Massingberd, H. (editor) *'Burke's Guide to the Royal Family'* (Burke's Peerage, 1973).

Naismith, R. *'The Origins of the Line of Egbert, King of the West Saxons, 802–839'* (English Historical Review, 2011).

Neubecker, O. *'Heraldry: Sources, Symbols and Meaning'* (McGraw-Hill, 1976).

Østergård, U. *'Nation-Building and Nationalism in the Oldenburg Empire'* in Berger, S. and Miller, A. *'Nationalizing Empires'* (Central European University Press, 2015).

Palmer, A. and Prince Michael of Greece. *'The Royal House of Greece'* (Weidenfeld Nicolson Illustrated, 1990).

Pastoureau, M. *'Traité d'Héraldique' (3ᵉ édition ed.)*, (Picard, 1997).

Plant, J.S. *'The Tardy Adoption of the Plantagenet Surname'* (Nomina, 2007).

Platte, H. *'Das Haus Oldenburg'* (Börde, 2006).

Plumb, J. H. *'The First Four Georges'* (Hamlyn, 1974).

Prestwich, M. *'The Three Edwards – War and State in England, 1272-1377'* (Routledge, 2003).

Rasmussen, C.P. *'The "Dukeries" around Sønderborg An Early-Modern Manorial Landscape Between Scandinavia and Germany'* in Finch, J. Frausing, M. and Boeskov, S. *'Estate Landscapes in Northern Europe'* (Aarhus University Press, 2019).

Riemer, D. *'Graf Huno auf der Spur'* in: Pauly, M. *'Die frühen Oldenburger Grafen'* (*On the Trail of Count Huno, in: The Early Oldenburg Counts*) (Isensee, 2008).

Riemer, D. *'Grafen und Herren im Erzstift Bremen im Spiegel der Geschichte Lehes'* (*The Counts and lords in the archbishopric of Bremen reflected in the history of Lehe.*) (W. Mauke, 1995).

Roberts, A. *'The House of Windsor'* (University of California Press, 2000).

Rowen, H.H. *'The Princes of Orange: the Stadholders in the Dutch Republic'* (Cambridge University Press, 1988).

Simms, B. Riotte, T. *'The Hanoverian Dimension in British History, 1714–1837'* (Cambridge University Press, 2010).

Sinclair, D. *'Two Georges: The Making of the Modern Monarchy'* (Hodder and Stoughton, 1988).

Starkey, D *'Henry'* (Harper Perennial, 2009).

Starkey, D. *'Monarchy'* (Harper Press, 2006).

Stokvis, A. *'Manuel d'histoire, de généalogie et de chronologie de tous les États du globe, depuis les temps les plus reculés jusqu'à nos jours'* (E.J. Brill Leide edición, 1890-93).

Van der Kiste, J. *'Kings of the Hellenes – The Greek Kings 1863-1974'* (Alan Sutton Publishing, 1994).

Van der Kiste, J. *'Northern crowns: the kings of modern Scandinavia'* (Sutton Publishing, 1996).

Van der Kiste, J. *'Kings of the Hellenes'* (Sutton Publishing, 1994).

Vickers, H. *'Alice, Princess Andrew of Greece'* (Hamish Hamilton, 2000).

Walker, I.W. *'Harold: The Last Anglo-Saxon King'* (Stroud: History Press, 2010).

Weir, A. *'Britain's Royal Families – The Complete Genealogy'* (Vintage, 2008).

Williams, K. *'Rival Queens – The Betrayal of Mary Queen of Scots'* (Hutchinson, 2018).

Windsor, The Duke of. *'A King's Story'* (Cassell and Co., 1951).

Woodhouse, C.M. *'The Story of Modern Greece'* (Faber and Faber, 1968).

Worsley, L *'Queen Victoria – Daughter, Wife, Mother, Widow'* (Hodder & Stoughton Ltd, 2018).

Ziegler, P. *'Princess Alice of Battenberg; married name Princess Andrew of Greece' in Matthew, H.C.G. and Harrison, B (eds.) 'Oxford Dictionary of National Biography'* (Oxford University, 2004).